AF790483

DEMOCRACY THROUGH REGIONAL INTEGRATION

Professor Katrin Nyman-Metcalf
Dr. Ioannis F. Papageorgiou

intersentia
Cambridge – Antwerp – Portland

Intersentia Ltd
Sheraton House | Castle Park
Cambridge | CB3 0AX | United Kingdom
Tel.: +44 1223 370 170 | Fax: +44 1223 370 169
Email: mail@intersentia.co.uk
www.intersentia.com | www.intersentia.co.uk

Distribution for the UK and Ireland:
NBN International
Airport Business Centre, 10 Thornbury Road
Plymouth, PL6 7 PP
United Kingdom
Tel.: +44 1752 202 301 | Fax: +44 1752 202 331
Email: orders@nbninternational.com

Distribution for Europe and all other countries:
Intersentia Publishing nv
Groenstraat 31
2640 Mortsel
Belgium
Tel.: +32 3 680 15 50 | Fax: +32 3 658 71 21
Email: mail@intersentia.be

Distribution for the USA and Canada:
International Specialized Book Services
920 NE 58th Ave. Suite 300
Portland, OR 97213
USA
Tel.: +1 800 944 6190 (toll free) | Fax: +1 503 280 8832
Email: info@isbs.com

Democracy through Regional Integration
© Katrin Nyman-Metcalf and Ioannis F. Papageorgiou 2015

The author has asserted the right under the Copyright, Designs and Patents Act 1988, to be identified as author of this work.

No part of this book may be reproduced, stored in a retrieval system, or transmitted, in any form, or by any means, without prior written permission from Intersentia, or as expressly permitted by law or under the terms agreed with the appropriate reprographic rights organisation. Enquiries concerning reproduction which may not be covered by the above should be addressed to Intersentia at the address above.

Cover image: Map reproduction courtesy of the Norman B. Leventhal Map Center at the Boston Public Library.

ISBN 978-1-78068-362-1
D/2015/7849/154
NUR 823

British Library Cataloguing in Publication Data. A catalogue record for this book is available from the British Library.

DEMOCRACY THROUGH REGIONAL INTEGRATION

CONTENTS

I. INTRODUCTION

I.1. OBJECTIVES

In recent years it can be observed that there are more and more examples where regional integration systems have prevented unconstitutional taking of power in various countries and parts of the world. This may be thanks to explicit tasks and powers set out in the constitutive documents of the regional integration system or it may be something the system develops *ad hoc* and in response to events. We can see examples such as Cote d'Ivoire, Honduras, Mali or Paraguay. Regional integration systems also exerted some influence – or attempted to do so – in Cambodia and Myanmar. Recently (May 2015) we see how African regional integration organisations reacted to the coup in Burundi. These interventions have something in common with one-another. They are instigated and organised by regional integration systems to prevent unconstitutional developments or to revert to the situation before such events. Such interventions are either based on mechanisms created by the constitutive documents of the regional integration organisations or their *ad hoc* decisions. Such action to preserve democracy happens despite the fact that most regional integration systems have economic cooperation aims rather than explicit democratisation aims. However, developments toward further regional integration in most parts of the world mean that the original aims and cooperation mechanisms tend to expand.

This book analyses possibilities for regional integration systems to act so as to transform into defenders or promoters of democracy, rule of law and the respect for human rights among their members. It also examines if and to what extent the promotion and protection of rights through a regional integration organisation can have a decisive importance for democratisation of member states of the regional body: can an organisation become greater than the sum of its parts and push these parts toward something that they may not otherwise, if the organisation did not exist, have achieved? The analysis covers the different ways in which regional integration systems can support positive developments in member states, potential (candidate) member states or in a wider context. The emphasis is on the explicit or implicit democracy-promoting role of the organisations, but seen in the context of actual actions rather than proclamations.

The book especially considers the role of institutions in regional integration systems[1]: how the system as such, through its institutions, in addition to action by its member states can exercise a positive influence in the region. The systems analysed are primarily those set up with an aim of regional integration rather than just for cooperation on more or less limited issues.[2] However, various kinds of regional systems are examined for comparative purposes and also for the reason that it is not just the regional systems with an explicit democracy promoting role that end up actually exercising such a role. The main question for analysis is if and how regional integration organisations and especially supranational elements of such organisations, expressed through the institutional structure of the integration system, can take on a role of their own in protecting and promoting democracy.

If such a role can be detected in regional integration organisations, the institutional mechanisms to achieve and support this role need to be understood. In particular, this includes mechanisms to ensure that member states follow the decisions of the organisation. This means that the possibility for any coercive or persuasive powers is especially significant. A comparative study helps to establish what factors enable an organisation to be successful in promoting a certain type of democratic development among its members.

The main issue for this book is thus whether institutions of regional integration can promote and strengthen democracy within component states and more generally how regional integration enhances and strengthens democracy in its region and, through that, in the world. The democracy-promoting role of regional integration is seen against the background of recent developments including governments overthrown by violence as well as violations if not always of the letter at least of the spirit of national constitutions, through abusing possibilities in the constitution with the aim to challenge separation of powers, term limitations or similar. This latter phenomenon could popularly be described as cheating without a coup d'état and seems to be becoming something of a norm in international politics nowadays, with many examples like e.g. Russia or Venezuela. Leaders attempt to amend the constitution by legal means and in doing so they go against the spirit of the constitution. We examine

1 This includes that the systems are restricted to a certain geographical region, although the exact interpretation of the extent of a region can vary. J. Klabbers, *An Introduction to International Organizations Law* (Cambridge University Press 2015), pp. 24–25.

2 In literature the term "regionalism" is sometimes used for project of regional cooperation, whereas "regionalisation" denotes trends based on trade, markets and other factors, pushing for closer cooperation. This term can also be used for developments within states, when regions gain importance. Regionalism is multifaceted and multidimensional. There is, however, no consensus on this terminology. In this book, the formal structures for regional cooperation are examined. See e.g. R. Higgott, "The theory and practice of region", pp. 17–38 in B. Fort and D. Webber (eds.), *Regional Integration in East Asia and Europe. Convergence and divergence.* (Routledge 2006), at pp. 21–24.

what if anything a regional integration organisation may contribute to support democratic principles against overt or covert abuse.

As in all academic research, it is important to define the terms used. By the term democracy we mean not just the holding of free elections but also the parliamentary system, respect for human rights, the landscape enabling free elections including the media landscape and the possibility for different candidates to put forward their message on more or less fair terms to be able to genuinely compete for votes. An electoral democracy presupposes the absence of fraud to be a real democracy. Democracy also includes a link to development and social justice as exemplified in relevant efforts of the Central American Integration System (SICA). The idea of democratic entitlement[3] with democracy as a legitimate expectation forms a backdrop to the discussion, although the extent of such democratic entitlement or the status of democracy as a principle of international law are not *per se* discussed. Theoretical aspects of democracy are outlined later in the book, although it does not purport to offer a comprehensive analysis of the many theories and discussions on this topic. The presentation of theoretical aspects of democracy, of federalism, of theories of human rights and constitutional law, are designed and delimited to provide the necessary background to the study of regional integration systems and the analysis of relevant factors of influence. Institutional structure or institutions in this book denote the formal bodies of the integration organisations.

The book provides examples of situations in which regional integration organs have managed to reinforce democracy or democratisation in some or all of their member states. Such influence may be seen in the most advanced regional integration system, the European Union (EU) both through the accession procedure that promotes democracy by demands it makes on candidates and through the financial and other support for democratisation that is given to potential members. In recent years the EU has been active in reacting against what has been seen as attempts at unconstitutional and/or undemocratic behaviour or actions in member states such as Hungary and Romania. Such pressure worked in the case of Romania whereas it led the Hungarian government to retract from only some of its more extreme objectives. Influence towards democratisation in its wider meaning is, however, also seen in most EU

3 T. Franck "The Emerging Right to Democratic Governance" in *American Journal of International Law* 86 (1992) was one of the first to discuss democracy as an evolving international legal obligation. The status of this is still under discussion but many commentators find that there are at least some aspects of democracy that have become an obligation under international law – this is seen in discussions on humanitarian intervention, where not just the emergency itself but also the form of government affect the decisions taken. The question of democracy as a norm of international law is still under discussion and viewpoints vary, see T. Christiano, "Self-determination and the Human Right to Democracy" (Chapter 25), pp. 459–480 and F. Peter, "A Human Right to Democracy" (Chapter 26), pp. 481–490 in R. Croft, S. M. Liao and M. Renzo (eds.), *Philosophical Foundations of Human Rights* (Oxford University Press 2015), especially pp. 488–489.

member states as many decisions taken by the EU have achieved a higher degree of public participation than national decisions, like decisions on infrastructure including new transport corridors (such as motorways or other Trans-European networks) and various environmental issues. The European pre-legislative debate may be less passionate but can be stronger and more vigorous than national debates on similar subjects. European guidelines oblige member states to open up for public participation and involvement. If specific procedures are necessary when the EU takes a decision, there is a clear tendency to adopt such procedures also for national decisions, even if the division of competence in the EU does not formally oblige the member states to apply such procedure for issues outside EU competence. Thus, the world's most advanced regional integration system – the EU – also in the context examined in this book, provides many examples. However, given the vast amount of research and literature on the EU, although several examples from the EU are used as illustrations and comparison, the main emphasis of the book lies on regional integration in other parts of the world.

Regional mechanisms for protection of human rights provide examples of regional enforcement of common principles. The book contains analysis of the human rights systems of the American and African continents and the much less developed Asian system, with Europe used as a background. These systems show evidence of special considerations regarding legitimacy and enforcement, which form part of democratic requirements.

In addition to explicit rules of the regional integration systems to promote democracy in decision-making and to protect human rights of individuals living in the member states, regional integration may have the effect of promoting peaceful coexistence of states by making them used to cooperate on non-contentious matters which helps to provide a framework also for more contentious matters – Central America shows examples of this. This role is linked to the strength of the organisation in question. However, how much of it is linked to an organisation or just to the links established anyway between states for trade or other reasons may be complicated to establish.

In general, many aspects of what is cause and effect in the activities of regional integration organisations are multi-facetted and require careful analysis, which is only touched upon in this book to a limited extent if it is essential for the core theme of the book. Various push and pull factors exist for the organisations but also for cooperation generally. In this context a problem with regional bodies is that countries in a region may have similar resources and production so in a global context they may be competitors and thus have less commercial interest to work together, as seen in Asia. In e.g. Mercosur there is an interest in mutual trade, which provides a natural reason to cooperate. In EU there is strong intra-EU trade so there is an interest to work together that is lacking in several other regional co-operation structures. In any case, there has to be some magnet of integration. If there is any form of interest – mainly economic but also of other nature, like communications or transport – the cooperation may work better for any issues, including democracy. If the interest in cooperation is great, states will have an incentive to submit to various demands made on them, including regarding their political system.

I.2. DELIMITATION

The systems studied are such that profess political integration as an explicit or implicit objective (*vocation d'intégration*). The book therefore does not in principle examine free trade associations or economic cooperation institutions such as e.g. the North American Free Trade Association (NAFTA). At the same time, it is a fact that many regional integration schemes started from modest economic objectives to spill over to other more political ones, which is why no integration schemes are fully excluded. However, the book does not deal with the question of the relationship between the local and the global level in economic relations in a globalised world or other issues linked specifically to economic cooperation.[4]

The book deals with regional integration systems globally, with special emphasis on the Central American Integration System (SICA), Mercosur, the Andean Pact, ASEAN as well as the African Union. Other systems such as the Caribbean Community (CARICOM) and the Arab League are studied albeit in a much more concise manner as these systems have played limited roles in practice. They are included in order to illustrate mechanisms that counter-indicate the possibilities of regional cooperation, rather than as study objects in their own right. Consequently the description of such systems, as well as some additional regional integration mechanisms of lesser practical importance, is more summarily. The EU, being by far the most advanced regional integration system is not described in any detail – given the vast amount of literature that exists on it – but rather used as a background against which other regional integration systems are analysed. This also means that the reader is assumed to have basic knowledge about the EU.[5]

Given the aim to study democratisation, organisations that consist of democracies or that at least purport to support democracy are primarily studied. At the same time, the influence of non-democratic states in organisations that nevertheless claim to support and promote democracy provides an interesting study object related to the relative weight of different factors promoting reform.

4 See on this topic e.g. D. Schneiderman, "Transnational legality and the immobilization of local agency" in *Annual Review of Law and Social Science* 2006. 2:387–408.

5 Writings on regional integration naturally often use the EU as the main study object, as well as the yardstick against which other integration systems are measured. Some commentators feel this is not always the best approach, as the EU is so far-reaching and advanced that it is difficult to measure other systems with the same tools and in any case, the EU model is not necessarily the only one and thus one that should be replicated. See e.g. Higgott (2006).

The book does not examine international democracy as such, in the meaning of analysing to what extent organisations or integration structures within themselves include democratic elements for international decision-making. At the same time, this matter is touched upon to some extent as it may be relevant in the way it influences issues of enforcement of decisions. The organisations and structures are examined in this book in their role as *promoters and supporters* of democracy *in the member states*. Consequently, the descriptive part deals with structures, decision-making procedures and statutes of each organisation. The aim of this is to provide the setting in which the influence of the organisation on its member states can be seen, rather than analysing and evaluating the democratic nature of the various regional bodies as such, with questions of possible democratic deficits or institutional failures.[6]

The book is written from a legal viewpoint although the analysis takes legal as well as political issues into account. The analysis of the institutional elements of integration is primarily a legal analysis enabling to draw political conclusions. However, the book does not deal predominantly with the role of courts, as this is analysed in *Regional Integration and Courts of Justice* (Intersentia 2005) by the same authors.[7]

I.3. METHOD

The authors are aware of the difference between words and acts and of the fact that in many regional integration systems there is a big gap between expressions of will and concrete actions. Consequently, the authors are not going to tire the reader by compiling declarations by heads of states and similar statements but rather emphasise concrete actions taken by the institutions in order to implement relevant acts.

As the book is written from a legal viewpoint, although theories of integration are mentioned if and when they directly relate to the issue of analysis, the book is not a survey or analysis of political science theories.[8]

---

6 For an analysis of international democracy see the Centre for Studies on Federalism, International Democracy Project, from January 2009. www.csfederalismo.it.

7 K. Nyman-Metcalf & I.F. Papageorgiou, *Regional Integration and Courts of Justice* (Intersentia 2005).

8 To mention only a few such studies discussing interesting theoretical points, theories of federalism are studied in various works by M. Burgess, like *Comparative Federalism, Theory and Practice* (Routledge 2006); supranationalism theories are studied by G. Majone, *Dilemmas of European Integration. The ambiguities and pitfalls of integration by stealth* (Oxford University Press 2005); neo-functionalism by e.g. B. Rosamond, *Theories of European Integration* in *The European Union Series* (eds. N. Nugent, W.E. Paterson and V. Wright; Palgrave Macmillan 2000) and sociological institutionalism by S. Stetter, *EU foreign and interior policies. Cross-pillar policies and the social constructions of sovereignty* (Routledge 2007).

In addition to academic sources of a legal, political science or other nature from which the facts and the academic views that form the basis for the authors' analysis are taken, media reports as well as material from international organisations are used as illustrations to the events and debates analysed. This allows reflecting also the wider debate on the topics discussed. Depending on the time and nature of the case studies, there is a lack of academic literature concerning some of the more recent events.

Most regional integration initiatives have an economic aim as well as any more profound integration aim. As pointed out above, this book analyses primarily those systems where something else than the economic integration aim is paramount. Indeed, economic integration has a logic of its own and needs to be analysed from a different perspective than such integration aspects that may promote democracy. However, given that the two aspects are in reality closely linked in many ways – like for example that a successful economic integration may be an incentive for integration in other fields and that democracy and human rights promotion can be linked to economic activities through conditionality requirements in trade agreements and sanctions – on occasion the book will also deal with economic factors driving integration, although such factors will not be specifically analysed.

II. REGIONAL INTEGRATION ORGANISATIONS

In this section, selected regional integration bodies are described. The description does not purport to be a full description of all aspects or activities of the bodies but concentrates on their mission of integration and on the role the institutions play in this mission. The comparative study consequently takes such aspects as its point of comparison. This part is of a predominantly descriptive nature. What are described are primarily elements (institutions, legal documents, procedures) that are essential for the integrational aim of the organisations and any structures that support this. The mission or aim of integration of the organisations is identified both based on the constitutive and other basic legal instruments, and on practice.

II.1. HISTORY AND BASIC ELEMENTS OF REGIONAL INTEGRATION

Voluntary regional integration schemes, uniting different states for a more or less limited purpose, date back to the early 19th century. Earlier integration systems were usually dominated by one state, not entirely voluntary or explicitly seen as steps on the way to form a unitary state. Even early regional integration systems without this initial aim in many instances eventually led to the creation of a state, like the German Reich, which was predated by a number of customs unions between different German states.[9] Switzerland was created through a similar process. Apart from such initiatives that led to new states, there were also ideas in the 19th century of alliances between independent states like a middle European customs union (Zollverein), including or having trading agreements with most major nations in the area.[10]

The Hague Peace Conferences in 1899 and 1907 illustrated a wish to transplant international arrangements into an institutionalised setting and away from just being straight-forward agreements between states. International conferences were seen as a first step to the creation of a more substantial international framework.[11]

---

9 Www.britannica.com/EBchecked/topic/657790/Zollverein.

10 W. Mattli, *The Logic of Regional Integration* (Cambridge University Press 1999) p 2.

11 R. Collins, "Constitutionalism as Liberal-Juridical Consciousness: Echoes from International Law's Past in *Leiden Journal of International Law* 22 (2009), pp. 251–287, at 262.

A different picture can be seen in Central America after the independence struggles of the 1820s where the idea was to form federal states, but where these later disintegrated to maintain only some elements of a weaker regional integration, like when the United Provinces of Central America was created – lasting until 1838. In later efforts of integration or cooperation, the aim of such a federal state remained to some extent.[12]

It is since the Second World War that international organisations have proliferated. This includes global as well as regional organisations, for specific topics or with a more general reach. Only few of these efforts can be called integration efforts in the sense of integrating a specific region, but to some extent all such organisations contribute to a certain integration of states. In selected geographical areas or regarding specific topics the integration may be far-reaching. Although such organisations have not prevented all problems between states, many commentators claim that links created between states both related to security and to economy have prevented large scale disasters, like those that befell the world in e.g. the earlier part of the 20th century such as the World Wars or the Great Depression.[13]

In the last quarter of the 20th century, regional organisations have become important alternatives to global organisations.[14] This is linked to the growing number of states making global organisations more unwieldy, but it also reflects trends of stressing local or regional characteristic as a counterweight to what is seen as excessive globalisation, dominated by a few powerful states.

Even if international organisations can be seen as successful to some extent, the question of representation remains: how to best determine who should be a member of certain select organisations (the G7 is an example[15]) or of their most important bodies (the UN Security Council)? These are questions that have been discussed actively especially in the last two or three decades as the global structures have become more multi-polar. Regional organisations have a place both in their own right, for dealing with regional issues, as they can have more far-reaching mandates and competences than global organisations thanks to the smaller number of essentially more similar members, and they can act as building blocks of global organisations or executors of decisions of such organisations.

The decision on what kind of organisation shall be founded and whether it should be global or regional will mainly depend on the tasks of the organisation. Many of the problems of the modern world such as climate change or terrorism

---

12 E. Torres-Rivas (ed.), *Historia General de Centroamérica*. 6 volumes. Sociedad Estatal Quinto Centenario, (FLACSO, Madrid 1993), pp. 104–106.

13 Mattli (1999) p. 2.

14 A. Orford, "Moral Internationalism and the Responsibility to Protect", *The European Journal of International Law* Vol. 24 No. 1 2013, pp. 83–108 at p. 101.

15 Reduced to G7 with the exclusion of Russia in March 2014, following the Russian annexation of Crimea.

have a global reach. The drawback of dealing with issues globally are the problems arising from having very large organisations. The World Trade Organisation (WTO) is a good illustration of an organisation that through its global character manages to influence world trade and through its decision-making mechanisms as well as its dispute-resolution system has real impact. However, the decision-making system is unwieldy and slow, exactly because it contains so many and so different states.[16]

There are different classifications of international organisations depending on their tasks, powers, independence and other criteria. Focarelli lists a number of criteria that show what it is that determines the autonomy and ability to impose the collective will on members. These are whether the decision-making organs are made up of independent individuals; whether the organisation can adopt legally binding decisions and can take majority decisions; if such decisions have direct effect and can be implemented in the member states; whether there is a judicial organ to monitor this; and whether there is some representation of the people of the member states and not just the states as states.[17] The regional integration systems tend to possess one or several of these characteristics and in addition encompass many different areas, as opposed to sector-specific international organisations that may have a large degree of autonomy but only in a limited sector (like the International Telecommunications Union, ITU, for example).[18]

II.2. THE AMERICAS

II.2.1. THE DEVELOPMENT OF REGIONAL INTEGRATION IN THE AMERICAS

The American continent can easily be divided into two separate groups, insofar as regional integration is concerned. Northern America (the United States and Canada) were early democracies and pursued policies of geographical expansion and democratization within the limits of their national territory. Regional cooperation for the US implied, already since the 19th century, political dominance over the American continent but also the sovereign right to enter or leave cooperation mechanisms. Canada, long oriented towards the colonial metropolis, was reluctant to enter any form of binding integration process with its southern neighbour, preferring to remain aloof from supranational

16 H. Horn, P.C. Mavroidis (eds.), *Legal and Economic Principles of World Trade Law* (Cambridge University Press, 2013).
17 C. Focarelli, *International Law as a Social Construct* (Oxford University Press, Oxford 2012), p. 179.
18 Y. Omerogobe, "Functionalism in the UPU and ITU" *International Journal of International Law* Vol. 27, 1987, pp. 50–62.

enterprises. Both countries considered any form of regional political integration with the other American states – most of which were for most of their time authoritarian regimes – as totally inconceivable.

The picture was different in Southern and Caribbean America.[19] Linguistic affinity and the common political and cultural background was a powerful integration tool in both cases. Already since independence from Spain in the early 19th century, what became later known as Latin American had a definite integration perspective – in letter if not in substance. Though the initial intentions of the fathers of the independence to establish wide federations in a continent-wide system of integration failed in the 1820s, Latin America continued to profess the goals of regional integration into the 20th century despite the rampant authoritarianism in most of the region.[20] The states of the Caribbean, as well, aware of the political exiguity and economic dependence, also sought to establish some form of regional cooperation[21] once the federal construction, immediately after independence from the UK collapsed under conflicting objectives between its entities.

After the Second World War, the first regional cooperation organisms were established – the most important one being the Organisation of American States (OAS); in the 1960s the continent saw its first regional integration organisations, the most prominent being the Andean Pact and the Central American Common Market. Without clear political integration goals, most of these organisms failed to sustain economic development, especially during Latin America's "lost decade" of the 1980s, the debt crisis and military regimes. In the 1990s, other regional integration schemes appeared, many of which are still active today. The most significant are the Mercosur, the Andean Community of Nations, the SICA and the Caribbean Community (CARICOM). The book also looks briefly into the OAS despite the fact of its being a mechanism for regional cooperation rather than an integration institution since the Inter-American Commission and Court of Human Rights depend on this latter institution.

Most regional integration schemes were set up without any reference to the respect of human rights or to democratic institutions: they focused on economic integration and free trade. Although almost all made reference to the common Bolivarian heritage and paid tribute to political integration, few if any references were made to the need for the protection of human rights or to the preservation of democratic institutions – and to the outcome for member states of failure to abide to these rules.

It was only gradually and after the 1980s that the link between regional integration and democratization was made, firstly implicitly and later on more

---

19 I. F. Papageorgiou, "The Role of Regional Parliaments in the Process of Regional Integration: The Case of the Central American Parliament" *The Federalist* 2002 XLIV(1), pp. 8–20.

20 E. Torres-Rivas (1993), pp. 104–106.

21 D. Berry, *Caribbean Integration Law* (Oxford University Press 2014).

and more explicitly in integration systems, as these latter evolved from the economic to the political and member states moved from authoritarianism to more open regimes.[22] The first such regional instrument was the Central American Integration System (SICA).

II.2.2. THE CENTRAL AMERICAN INTEGRATION SYSTEM

Central American integration has been one of the few integration schemes in the region not limited to economic objectives alone and includes, at least in theory, ambitious political goals. Indeed, the present integration organism, called Central American Integration System (henceforth SICA from its Spanish acronym), has among its goals the establishment not only of a free-trade zone, but also of a common market and, in the long-run, of a political union. Also it presents a number of original characteristics, not the least of which is the fact that modern-day integration started from the establishment of a directly elected parliamentary body, the Central American Parliament (henceforth Parlacen from its Spanish acronym of *Parlamento Centroamericano*)[23] and that the original purpose of integration – not unlike the early efforts in European integration – was internal and regional democratization. Furthermore, SICA's judicial organ, the Central American Court of Justice, is entrusted with supranational powers and, at least in theory, enforceability of its rulings.[24]

The five countries that traditionally compose the Central American isthmus (Guatemala, El Salvador, Honduras, Nicaragua and Costa Rica)[25] share a long common past as part of the Mayan cultural zone and, following the Spanish Conquest, became a separate administrative unit (the General Captaincy of Guatemala). During the independence struggles of the 1820s, Central America, after a brief annexation to the Mexican Empire, declared its independence and formed a federal state, the United Provinces of Central America. However, internal fighting between rival political factions and among provinces led to the dissolution of the Federation in 1838. Notwithstanding this initial

22 D. Altman, "Bringing direct democracy back in: toward a three-dimensional measure of democracy", pp. 615–641 in *Democratization* 2013 Vol. 20 No. 4, pp. 615–641, at 625–626 and 641.

23 Papageorgiou (2002), pp. 16–19.

24 Nyman-Metcalf & Papageorgiou (2005), pp. 45–49.

25 Geographically, Central America also includes Panama, which became an independent State, carved out of Colombia in 1903 – with the active U.S. help, in order to facilitate the construction of the Panama Canal – and English-speaking Belize, formerly British Honduras. Historically, though, neither country was oriented towards Central America, while Belize had a long-standing feud with Guatemala, which considered it as part of its territory. Both countries have gradually come to a rapprochement with the other Central American states – Panama is now a full member of almost all regional integration institutions and even Belize became a member of SICA in 2000.

failure, the dream of Central American union, "*the patria grande*" guided a number of attempts to reconstruct the Federation throughout the 19th and the 20th centuries. Each of them failed for similar reasons to those that led to the demise of the Federation: local antagonism, lack of communications, absence of democratic traditions, insufficient economic and political development and foreign intervention.[26]

Only after the Second World War did a successful integration scheme, the Central American Common Market (CACM)[27] appear. Founded in 1960, it aimed at creating a customs union and, later on, a common market, while at the same time co-ordinating the region's industrialisation and economic development. An integrated executive organ (the SIECA)[28] was entrusted with the implementation of the common rules adopted and the monitoring of the states' abiding to them; gradually it acquired an existence of its own. Indeed, at that time Central America became a prime example of the neo-functionalist theories of integration, which saw in it a fertile ground for their theory.[29] Still, though one of the most successful examples of economic integration in the 1960s, the CACM failed to transform economic performance into genuine prosperity:[30] The unwillingness of member states to allow for more democracy in the region – at the time, all member states, with the exception of Costa Rica, were ruled by authoritarian regimes – the disparity between the "beneficiaries" and the "victims" of integration and the reluctance to advance towards deeper integration[31] led to the eventual exhaustion of the Common Market in the early 1970s, while the region foundered in a series of civil conflicts.

Throughout that decade and into the 1980s, civil wars in Salvador and Nicaragua and external intervention put the region in the centre of the East-West conflict. Amid concerns that the military escalation might lead to a generalised regional war, regional integration came again to the forefront as a way out of the crisis. After all external efforts to reduce tension (mainly those undertaken by the Contadora group[32]) failed to produce results and with a military stalemate,

---

26 E. Torres-Rivas (1993), pp. 104–106.

27 Mercado Común Centroamericano (MCCA) in Spanish.

28 Secretaría de Integración Económica Centroamericana (Secretariat for Central American Economic Integration).

29 P. C. Schmitter, "Central American Integration: Spill-Over, Spill-Around or Encapsulation?" in *Journal of Common Market Studies* 1970 Vol. 9, No. 1, p. 19.

30 R.R. Loucel, "Integración centroamericana: evolución y perspectivas" in *Integración latinoamerican*, Vol. 19, No. 201 (1994) p. 54.

31 J. Dosch, "Asia-Pacific Multilateralism and the Role of the United States" in J. Dosch and M. Mols (eds.), *International Relations in the Asia-Pacific* (St. Martin's Press, New York 2000), pp. 87–110 at p. 90.

32 Composed of four Latin-American countries – Mexico, Colombia, Venezuela and Panama – the group, which took its name from the Panamanian island of Contadora where their Foreign Ministers met for the first time in 7 and 8 January 1983, coordinated initiatives to achieve direct negotiations among the states and the parties in the conflict in Central America. The group represented the first attempt to solve the Central American conflicts outside the East-

newly-elected Presidents Oscar Arias Sanchez of Costa Rica and Vinicio Cerezo of Guatemala proposed a peace plan based on confidence-building, internal democratisation and the holding of free elections;[33] the Esquipulas-I plan was adopted in the Guatemalan city of Esquipulas in July 1986 during the first meeting of all Central American Presidents for a generation. The plan included the call for the creation of a directly-elected regional parliament, the Central American Parliament (Parlacen) as a focal point for the reconciliation and peace in the region.[34] For the first time, Central American leaders recognised the link between pacification and internal and regional democratic consolidation. Breaking with the tradition prevailing elsewhere in Latin America, they opted for a regional tool to facilitate and measure democratic progress nationally and admitted that national and international democracy could not be separate.[35]

Furthermore, this step marked a turning point for regional integration in the Americas. Up till then, the parliamentary dimension in regional integration was neglected, even ignored. Since the majority of regional integration schemes were, in any case, limited to economic goals, parliamentary institutions played hardly any role in them. At the same time, popular participation to integration processes was not only undesirable but even actively discouraged. In the context of the authoritarian or semi-authoritarian regimes that constituted the norm in Latin America, popular involvement was not required. The few regional parliamentary assemblies that existed were either isolated from any integration scheme (like the Latin American Parliament) or constituted mere consultative instruments created in the wake of the European experiment (for instance, the various transformations of what is called now the Andean Community of Nations).

On the contrary, the direct election of the Central American Parliament not only introduced citizenship directly in the integration process, but also expanded the integration objectives into the political sphere, by linking regional integration to democratisation and peace.[36] From this aspect, it is interesting to recall the similarities with the foundation and the subsequent enlargement of the European Communities (EC): it was to avoid another war and to consolidate

West context – the U.S. were not involved and even shunned, initially, the initiative – and aimed to promote negotiations and assist in the "conclusion and implementation of a regional multilateral and complete treaty which could satisfy the interests and overcome the fears of all interested parties" as stated in the relevant Contadora Declaration. See Dossier IRELA, N° 11 " El plan Arias: una salida para el proceso de paz centroamericano?". IRELA. Madrid. February 1988. p. 11.

33 A. Opazo Bernales & R. Fernandez Vázquez, *Esquipulas II – una tarea pendiente* (EDUCA 1990), pp. 134–143.

34 C. Kissling, "The legal and political status of international parliamentary institutions" (Chapter 3) in L. Levi, G. Finizio, N. Vallinoto, *The Democratization of International Institutions* (Routledge 2014), pp. 25–52 at 28–29.

35 Opazo Bernales & R. Fernandez Vázquez (1990), pp. 134–143.

36 Papageorgiou (2002), pp. 16–19.

democracy in Germany that Europeans built their first supranational structures; it was to avoid the return of dictatorship that the southern European states (Greece, Spain and Portugal) joined the EEC later. The same objective – as well as economic and geopolitical considerations – was also evident in the 2004–7 enlargements of the EU to Central and Eastern European countries: economic arguments were accompanied by the conviction that joining a larger European family would strengthen democratic institutions.[37]

Despite these promising premises, the subsequent development in Central America did not fulfil the expectations: the new Parliament, despite its direct election, was devoid of any effective powers;[38] the only genuinely democratic state of the region, Costa Rica, refused to join it – as well as to surrender sovereign competences to it. As a result, it was a rump Parliament, composed by deputies from Guatemala, Salvador and Honduras, that was eventually installed on October 28, 1991.

This relative failure, though, did not prevent further and deeper forms of integration in the early 1990s. The gradual normalisation of the political situation as well as external factors (international pressure, in particular the increasing role of the European Community, and the dominant trends of economic globalisation) contributed in taking conscience of the fact that the region's structural problems and its economic under-development should be fought with regional coordination rather than national measures. This led to a renewed interest in political rapprochement and economic integration. In this way, after 1986, the region witnessed a large number of projects aiming to (re-) establish and strengthen political cooperation and economic integration.

Between 1986 and 1990, the region re-established many pre-existing integration institutions and created new ones. The "old" institutions had started operating at various stages of the integration process and included a blend of neo-functionalist institutions and of traditional sectorial inter-state cooperation organisms.[39] It was obvious that they needed coordination and the setting of specific priorities. Gradually, the countries felt the need for an organism to serve as an "umbrella" for all dispersed integration activities and to provide the necessary impetus to a more coherent, political direction of regional integration.[40] Despite certain proposals for a totally new and

---

37 D. Dobrovoljec & K. Nyman-Metcalf, "Enlargement of the European Union – A Regatta with Moving Goal Posts?" *European Journal of Law Reform* 2001 3(2), pp. 131–147.

38 Kissling (2014), pp. 28–29.

39 The integration constellation in Central America included the institutions of the Central American Common Market which were revitalised after the political normalisation, a number of other sectoral institutions, which often dated back to the 1950s and 1960s as well as the institutions created by the Constitutive Treaty of the Parlacen.

40 This aim was first expressed in the ministerial meeting of the ministers responsible for economic integration (an organ of the CACM which started functioning again in the late 1980s) in San Pedro Sula (Honduras) on 7 October 1989 and became official in the Meeting of Presidents at Antigua (Guatemala), in July 1990. The final declaration of this meeting

comprehensive integration treaty, it was finally decided that the best framework was the institutional setup of the earlier regional cooperation scheme called the Organization of Central American States (ODECA).[41]

Even though inactive since the 1970s, the ODECA was from a legal point of view operative. Thus, in 1991, the six presidents of the region[42] signed the Tegucigalpa Protocol which reformed the Charter of the ODECA and established the Central American Integration System (*Sistema de integración centroamericano* – SICA). The SICA should constitute the "region's organic structure aiming to achieve integration in all its aspects (...) in the perspective of the transformation of Central America into a region of peace, freedom, democracy and development".[43] The meeting also decided to set up a preparatory commission for the implementation of the necessary institutional modifications. The Protocol entered into force on 1 February 1993.

The Protocol defines a number of new goals for member States: the first was the consolidation of democracy. It also includes such objectives as the reinforcement of elected and democratic institutions, respect of human rights, the establishment of a new model of regional security; the creation of a regional system for prosperity and economic and social justice, pursuing the construction of a regional economic bloc; reaffirming the self-determination of Central America in foreign affairs, promoting a sustainable development and protecting the environment by the establishment of a new regional ecological order.[44] The Protocol put under the same umbrella the various regional integration schemes and organisms and created a system that draws a lot from

underlined the decision of Presidents to "restructure, reinforce and reactivate the process of integration (...) by adapting or redesigning its legal and institutional framework". (Point 26 of the final declaration).

41 The ODECA (*Organización de Estados Centro-Americanos* – Organization of Central American States) was a regional cooperation organization, founded in 1951 by the five countries of the region with the Charter of San Salvador. Its objectives and institutional setting emulated those of the UN and the Organisation of American States (OAS) and it was not provided with any supranational institution. It became inactive almost from its inception and was re-shaped in 1962, on the wake of the establishment of the CACM, by the Panama Charter. Despite the fact that the Charter spelled out ambitious objectives (among them, to create "an economic and political community [aspiring to] Central American integration" in order to "ensure economic progress [for States parties], to eliminate the barriers [dividing them], to improve (...) living conditions for its peoples, to guarantee stability and growth of the industry and to confirm solidarity among Central Americans" as stated in the Preamble of the Charter) and a complex institutional framework (not less than eight principal organs, among which a meeting of Presidents, a legislative Council and a Court of Justice) it never took off, its competences being vague and competing with those of the CACM and its powers being overwhelmed by the need for consensus in all decisions. It remained inactive during the entire 1970s and 1980s and its organs were never convoked during that period.

42 The presidents of the five member states of the ODECA and the president of Panama.

43 Point 4 of the "Tegucigalpa Declaration." Final Communiqué of the Meeting of Central American Presidents. 13 December 1991.

44 Article 3 of the Tegucigalpa Protocol I 1991.

the European Union institutional system (for instance, its institutions include the Meeting of Presidents, a Council of Ministers, an Executive Committee, a General Secretariat as well as a Court of Justice and the Parliament). It also sets a wider goal for integration. The SICA no longer has exclusive economic objectives; rather, it represents the bridge between the traditional system of intergovernmental co-operation and the more advanced "community" legal order, recognising the indivisible character of development, peace, democracy and integration and the use of regional means to achieve them.

The Protocol does not contain specific democratic or rule of law provisions for being or remaining members thereof. Its spirit, though, and its entire conception (in particular Articles 3 on the objectives and 4 on the aims of the Protocol), make participation in it incompatible with at least not formal multi-party democracies In addition, the SICA member states adopted in 1995 a specific Treaty on Democratic Security[45] which is an integral part of the SICA system. This Treaty further specifies that the region aims to establish democratic institutions and to allow for the rule of law and the end of military involvement in political life, but still, fails to create a correlation between democratic institutions and regional integration.

Despite the various reversals suffered by the regional integration process in Central America – the permanent strife between the supranational and the intergovernmental model of integration, the refusal of member states to effectively surrender competences to the integrated organisms, the discrepancy, common throughout the Latin American sub-continent, between state commitments and delivering – the SICA is today one of the furthest reaching regional integration schemes of the region. From that point of view, it is interesting to examine its impact on the democratisation of the member states.[46]

As mentioned before, Article 3 of the Tegucigalpa Protocol specifies that "the fundamental objective of the Central American Integration system is to bring about the integration of Central America as a region of peace, freedom, democracy and development" and that "to that end [it reaffirms] the objective... to consolidate democracy and strengthen its institutions on the basis of the existence of Governments elected by universal and free suffrage with secret ballot, and of unrestricted respect for human rights".[47] Article 4 goes further and states that "to attain the above objectives, the Central American Integration System and its members shall proceed in accordance with the following fundamental principles:

45 Framework Treaty on Democratic Security in Central America, San Pedro Sula, Honduras, 15 December 1995.

46 Nyman-Metcalf & Papageorgiou (2005).

47 Article 3 of the Tegucigalpa Protocol I 1991.

(*a*) The protection of, respect for and promotion of human rights shall constitute the fundamental basis of the Central American Integration System;
(*b*) Peace, democracy, development and freedom constitute a harmonious and indivisible whole which shall guide the acts of the States Members of the Central American Integration System."[48]

The Protocol does not include any mechanism for sanctioning or expelling a member that does not abide to these principles, but Articles 5 and 6 (on the membership) stipulate that "the Members of the Central American Integration System shall be those Central American States that fully accept the obligations set forth in this Charter ..., and that implement this Charter in accordance with the provisions of article 36 hereof" as well as that "member States shall undertake to abstain from the adoption of any unilateral measure that may endanger the attainment of the objectives and compliance with the fundamental principles of the Central American Integration System".[49] Interestingly these provisions were not invoked when Honduras' participation was questioned following the June 2009 coup.

II.2.3. THE ANDEAN COMMUNITY OF NATIONS

The Andean Community of Nations (henceforth CAN from its Spanish acronym *Communidad Andina de Naciones*) is the last transformation of the oldest existing integration system in Southern America. Founded in 1969 as the Andean Pact (or the countries of the Cartagena Agreement) it has been justly described as the integration "phoenix".[50] It was established on the wake of the economic integration impetus in Latin America in the 1960s and came as a result of an increasing uneasiness among these Latin American countries which felt that they were being left behind in the regional economic cooperation schemes promoted in the 1950s and 1960s by the UN Economic Commission for Latin American and the Caribbean (CEPAL) and its drive towards the "import-substitution development". This uneasiness led these countries of "moderate development" (Colombia, Peru, Ecuador, Bolivia, Chile and, later on in 1973, Venezuela) to establish a distinct sub-regional integration scheme which emphasized the gradual integration and took more into account the specific level of development of each country.[51] The negotiations led to the signature of the Cartagena agreement, signed in Bogota in May 25, 1969 and

---

48 Article 4 of the Tegucigalpa Protocol I 1991.
49 Articles 5 and 6 of the Tegucigalpa Protocol I 1991.
50 F. Barthelemy, *Un continent en quête d'unité – l'au-delà du rêve* (Les éditions ouvrières, Paris. 1991), p. 67.
51 *Ibid.*

the establishment of the Andean Pact, which entered into force on 16 October 1969.[52]

The objectives of the Pact were exclusively economic: it provided for the establishment of a free trade area, and, later on, of a customs union with a common external tariff and the coordination of national economic policies stressing the need for a state-led industrialisation of the region and the setting up of strong ties of economic inter-dependency between member states. The integration model promoted by the Andean Pact was based on two main principles: on the one hand, "closed regionalism" that is an integration model that relied on market expansion through common industrial and commercial policies and protection from third countries; and on the other, an emphasis on institutionalism, that is the adoption of the neo-functionalist theories of integration which stressed the role of institutions in the integration process.[53] All through its existence, the Pact suffered from the development asymmetries and the ideological, political and economic tensions among its members, which constituted a permanent centrifugal element. Indeed, even today the Andean Community is considered a territory expressing most crudely the tensions between the various conceptions of integration in Latin America.[54] The economic objectives of the pact were not fulfilled,[55] and intra-zonal trade remains low.[56] On 31 December 2005 and following many years of delays, the Community achieved the free trade area (following the total re-incorporation of Peru, which had withdrawn from the Pact in 1992 and joined it again 1997), which still faces, though, some implementation problems. On the other hand, it still lacks an effective customs union, despite more than 40 years of efforts. Although, in theory a common external tariff exists since 1995 (with the adoption of Decision 370), the customs union has never been implemented

52 Membership in the Andean integration system has changed over time. The five founding members of the Andean Pact were joined by Venezuela in 1973. Chile withdrew from the Pact in 1976 after the military coup of 1973. In 2006, President Hugo Chavez withdrew Venezuela from the Andean Community, and Chile re-joined as an associate member. Following a cooperation agreement between Mercosur and the Andean Community, all Mercosur members gained associate status in the CAN.

53 D. Sanchez Rodriguez, "The Andean Community" in L. Levi, G. Finizio, N. Vallinoto (eds.), *The Democratization of International Institutions – First International Democracy Report* Routledge, 2013.

54 L. Gil, D. Paikin, "Mapa de la integración Regional en América Latina." *Procesos e instituciones. Nueva Sociedad. Revista latinoamericana de ciencias sociales.* Policy Paper. September 2013 in www.nuso.org/upload/articulos/Analisis_mapa_de_integracion_regional.pdf.

55 See R. Pachon, "La CAN y sus relaciones con Europa y Suramérica" in *Revista de la Integración No 2 – La construcción de la integración suramericana.* July 2008. Edition of the General Secretariat of the Andean Community, p. 42.

56 Intra-zonal trade in the Andean Community has consistently been less than 10% of total trade of its member states. In 2012, exports from the four full members of the Community (Ecuador, Peru, Colombia and Bolivia) amounted to 137.991 million US dollars while intra-community exports were 10.349 million US dollars. Source: Indicadores economicos de la CAN in http://estadisticas.comunidadandina.org/eportal (last access 10/6/2015).

in practice due to the member states' reluctance or incapacity to abide to the customs union requirements.[57]

As pointed out above, the phoenix-like condition of the Community was further enhanced by its re-organisation, in particular the adoption, in 1996 of the Trujillo Protocol.[58] The Protocol renamed the Andean Pact into the Andean Community of Nations and further reinforced its already impressive institutional framework, in particular following its initial re-organisation, in 1979. The Trujillo Protocol provided CAN with a more political objective[59] and an institutional structure that emulates the European Union's institutional mechanism. It is thus composed of a supreme political organ (the Andean Presidential Council, entrusted with taking the major political decisions), a permanent executive organ, the General Secretariat (formerly the Junta), a permanent body entrusted with the Community's foreign relations and the coordination between the various integration organs (the Council of Ministers of Foreign Affairs), a legislative organ (the Commission, composed of the trade ministers, or their representatives, of member states), a parliamentary body (the Andean Parliament) with a consultative role and a regional court of justice (the Andean Tribunal) aiming to rule on issues of application of integration law.[60]

As mentioned above, the Andean Pact faced from its beginnings serious cohesion problems. Intra-zonal trade remained secondary and integration did not increase substantially its volume. Already in 1976, Chile, its most economically advanced member, withdrew as a result of the different economic and political path followed by the then ruling military junta. Bolivia was gradually dragged towards the orbit of Mercosur, trying to find a way to sit between or in both organisms. The Andean Pact was soon reduced to its Andean members; even they did not seem to give priority to establishing a strong Andean Community, preferring bilateral free-trade agreements with the major economic powers, in particular the US. Border disputes – and even wars – arose often

57 The customs union was effectively abandoned in 2007 by means of Decision 624, which stated that Bolivia, Colombia, Ecuador and Peru could fix their own national tariffs within the limits set by the World Trade Organization (WTO).In addition, an extra problem is the fact that member states are allowed, by means of Decision 598 adopted in 2004, to negotiate trade agreements with third countries or country groups. This possibility increases centrifugal tensions in the Community and renders even more difficult the adoption of common tariff policies.

58 *Protocolo Modificatorio que crea la Comunidad Andina y establece el Sistema Andino de Integración* adopted during the 8th Meeting of the Presidents of the Andean Pact in the city of Trujillo on March 10, 1996 (Protocolo de Trujillo).

59 The preamble of the Trujillo Act provides that "...the Andean Presidents have decided to consolidate and promote closer ties of cooperation by strengthening their democracies, eradicating poverty, promoting sustainable development and environmental conservation, opening up their markets and coordinating their positions in various international negotiating forums".

60 In addition, the Protocol of Trujillo established a number of accessory consultative bodies (among them, the Andean Enterprise Consultative Council and the Andean Labour Consultative Council), the Simon Bolivar Andean University etc.

between its members (between Ecuador and Peru in 1981 and again in 1995, a Colombian air raid to Ecuador by Colombia in 2008 pursuing FARC rebels, and skirmishes between Colombia and Venezuela in 2009). The mediation was rarely provided by the Andean system – it was rather the Organisation of American States (OAS) or other external parties that tried to defuse the problems.

Although the Cartagena Agreement already stated in its preamble that their enterprise was founded in the principles of "equality, justice, peace, solidarity and democracy", there was little done for regional democracy in the following years – a pattern common to all regional integration mechanisms of the continent at the time. It was only in 1980, when all Andean Pact countries had returned to civilian governments that the Presidents of the member states signed, in Riobamba (Ecuador) a Charter of Conduct (*Carta de Conducta*) which stated that Andean Pact countries should be democratic and respect human, political, economic and social rights as a fundamental rule in their internal behaviour.[61] The document established a number of indicators defining the democratic character of the member countries, and provided that respect for human rights, constitutes a fundamental rule for internal conduct of member states, while defence of these rights is an international obligation. Still, such declarations lacked any significant effect, constituting mere proclamations of good intentions. In 1998, though, member states signed in Bogota a Declaration on Democracy and Integration.[62] This was followed by the signature of the "Additional Protocol to the Cartagena Agreement" on the 'Andean Community Commitment to Democracy' signed in Oporto (Portugal) in 1998. The Protocol stated that democratic order and legally constituted states constitute prerequisites for the Andean integration. It provided in Article 1 that "Democratic institutions and a constitutional state that are fully effective are essential to the political cooperation and the process of economic, social, and cultural integration carried out within the framework of the Cartagena Agreement and of other instruments of the Andean Integration System" and that the provisions of the Protocol would "be applicable if the democratic order is disrupted in any of the member states".[63]

The Protocol sets a series of institutional responses in "the event of developments that could be considered a disruption of the democratic order in any member state".[64] To that end, it provides for consultations between the other member states and "if possible, with the country involved in order to examine the nature of those developments", the holding of a meeting of "the Council of Foreign Ministers" to "ascertain whether the developments in question constitute a

61 Barthelemy (1991).

62 "*Declaración del Consejo Presidencial Andino sobre Democracia e Integración*". It was signed in Bogotá on 7 August 1998, on the occasion of the installation of the new Colombian President, Andres Pastrana.

63 "Additional Protocol to the Cartagena Agreement on the Andean Community Commitment to Democracy', Oporto, 1998.

64 *Ibid.*

disruption of the democratic order" and specific sanctions "in accordance with the seriousness and the evolution of political developments in the country in question". These sanctions include the "suspension of the member state's participation in any of the bodies of the Andean Integration System" its suspension from "the international cooperation projects carried out by the Community", the extension of the suspension to other System bodies, such as "its disqualification by Andean financial institutions from obtaining access to facilities or loans" and "other measures and actions deemed relevant in accordance with international law".[65] These measures shall be adopted by the Andean Council of Foreign Ministers through a Decision, without the participation of the Member state involved. It also provides that the Community shall "continue to take diplomatic steps to bring about the reestablishment of democratic order in the Member state in question and that such measures "shall cease through a Decision once the Andean Council of Foreign Ministers ascertains that democratic order has been reestablished".

The Protocol sets the democratic clauses of the integration process and is the most far-reaching provision directly linking regional integration and democracy in the American continent and even foreseeing sanctions in case of democratic breach. In another text, the 2002 Andean Charter on the Promotion and Protection of Human Rights[66] the Community further enhances the democratic character of integration; the Charter provides in article 4 that member states commit themselves to the "preservation, protection and defense of democracy" and in Article 5 to respect the rulings of the Inter-American Court of Human Rights. More significantly, Article 16 commits member states to "defend the democratic order in the Andean region".

Most of these documents, however, remain of a declaratory nature. Although democracy and rule of law are considered essential conditions for integration, they have not proven to be particularly effective in their implementation. As elsewhere in the Americas, regional integration organisms lack the effective capacity, and legitimacy, to intervene in favour of democratic principles in case a member breaches democratic rules.

II.2.4. MERCOSUR

Mercosur (from the Spanish acronym *Mercado Común del Cono Sur*) is the last and perhaps most significant sub-regional integration scheme in Latin America. It was established in 1991, by the Treaty of Asunción, or Treaty establishing a common market between Argentina, Brazil, Paraguay and

65 *Ibid.* Sanchez Rodriguez (2013).

66 Andean Charter on the Promotion and Protection of Human Rights, Guayaquil, 23 July 2002.

Uruguay[67] after a number of bilateral economic integration initiatives had already allowed for a rapprochement between Argentina and Brazil. The two major countries of Southern America had followed completely different paths since independence[68] and maintained rather distant relations[69] throughout the 20th century. The fall of the military regimes in both countries more or less at the same time, in the mid-1980s,[70] and global economic developments persuaded their newly elected democratic leaders to move towards closer economic relations which eventually led to the establishment of a number of bilateral agreements. The association in the process of Paraguay and Uruguay, two small countries highly dependent on both Argentina and Brazil, which had, nonetheless, the ability to dilute the risk of any direct confrontation of the two "big" member states, allowed for the creation of the biggest trade bloc in South America.

Mercosur has been described as an intergovernmental structure with community objectives.[71] Although its objectives – the gradual instauration of a common market – remind a lot the early objectives of the European Economic Community (EEC), it opted, during a transitory period, for a "light" institutional structure including only three intergovernmental institutions (the Common Market Council, the Common Market Group and the Mercosur Trade Commission) whose specific competences were not totally clear. It was later, in 1996[72] with the Ouro Preto Protocol[73], that it acquired its final institutional makeup: this remains, to a large extent, that of an intergovernmental organism.

---

67 The group's membership increased in the event. Chile, Bolivia, Peru, Colombia and Venezuela became associate members while this latter country signed in 2006 a Protocol allowing for its full membership. Ratification of this Protocol was stalled by Paraguay on the grounds that the country did not respect the democratic principles. In July 2012, after Paraguay's suspension from membership, the other Mercosur member states announced the formal integration of Venezuela in the group.

68 While in Argentina federalists and centralists fought for power following the departure of the Spanish, in Brazil, monarchy managed to maintain the colonial era unity of the country. In the early 20th century, Argentina opened up to European emigration and turned into one of the richest countries in the world while Brazil failed to overcome domestic social and political conflicts. When Brazil started finding its way to development and became a regional power, Argentina was falling into a steady decline, unable to complete its economic modernization.

69 Relations between the two was also described as 'rival' but efforts to cooperate were also numerous and sometimes outnumbered those of rivalry. See G.L. Gardini, *The Origins of Mercosur. Democracy and Regionalization in South America* Series Studies of the Americas (Palgrave Macmillan February 2010), p. 18.

70 Argentina became again a democracy in December 1983, while Brazil in March 1985.

71 J.A.E. Vervaele, "Mercosur and regional integration in Southern America" in *International and Comparative Law Quarterly* vol. 54. April 2005, pp. 387–410.

72 Article 18 of the Treaty provided that "Prior to the establishment of the common market on 31 December 1994, the States Parties shall convene a special meeting to determine the final institutional structure of the administrative organs of the common market, as well as the specific powers of each organ and its decision-making procedures".

73 Additional Protocol to the Treaty of Asunción on the Institutional Structure of Mercosur, Protocol of Ouro Preto, 17 December 1994 (entry in force 1996).

According to article 1 of the Ouro Preto Protocol "the institutional structure of Mercosur has the following organs:

I – The Common Market Council (CMC);
II – The Common Market Group (GMC);
III – The Mercosur Trade Commission (CCM);
IV – The Joint Parliamentary Commission (CPC);
V – The Social and Economic Forum (FCES);
VI – The Mercosur Administrative Secretariat (SAM).[74]

The Common Market Council (*Consejo del Mercado Comun*) is "the highest organ of Mercosur which bears the political leadership of the integration process and decision-making to ensure the fulfilment of the objectives set by the Treaty of Asunción and to achieve the final constitution of the common market" (Article 3). It is composed of Ministers of Foreign Affairs and of Economy, while at least once a year, it will meet with the participation of presidents of member states (Article 6). It is assisted in this task by the Common Market group (*Grupo Mercado Comun*), which is the executive branch of the organization; it consists of four full and four alternates members for each country, appointed by their respective governments, and coordinated by the Ministries of Foreign Affairs. Among its tasks are to propose decisions to the Common Market Council and to implement this latter's decisions while it also runs working and other ad hoc groups as well as holding specialized meetings. A Mercosur Trade Commission (*Comisión de Comercio del Mercosur*), under the authority of the Group, is competent for trade and competition issues as well as entrusted with dispute settlement in these areas.[75]

The Ouro Preto Protocol introduced three new organs in its institutional structure, which were absent from the original Treaty.[76] The Joint Parliamentary Commission, a consultative organ representing national parliaments, the Social and Economic Forum, representing the organised social and economic forces of each country and the Mercosur Administrative Secretariat "operating as a support body [and]… responsible for providing services to the other organs of Mercosur" established in Montevideo. The Protocol also provided legal personality to the organization (Article 34) which was not foreseen in the Asunción Treaty, while Article 38 set an explicit obligation to enact decisions taken by stipulating that "States Parties undertake to adopt all necessary measures to ensure, in their respective territories, compliance with rules issued by the Mercosur organs".

---

74 *Ibid.* Article 1.

75 The Ouro Preto Protocol (www.sice.oas.org/trade/mrcsr/ourop/ourop_e.asp), also Vervaele (2005).

76 For a detailed analysis of the history and institutional structure of Mercosur, see M. Luna Pont "Southern American Common Market (MERCOSUR)" in L. Levi, G. Finizio, N. Vallinoto (eds.), *The Democratization of International Institutions* (Routledge 2014), pp. 261–285.

A further institutional revision came about with the Olivos Protocol, adopted on 18 February 2002,[77] which established, in Asunción, the Permanent Court of Review of Mercosur (*Tribunal Permanente de Revisión – TPR*).[78] The Court is a principal organ of the Mercosur system[79] and is entrusted with the examination and solution to appeals against the rulings of the Ad Hoc Arbitration Tribunals. In addition it can act as a single jurisdictional instance if so requested by the parties and when member states request the urgency procedure;[80] it emits consultative opinions following a relevant request by the member states or decision-making organs of Mercosur or by the supreme courts of member states, or even by the Mercosur Parliament. The Protocol explicitly provides that the rulings (both of the Ad hoc Arbitration tribunals and of TPR) are compulsory for the States Parties in the dispute and will have the force of *res iudicata*.[81] The Protocol also established an Administrative-Labor Court (*Tribunal Administrativo-Laboral* TAL) to hear and resolve disputes related to labour matters arising between the Secretariat of Mercosur and its staff.

As stated above, the initial objective of Mercosur was simply to allow for economic integration. Nowhere in the fundamental texts of the organisation were there any references to democratic institutions – although implicitly it was acknowledged that authoritarian regimes were not able to provide for the regional political openness necessary to establish a common market. Gradually though, and as Mercosur acquired some political features – notably while trying to secure a free trade agreement with the EU, which required explicit commitment to democratic institutions[82] – it adopted more rules on guaranteeing democratic rule among member states. Thus the Declaration of the Presidents' Meeting in Las Leñas (Argentina) in June 1992, stated for the first time that "the Presidents reaffirmed that the full exercise of democratic institutions

---

77 The Protocol entered in force on 1 January 2004. The Court started operating on 13 August 2004.

78 Originally, the Treaty of Asunción did not provide for a way to solve disputes among member states. In 1991, the Brasilia Protocol (Common Market Council Decision N° 01/91 *Protocolo de Brasilia Para la Solucion de Controversias*) established a dispute settlement system, based on ad hoc Arbitration tribunals.

79 Member states initially wanted to avoid a regional court, supposedly expensive and politically annoying; the need for a court of Mercosur, though, became evident as it advanced into various areas of activities and disputes arose on the interpretation of decisions. In this context it is interesting to mention that the preamble of the Olivos Protocol mentioned "the need to guarantee the correct interpretation, application and respect of the basic instruments of the integration process and all normative texts of Mercosur in a consistent and systematic manner".

80 The urgency procedure was, in fact, requested by Paraguay following the Mendoza Summit decision to suspend the country's membership in Mercosur. See below.

81 It must be pointed out, nevertheless, that the Court is not a supranational court, insofar as access to the Court is not allowed to individuals or moral persons. See Luna Pont (2014), p. 267.

82 B. Andreosso-O'Callaghan, "Market Access and Trade Facilitation" (Chapter 16) in T. Christiansen, E. Kirchner and P. Murray, *The Palgrave Handbook of EU-Asia Relations* (Palgrave Macmillan 2013), pp. 263–276 at p. 266.

is an essential course for the existence and development of Mercosur".[83] In June 1996, a further step was taken with the Presidential Declaration on the Democratic Commitment in Mercosur[84] which reiterated the need for an "effective application of representative democracy" among Mercosur member states and the "incompatibility of alterations to the democratic order with the continuation of the integration process for the member state concerned".[85] This commitment took a more formal expression in the so-called Ushuaia Protocol on the Democratic Commitment of Mercosur.[86] The Protocol was, at the time, the most advanced text in the field of democratic values in Mercosur and, indeed, throughout Latin America. It reiterates the principles of the Treaty of Asunción and, in Article 1, it stipulates that "the full exercise of democratic institutions is an essential condition for the development of integration processes between States Parties to this Protocol". However, in difference with other similar texts, the Protocol provides for possible sanctions. Article 3 warns that "any breach in the democratic order in one of the States Parties to this Protocol shall lead to the application of the procedures foreseen" in the Protocol. Initially the procedures shall include consultations between the State affected and the others; in case consultations fail to produce results, the other states shall "examine the nature and scope of the measures to be applied, taking into account the gravity of the situation…such measures will start with the suspension of the right to participate in the institutions of the various integration processes till the suspension of the rights and obligations arising from such processes".[87] Any such measure shall be decided by consensus of the remaining states parties and shall cease, again by consensus, when the states verify that there has been a "complete restoration of the democratic order".[88] The Protocol is binding for the Mercosur member states and it also has to be adopted by those states that wish to get associate status.[89]

Adherence to the Ushuaia Protocol became a prerequisite for membership in Mercosur and a rare occasion where it mattered was the accession of

83 Presidential Declaration of Las Leñas, point 2. 26–27 June 1992, in the electronic site of the organization www.mercosur.int/innovaportal/v/273/1/secretaria/estructura_institucional_del_mercosur.

84 Presidential Declaration of Potrero de Los Funes (San Luis). 25 June 1996. In www.urjc.es/ceib/espacios/observatorio/gobernabilidad/documentos/democracia/Gob-I-03.pdf.

85 It should be noted that this commitment was adopted in conjunction with the failed attempt of a coup in Paraguay on April 1996; on that occasion, the foreign ministers of the other Mercosur member states visited Asunción in order to demonstrate their commitment to maintaining democratic institutions in the country. See E. González Urrutia, "*Mercosur y la Clausula Democratica*" in www.nuevamayoria.com/ES/ANALISIS/urrutia/070306.html. March 6, 2007.

86 Ushuaia Protocol on democratic commitment in the Mercosur, the Republic of Bolivia and the Republic of Chile. Ushuaia, 24 July 1998. Entry into force: 17 January 2002. No 37341. UNTS. Treaty series. March 2002.

87 Article 5 of the Ushuaia Protocol.

88 Article 7 of the Protocol.

89 Decision 18/04 of the Common Market Council (CMC) stipulated that all ALADI member states that are interested in associating themselves with Mercosur must adhere to the Protocol as well as the 1996 Presidential Declaration on the Democratic Commitment in Mercosur.

Venezuela to Mercosur. Venezuela, an associate member since 1998, applied for full membership status in 2005 and accession negotiations started almost immediately.[90] Though the negotiations were concluded quickly (the Accession Protocol was signed already in 2006), Paraguay did not ratify the Protocol: the objection came from the Senate of the country, where the opposition to the then President, Fernando Lugo, held the majority, which alleged that the government of Venezuela did not abide with the Ushuaia Protocol in terms of respect of human rights.[91] Although this position was determined by national and ideological reasoning (the Conservative Senate wanted to obstruct the President's left-leaning positions in favour of Venezuela), the debate brought to international attention the provisions of the Ushuaia Protocol and incidentally almost broke Mercosur's general rule on adoption of decisions by consensus.[92]

The provisions of the Ushuaia Protocol were invoked in order to suspend Paraguay from Mercosur in June 2012, following the hasty impeachment and destitution of President Lugo by the Paraguay Congress. Alleging that the destitution of the President constituted a breach of the democratic order and on the basis of the Protocol, the other member states, by means of a Declaration prior to the Mercosur Summit in Mendoza on 29 June 2012, decided to apply the sanctions and suspend the country's membership in Mercosur.[93] This decision – clearly politically motivated – was widely considered of doubtful legality.[94] It remains, nonetheless, the only case in Latin America of the use of a democratic

---

[90] Decision 29/2005 of the CMC.

[91] Such opposition was not limited in Paraguay alone. The Brazilian Senate also had misgivings and delayed ratification on human rights grounds. A Brazilian senator even qualified, in this context, the government of Venezuela as a "dictatorial government practicing a totalitarian democracy". See www.montevideo.com.uy/notnoticias_98349_1.html on 10.12.2009.

[92] The President of Uruguay, Jose Mujica, had suggested, before the Mercosur Presidential Summit of December 2011, that Mercosur obviates from the rules of unanimous ratification in the case of Venezuela, suggesting instead, that the presidential consent (in this case, Paraguay's president) would be sufficient for accession. This, obviously, illegal "formula" as it was called was finally abandoned. See www.elobservador.com.uy/noticia/215368/mercosur-intenta-desenredar-la-compleja-entrada-de-venezuela/ from 19.12.2011.

[93] The final common communiqué of the Presidents stated that "5. [They] Reiterated their condemnation of the breach of democratic order produced in [...] Paraguay, stressed that the restoration of democratic institutions is essential to the development of the integration process and decided to suspend, under the Protocol of Ushuaia [...], the right of that country to participate in the organs of MERCOSUR". The communiqué insisted that "the application of this measure" should not "cause injury to the Paraguayan people" and confirmed that suspension "shall cease when, according to the provisions of Article 7 of the Protocol of Ushuaia, the full restoration of democratic order in the party concerned is verified". See the final communiqué in www.dipublico.com.ar/9407/cumbre-del-mercosur-mendoza-2012-comunicado-conjunto-de-los-presidentes-de-los-estados-partes/. At the same time, the three presidents decided to seize the occasion to allow the entry of Venezuela to MERCOSUR and "called a meeting for the purpose of the official admission of Venezuela to MERCOSUR on July 31, 2012" in Rio de Janeiro.

[94] See in particular A. Pastori, "*Inconsistencias jurídicas internas del Mercosur posteriores a la suspensión de Paraguay y a la Adhesión de Venezuela: ¿qué le hace una mancha más al tigre?*", Study n. 6/2013. September 2013. Consejo Uruguayano para las Relaciones Internacionales.

clause to condemn a violation of democratic rules in a member state. Eventually, Paraguay was admitted again in Mercosur, after the newly elected President, Horacio Cartes, was sworn in, in August 2013,[95] and its Congress ratified Venezuela's accession to Mercosur in December 2013.[96]

Before this event, Mercosur advanced further in adopting democratic rules for its member states with the negotiation and adoption of the Montevideo Protocol on the Commitment for Democracy (also known as Ushuaia II Protocol).[97] The election of left-wing presidents in Uruguay and in Paraguay allowed for a stronger emphasis on human rights (which to a large extent covered for the lack of progress in achieving the objectives of Mercosur). As a result the Montevideo Protocol came into being. The text is not very different from the text of the Ushuaia Protocol although it contains more specifics and expands its scope, but in fact replicates the provisions of Unasur's "Additional Protocol to the constitutive Treaty of Unasur on Democratic Commitment" adopted in Georgetown, Guyana, some months earlier, on 26 November 2010.[98] Thus the provisions of the Protocol shall apply, not only when there is a "breach in the democratic order in one of the States Parties" but also when there is "a breach or threat of breach of the democratic order, a violation of the constitutional order or any situation that jeopardises the legitimate exercising of power and the application of the values and principles of democracy".[99] In the event of such a situation, the Presidents (or in their absence, the Foreign Ministers) of the remaining member states shall meet, at the request of the affected member state or any other Mercosur member, in an extraordinary enlarged meeting of the Common Market Council to be held in the country that is holding the rotating presidency of the organisation. The Presidents shall promote immediate consultations with the authorities in the affected country, will "use their good offices and take diplomatic steps to promote the restoration of democracy in the affected country". If such consultations fail to produce results or if the constitutional authorities of the affected country are prevented from holding them, the remaining states "shall consider, by consensus, the nature and the scope of the measures to be applied".[100] The Protocol provides that the constitutional government of a member state may, when it considers that it faces one of the situations mentioned above, request the member states' cooperation in order to

95 See www.la-razon.com/mundo/Mercosur-confirma-reintegro-Paraguay-Cartes_0_1868213259.html. 12.07.2011.

96 See www.telam.com.ar/notas/201312/45200-el-congreso-paraguayo-aprobo-el-ingreso-de-venezuela-al-mercosur.html. 18.12.2013.

97 *Protocolo de Montevideo sobre el Compromiso con la Democracia en el Mercosur* (Ushuaia II). In www.mercosur.int/innovaportal/file/4827/1/protocolo_de_montevideo-ushuaia_ii_es.pdf. Adopted on 20 December 2011. It has not entered into force yet.

98 See the relevant chapter on Unasur. The English text of the Additional Protocol can be found in www.sela.org/attach/258/EDOCS/SRed/2011/06/T023600004782-0-PROTOCOL_TO_THE_CONSTITUTIVE_TREATY_OF_UNASUR_ON_COMMITMENT_TO_DEMOCRACY.pdf.

99 Montevideo Protocol, Article 1.

100 *Ibid.* Article 3.

strengthen and preserve the country's democratic institutions. In such a case, and with the consent of the requesting government, Mercosur may provide committees of support, cooperation and technical assistance of public commissions to assist the dialogue among the involved political, social and economic actors in the country concerned.[101]

Article 6 of the Protocol also provides for specific measures to be taken – only if there is a breach or threat of breach of the democratic order in the affected country: as in the case of the Unasur Georgetown Protocol, these measures include the suspension of the right to participate in the various Mercosur organs; partial or complete closure of land borders, including the suspension and/or limitation of trade, air and maritime traffic, communications and provision of energy, services and supplies; the suspension of the rights and benefits enjoyed under the Mercosur treaty; advocacy to suspend this state's membership and trade links with other regional or international organisations and bilateral agreements; support of efforts by international or regional organisations, in particular the United Nations to resolve in a peaceful and democratic way the situation; and the adoption of additional political and diplomatic sanctions. All such measures should be proportional to the gravity of the situation and would go together with continuous diplomatic efforts from the part of Mercosur to solve the situation.

Article 11 provides that the Protocol shall enter in force after its ratification by the fourth member state. At the time of the writing of this book (June 2015), the Protocol was ratified only by Venezuela,[102] while it was rejected by the Assembly and the Senate of Paraguay in 2012,[103] in the wake of Paraguay's suspension from Mercosur.

In addition to the Ushuaia and Montevideo Protocols, Mercosur established, in 2004, a Centre for the Promotion of the Rule of Law (*Centro MERCOSUR de Promoción del Estado de Derecho,* or CMPED)[104] in order to reinforce the development of the rule in the organisation. According to the decision, CMPED will "analyse and support the development of the state, democratic governance and all aspects related to the regional integration processes, with special emphasis on Mercosur" and, to this end, it shall undertake scientific research, conferences and other dissemination activities, meetings with academia and civil society etc. The Centre operates in the seat of the Permanent Review Tribunal of Mercosur, in Asunción. In the same

101 *Ibid.* Article 5.

102 State of ratifications and entries into force of treaties, protocols and conventions of Mercosur, in www.mercosur.int/t_generic.jsp?contentid=4827&site=1&channel=secretaria.

103 See www.noticias24.com/internacionales/noticia/46593/paraguay-rechaza-protocolo-ushuaia-ii-invocado-por-el-mercosur-para-suspenderle/.

104 Decision 24/2004 of the Common Market Council. In www.mercosur.int/innovaportal/v/580/1/secretaria/decisiones_2004.

context was established, in 2007, an Observatory for Democracy[105], entrusted with contributing to the reinforcement of the objectives of the Ushuaia Protocol, following the electoral processes in member states, coordinating the activities of the Mercosur Body of Election Observers and with undertaking other activities related to the consolidation of democracy in the region. The Observatory operates in association with the Centre for the Promotion of the Rule of Law in Asunción.

As already mentioned above, the Ouro Preto Protocol established a Joint Parliamentary Commission, appointed by the respective national parliaments, with the objective "to endeavour to speed up the corresponding internal procedures in the States Parties in order to ensure the prompt entry into force of the decisions taken by the Mercosur organs [... and to...] assist with the harmonisation of legislations, as required to advance the integration process". Later on, by the Constitutive Protocol of the Mercosur Parliament,[106] in December 2005, which entered into force in 2007, the Commission was replaced by the Mercosur Parliament, which started meeting in May 2007.[107] Although the Parliament's role is mostly consultative,[108] with the right to issue opinions over matters linked to the development of the integration process, it has specific competence to watch over the "preservation of the democratic regimes in States Parties" and "to prepare and publish an annual report on the situation of human rights in the States Parties".[109]

Following the establishment by Mercosur of the Observatory for Democracy, the Parliament also established its own observatory (*Observatorio de la Democracia en el Parlamento del MERCOSUR-ODPM*)[110] which expressed the Parliament's need to be actively involved in the protection of democratic institutions in member states. The ODPM is not an institution but rather a parliamentary commission, and its objectives coincide, to a large extent with

---

105 '*Observatorio de la Democracia del MERCOSUR*'. Decision 05/07 of the Common Market Council in www.mercosur.int/msweb/Normas/normas_web/Decisiones/ES/2007/DEC%20005-2007_ES_Observatorio.pdf.

106 *Protocolo Constitutivo del Parlamento del Mercosur* (decision of the Common Market Council 49/04) in http://archivo.presidencia.gub.uy/_Web/proyectos/2006/02/43%20RPOTOCOLO_06%2002%202006_00001.PDF.

107 The Parliament is composed of 18 members per member state, appointed by their respective national parliaments. Although both the Constitutive Treaty and later presidential meetings as well as the Parliament's resolutions provided for the direct election of its members – the latest such decision provided for an election during the year 2014 – and the Parliament has adopted a decision on its composition that forfeits parity between member states in favor of a degressive proportionality – each timetable is postponed; only Paraguay has proceeded so far to the election of its members.

108 C. Dri, "At What Point does a Legislature Become Institutionalized? The Mercosur Parliament's Path". *Brazilian Political Science Review* (BPSR) Vol. 2 n. 2 (2009).

109 Article 4 of the Constitutive Treaty.

110 Disposal (a disposal – in Spanish *Disposición* – is an internal decision of the Parliament) 26/2008.

those of the Observatory for Democracy.[111] It is composed of 3 Mercosur parliamentarians per state. Though these Observatories do not produce major results, they are used in cases of crisis and the electoral monitoring aspect is quite used by now among the members of the bloc.[112]

Mercosur, more than 20 years after its creation, is still trying to set its pace and its objectives. The initial economic integration objectives are not fulfilled. Successive economic and political crises have prevented the full establishment of a common market and intra-zonal trade is still rather limited. The Brazilian financial crisis in 1998 and Argentina's default in 2002 hindered efforts for further integration under the original 'open regionalism' model, at the same time as Brazil, its biggest member, opened up to the world markets on its own. The return of left-leaning governments in all Mercosur members after 2000 (including Paraguay after 2008) allowed for the group to reinvent itself, less as an economic integration organisation and more as a political concentration one. Thus, it gave more emphasis on non-economic elements, such as the promotion of democratic principles and rule of law. In this context, it adopted a number of instruments and institutions to protect democratic institutions and constitutional order in its member states. Although direct military intervention is currently less of a threat to Latin American democratic institutions compared to increased authoritarian populism, the emphasis on democratic principles can be used as an extra protection to member states and their societies.

II.2.5. UNASUR

UNASUR (Union of South American Nations, in Spanish *Unión de Naciones Sudamericanas*) is one of the most recent multilateral organisations of Latin America. It is not properly speaking an integration organisation[113] but rather an organisation that fosters cooperation between South American states, in the line of the long series of other similar efforts (the Contadora and the Rio Groups)

111 See the disposal 07/09 of the Parliament on the rules of procedure of the Observatory in www.parlamentodelmercosur.org/innovaportal/file/169/1/disp._07.09.pdf.

112 It was, for instance, used in the electoral process in Venezuela in February 2014. See www.telam.com.ar/notas/201402/52158-el-parlamento-del-mercosur-condeno-la-violencia-en-venezuela-y-activara-un-observatorio.html.

113 Although the Constitutive Treaty of Unasur provides, in Article 2 (Objective) that "the objective of the South American Union of Nations is to build, in a participatory and consensual manner, an integration and union among its people" it goes on to explain that this will be done by "...prioritizing political dialogue, social policies, education, energy, infrastructure, financing and the environment, among others...within the framework of strengthening the sovereignty and independence of the States". In addition Article 3 "Specific objectives" enumerates a series of social and economic objectives to attain with an emphasis on cooperation between members rather than some form of political or economic integration and does not pretend to any transfer of sovereign competences to common institutions. See Unasur Constitutive Treaty in www.comunidadandina.org/ingles/csn/treaty.htm.

to establish forms of multilateral cooperation excluding the United States. Similar to ALBA (*Alianza Bolivariana para los Pueblos de nuestra América*) it is set in the trend of the 'post' or 'anti-liberal' tendency of the end of the 1990s and early 2000s when left-leaning or populist governments in the region looked for an alternative to the so-called 'open regionalism' established in the wake of the 'Washington Consensus' and represented by the traditional integration organisms which emphasized neo-liberal economic integration policies.[114]

Its origin has to do with the re-orientation of the regional policy of Brazil following the election of Luiz Inácio Lula da Silva as president of the country in 2002 and the gradual retreat of Mexico from Latin American politics in favour of a more active relationship with the United States. A number of earlier presidential meetings culminated in the Cusco Declaration of the 3rd South American Summit of 8 December 2004[115] which set the foundations of the then South American Community of Nations. The Declaration was a brief and general document, which stated three basic aims for the new organization:

- concerted and coordinated political and diplomatic efforts that will strengthen the region as a differentiated and dynamic factor in its foreign relations;
- the deepening of the convergence between MERCOSUR, the Andean Community and Chile [with the participation of Guyana and Surinam] through the perfecting of the free trade area… and
- the physical integration and integration of energy and communications in South America.

Interestingly, the Declaration stated already the need for a "sharing of democratic systems of government and of a conception of governance resting on the people's participation…and exercise of power with strict adherence to the state of law". Following a long process of negotiations[116], the Constitutive Treaty of Unasur was signed in Brasilia, on 23 May 2008, at the 3th South American Summit.[117] The Treaty reflected the differences between the Venezuelan and the Brazilian visions of this project, namely the emphasis on Unasur as an alternative to the "neo-liberal" model of integration promoted by the Andean Community and

114 J.A. Sanahuja, "*Multilateralismo y regionalismo en clave suramericana: El caso de UNASUR*" in *Los desafíos del multilateralismo en América Latina. Pensamiento proprio*. No. 33. Year 16. January-June 2001.(Edicion Cries 2001), pp. 120–1.

115 *Declaración del Cusco sobre la Comunidad Sudamericana de Naciones*. III Cumbre Presidencial Sudamericana. Cusco, 8 de diciembre de 2004. www.iirsa.org/admin_iirsa_web/Uploads/Documents/oe_cusco05_declaracion_del_cusco_eng.pdf.

116 For a detailed analysis of the early history and institutional structure of Unasur, see N.M. Comini "Union of South American Nations" in L. Levi, G. Finizio, N. Vallinoto (eds.), *The Democratization of International Institutions* (Routledge 2014), pp. 286–295.

117 Following the Cusco Declaration, summits held under the auspices of the South American Community of Nations were re-numbered.

Mercosur or as an "umbrella" organisation for these two integration schemes.[118] As a result, it avoided any reference to the economic integration objectives. In general, the free trade component of Unasur retreated in the final text in favour of a more "political" approach of the organization, allowing it to be characterized more as a "political cooperation organization".[119] It is composed of 12 members (all the Andean Community and Mercosur member states as well as Chile, Suriname and Guyana).

According to the Treaty, Unasur's institutional structure comprises a Council of Heads of State and Government, a Council of Ministers of Foreign Affairs, a Council of Delegates and a General Secretariat.[120] The Treaty also establishes a rotating (*Pro Tempore*) Presidency, entrusted with preparing, calling and chairing the meetings of the different bodies, submitting the annual program of activities of Unasur to the Council of Ministers of Foreign Affairs and the Council of Delegates as well as representation tasks. Real power in Unasur lies with the Council of Heads of State and Government, which establishes policy guidelines and decides on the priorities to be implemented, summons sectoral Ministerial meetings and creates Councils at Ministerial level, decides on the proposals presented by the Council of Ministers of Foreign Affairs and adopts the political guidelines for relations with third parties.[121] The Council of Ministers of Foreign Affairs is basically entrusted with the implementation of the guidelines and decisions of – as well as proposal of decisions to – the Council of Heads of State and Government. Finally, the Council of Delegates is a coordinating body, meeting more frequently, with tasks of preparation and implementation of decisions. The General Secretariat is the only supranational body of Unasur, but its responsibilities are limited to the execution of the tasks conferred upon it by the organs of Unasur and to the coordination and support of the activities of the organization. Its headquarters were fixed in the city of Quito, Ecuador.[122]

Unasur operates on the basis of the consensus among member states. Article 12 provides that all norms should be adopted by consensus.[123] Legislative

---

118 Sanahuja (2001), p. 128.

119 *Ibid.* p. 129.

120 Article 4 of the Constitutive Treaty.

121 *Ibid.* Article 6.

122 The first person appointed to be General Secretary, former Ecuador president Rodrigo Borja, rejected the position, due to the absence of reference to the role of Mercosur and the Andean Community in the Treaty as well as the scarce powers and the strong intergovernmental character of Unasur. Following this, Unasur remained without a General Secretary for two years, when the post was assumed by the country holding the rotating Presidency. In May 2010, Argentine President Néstor Kirchner took over as secretary-general. Following his death, the post remained again vacant and in 2011 it was taken over by a twin mandate of a Colombian and a Venezuelan former ministers. The current General Secretary is former Colombian president, Ernesto Samper. Comini (2014) p. 291.

123 It should be noted that the preamble of the Treaty specifies that "South American integration and South American union are based on the guiding principles of unlimited respect for the sovereignty and territorial integrity and inviolability of States ...".

measures adopted by Unasur shall be binding on Member States once they have been incorporated into each Member State's domestic law, according to its respective internal procedures. Finally the Treaty foresees the creation, subject to an Additional Protocol to the Treaty, of a regional parliament to be set in Cochabamba (Bolivia) and proclaims the full participation of citizens in the process of South American integration.

The existence of democratic institutions in member states was only obliquely mentioned in the Treaty: among the guiding principles of the Treaty, as stated in its preamble, were democracy, citizen participation and pluralism, as well as universal, interdependent and indivisible human rights. In addition, the last paragraph of the preamble proclaimed that "fully functioning democratic institutions and the unrestricted respect for human rights are essential conditions for building a common future of peace, economic and social prosperity and for the development of integration processes among the Member States". Strengthening democracy was also stated among the objectives of the Treaty in Article 2.

Given that Article 26 of the Constitutive Treaty provided that the Treaty would enter into force following the ratification by nine of its 12 members, it took Unasur almost two years to become operative. Its treaty entered into force in March 2011, after Uruguay ratified it on 30 November 2010. However, even before it started formally to exist it had to face a major issue of democratic stability among its member states, in September of 2008, on account of the political trouble in one of its members, Bolivia.[124] On that occasion, Chile, as the rotating presidency of the group, called for an emergency summit of the Unasur heads of state in Santiago, on 15 September 2008. This was held amid divergences among its members, notably Venezuela, which wanted to support the Bolivian president against the secessionist departments and alleged U.S. interference and Brazil and Chile, which considered that such a Unasur position would risk to exacerbate the conflict. On that occasion, Unasur tried to avoid the escalation of violence, the risk of division of the country and, also, to avoid a US implication, either directly or through the OAS.[125] For these reasons, it decided to set up a Commission of Inquiry and to send a delegation to Bolivia in order to establish a dialogue and prevent the deterioration of the situation in the country.[126] The presence of the delegation and the conclusions of the Commission that the events in Pando were a 'crime against humanity' promoted by the state apparatus in that department played an important role in reducing tensions and avoiding an escalation.

124 In August and September 2008, a major political and institutional crisis escalated in Bolivia following the revocation referendum of President Evo Morales, leading to peasants and students being killed in the department of Pando, the proclamation of the state of emergency by the central authorities and a serious risk of civil war in the country.

125 Sanahuja (2001) p. 140.

126 "*Declaración de la Moneda*". In www.comunidadandina.org/unasur/15-9-08com_bolivia.htm.

It must be stressed that this early crisis in Unasur's life – the organization was not even legally existing at the time – is a demonstration of what Unasur's role could be in South American politics: an organization that, through multilateral actions, could avoid both the direct or indirect implication of the United States, could reduce the resistance to possible Brazilian unilateral involvement and could challenge the sacrosanct principle of non-interference into domestic matters. It should be recalled that this initiative was the first one, after the Contadora group of the 1980s, where Latin American countries tried in an organised way to avoid involving U.S. into Latin American matters while at the same time taking initiative to restore peace and democracy through non-violent means.

Another crisis faced by Unasur was the political crisis that sparked in Ecuador, in September 2010, following riots and a refusal to obey orders by part of the police force and rumours of an attempted coup and an attempt to assassinate the Ecuadorian President Rafael Correa. On that occasion, too, the presidents of the Unasur member countries met on 1 October in Buenos Aires to deal with the situation. The declaration adopted in that meeting[127] confirmed Unasur's "strong commitment to the preservation of democratic institutions, rule of law, constitutional order, social peace and full respect for human rights," as "essential conditions for the regional integration process"[128] and condemned the attempted coup against Ecuador's constitutional president. In addition, though, the Summit declared that Unasur would not "tolerate, under any circumstances, any further challenge to the institutional authority or any attempted coup against the civilian power elected legitimately" and that, in such case, Unasur would "take concrete and immediately measures, such as closing the borders and suspending trade, air traffic and the provision of energy, services and other supplies".[129] It is not clear to what extent Unasur' s intervention had an effect on the situation in Ecuador, which to a large extent was exaggerated by Rafael Correa for domestic purposes. It had an effect, though, on the decision of Unasur to adopt a "democratic clause" for its members. In fact, the last paragraph of the Buenos Aires declaration provided to adopt during the "next ordinary meeting of the Council of Heads of State ... an Additional Protocol to the constitutive Treaty of Unasur on Democratic Commitment".[130]

As a result, Unasur adopted, in the 4th Ordinary Meeting of the Council of Heads of State and Government of Unasur, in Georgetown, Guyana, on November 26, 2010, an additional protocol to the Constitutive Treaty, the "Additional Protocol to the constitutive Treaty of Unasur on Democratic

127 '*Declaración de Buenos Aires sobre la situación en Ecuador*' in www.sela.org/attach/258/EDOCS/SRed/2010/10/T023600004362-0-Declaracion_de_Buenos_Aires_sobre_la_situacion_en_Ecuador_-_Unasur_-_1_de_octubre,_2010.pdf. Last access 10/06/2015.

128 *Ibid.*

129 *Ibid.*

130 *Ibid.*

Commitment", adding a so-called "democratic clause" to the charter of the organization.[131] The Protocol includes language similar to other "democratic clauses" texts in South American regional organisms and makes explicit the relationship between membership of Unasur and democratic values. In its preamble it reiterates that "commitment to the promotion, defence and protection of democratic order, Rule of Law and its institutions, Human Rights and fundamental freedoms" are "essential and indispensable conditions for the development of [member states'] integration process and a vital requirement for their participation in Unasur".[132]

Article 1 of the Protocol provides that it shall "apply in the event of a breach or threat of breach of the democratic order, a violation of the constitutional order or any situation that jeopardises the legitimate exercising of power and the application of the values and principles of democracy" and provides for the Council of Heads of State and Government to adopt a number of measures "for the purpose of re-establishing the democratic institutional political process"[133]: these measures include suspension of membership, partial or complete closure of land borders, including the suspension and/or limitation of trade, air and maritime traffic, communications and provision of energy, services and supplies, adoption of additional political and diplomatic sanctions and advocacy to suspend this state's membership and trade links with other regional or international organisations and bilateral agreements.[134] The text provides that Unasur, in addition to sanctions, "shall use its good offices and take diplomatic steps to promote the restoration of democracy in the affected country".[135]

It has to be recalled that all these processes took place while Unasur was, still, not officially in force – which only took place in 2011. The Additional Protocol entered into force on 19 March 2014, 30 days after the receipt of the ninth instrument of ratification – by Uruguay – by Ecuador's Ministry of Foreign Affairs entrusted with the keeping of the relevant instruments of ratification.[136]

It is obvious that Unasur, as a recent organisation, is still unclear as to its objectives and means of actions. It has been marred by tensions between the two big powers of the region, Brazil and Venezuela. Venezuela has tried to use it as a platform to condemn the USA but this has been headed off by other members, although it has threatened to disrupt the organisation's summits. As a result of this ambiguity, as well as the lack of funding and operational

131 The text in English of the Additional Protocol can be found in www.sela.org/attach/258/EDOCS/SRed/2011/06/T023600004782-0-PROTOCOL_TO_THE_CONSTITUTIVE_TREATY_OF_UNASUR_ON_COMMITMENT_TO_DEMOCRACY.pdf. Last access 10/06/2015.
132 *Ibid.*
133 *Ibid.*
134 *Op. cit.* Article 4 of the Additional Protocol.
135 *Ibid.*
136 See http://cancilleria.gob.ec/entro-en-vigencia-clausula-democratica-de-unasur-y-colombia-deposita-instrumento-de-ratificacion/. Last access 25/11/2014.

support (the failure, for a long time, to appoint a secretary-general is indicative thereof) prevents it from playing a major role in South American politics. Although it has acquired a number of other institutions as it consolidated its position,[137] and discussions have taken place about the establishment of a South American Parliament,[138] no specific objectives have been adopted. Unasur seems to be a new form of "soft" integration based on multilateral cooperation with a weak institutional structure. Even its "democratic clause" is less forceful that similar provisions in other regional mechanisms. For instance, in the Paraguay crisis of 2012, Unasur applied the Additional Protocol, though still not in force, to impose sanctions on Paraguay, but it was Mercosur's sanctions and pressure that led to the gradual normalisation of relations. Unasur may change in the future, for the time being, though, it is more an organism promoting multilateral cooperation in South America than an integration tool.

II.2.6. NAFTA

The North American Free Trade Agreement (NAFTA) is interesting as it includes industrialised countries and a developing country and is the furthest-reaching economic integration project between such different parties. NAFTA was agreed in 1992 and entered into force in 1994, building to some extent on earlier US-Canadian integration. Mattli in 1999 predicted success for NAFTA as it meets both supply and demand conditions. The economic gains are potentially high and have entailed a strong lobby for the free trade. Mattli sees the undisputed leading position of the USA as a benefit for clarity and coordination but also recognises the importance of institutions like a novel dispute-solving mechanism. The trade in the region was big before the Agreement and is likely to remain strong and grow.[139] NAFTA has, however, not proven to be particularly successful and it may be speculated if this is linked to its weak institutional structure, which may have meant that there was no possibility to profit from the apparent positive indicators for cooperation. Notably, NAFTA has not moved outside of its purely economic aims to influence governance.

A regional integration body may serve to bind successor governments to a certain policy that it will be difficult to abandon if it is part of a system with many components. Authors suggest the Mexican government saw NAFTA as a way to ensure that future governments would not regress on economic

137 Among others, a Council of Ministers on Energy, on Defense, on Social Development and on Health and Education. Comini (2014) p. 292.

138 *Ibid.*

139 Mattli (1999), p. 179.

openness.[140] Thus in an indirect fashion also an organisation such as NAFTA may have some impact on governance and also democratisation.

II.2.7. ORGANIZATION OF AMERICAN STATES (OAS)

The Organization of American States (OAS) is the oldest and most representative cooperation organism on the American continent. It is an international regional agency according to Article 52 of the UN Charter, set up by the nations of the Western Hemisphere "to achieve an order of peace and justice, to promote their solidarity, to strengthen their collaboration, and to defend their sovereignty, their territorial integrity, and their independence".[141] The OAS was established after the Second World War, similar to other cooperation organizations in Europe and elsewhere in the world.[142] The objectives, structure and operation of the OAS are set out in its constitutive text, the Charter of the OAS, which was substantially amended by the 1967 Protocol of Buenos Aires, which added a number of new objectives for OAS.

The Ninth International Conference of American States, which adopted the Charter of the OAS adopted as well the American Declaration of the Rights and Duties of Man, the first regional document listing and protecting universal human rights on the American continent.[143] The Declaration, unlike its United Nations counterpart, the Universal Declaration of Human Rights, includes both human rights that need to be protected along with duties that individuals have to society. Although, as indicated by its very name, the Declaration was originally supposed to be merely a solemn text, not binding for the signatory States, both the Inter-American Court on Human Rights and the Commission on Human Rights have constantly, in their case law, accepted that the Declaration is also a source of legal obligations for the OAS member states.[144]

The OAS is, first and foremost, an intergovernmental structure, almost completely lacking any supranational element. Major decisions are all taken by

140 D. Nicol, "Business Rights as Human Rights" in T. Campbell, K.D. Ewing and A. Tomkins, *The Legal Protection of Human Rights. Sceptical Essays (Oxford University Press 2011)*, pp. 229–243 (Chapter 11) at p 232.

141 Article 1 of the Charter.

142 The Charter was signed on 30 April 1948 and entered into force the 1st of December 1951.

143 The Declaration is prior by some months to the Universal Declaration of Human Rights and it is considered to be the first such international human rights text. See Henkin, Pugh, Schachter-Smit, *International Law Cases and Material* (American Casebook Series, St Paul Minnesota. 1982), p. 823.

144 See the advisory opinion of the Court, dated 14 July 1989 (OC-10/89). According to the Commission on Human Rights, on the basis of Article 20 of its Statute and Article 64 of the Convention, it has the power to examine communications concerning the violation of the Declaration based on the OAS Charter and its Statute. According to this opinion, the Commission is able to examine cases of violations committed even by States that have not yet adhered to the Convention.

consensus and the cornerstone of its operation is the respect of the principles on non-intervention in the internal affairs of a State and the complete respect for national sovereignty. Still, the Charter of the OAS made reference to an Inter-American Commission on Human Rights.[145] This provision was strengthened by the Buenos Aires modification of the Charter and was the legal basis for the start of the operation of the Commission in 1959. The Charter provided, from the start, for the adoption at a later stage of a Convention on human rights. The Commission, based in Washington, started its operation in 1959.

The supranational protection of human rights became binding through the signature, on 21 November 1969 in San José (Costa Rica), of the American Convention on Human Rights.[146] The Convention, also known under the name of the San José Pact, is a classical text for the international protection of individual rights and freedoms. It draws its inspiration partly from the preceding experience of other similar regional treaties, but also from the Charter of the Organisation of American States, the American Declaration of the Rights and Duties of Man, the Universal Declaration of Human Rights and the International Pact on Civil and Political Rights. The Convention entered into force on the 18th of July 1978. Although not all States parties to the OAS have signed the San José Pact[147] the case-law of the Inter-American Commission on Human Rights has, furthermore, constantly upheld the Commission's right to control these States that have not ratified the Pact, based on the obligations imposed upon the States by the Charter.

II.3 AFRICA

II.3.1. THE ORGANISATION OF AFRICAN UNITY AND OTHER EARLIER INTEGRATION EFFORTS

The idea of African unity has quite a long history, at least from the time when former colonies in Africa started to become independent (the first being Sudan in 1956 and Ghana in 1957). Several African thinkers felt that the colonial borders were not appropriate for independent African states and that creation of new

145 Article 106 of the OAS Charter stipulates that "there shall be an Inter-American Commission on Human Rights, whose principal function shall be to promote the observance and protection of human rights and to serve as a consultative organ of the Organization in these matters". It goes on to foresee the adoption of a convention on human rights as well as the creation of "other organs responsible for these matters". This last phrase constituted the legal basis for the establishment, later, of the Inter-American Court on Human Rights.

146 The Convention was signed during a special conference of the OAS on Human Rights, held in San José from 7 to 22 November 1969.

147 The most notable example is the United States, which has not ratified any inter-American text on human rights since 1948. The United States have signed the Convention of San José during the Jimmy Carter administration, but have never ratified it.

units or at least close cooperation across these borders was more suitable for the post-colonial time. As it would be very hard to create new states with new borders while at the same time the colonial African borders in many instances had no traditional basis, commentators suggested pan-African unity might be a solution to inappropriateness of the borders. This way the *uti possidetis* principle could be accepted (and at the first ordinary session of the Organisation of African Unity (OAU) in 1964 the organisation indeed reasserted this principle and the existing borders[148]) but potential negative effects minimised. The borders have since then at times been questioned[149] but there have also been proponents for them, stating that even if many borders were not made by Africans they still were not arbitrary.[150]

In the 1960s the first president of Ghana, Kwame Nkrumah, presented his vision of a united Africa as the way out of poverty, colonial domination and other ills of the continent. The Organisation of African Unity (OAU) was created in 1963, with the Charter signed on 25 May 1963. OAU was until the African Union the largest and oldest – although not the only – organisation of regional integration in Africa. This was also the organisation under whose auspices independence was achieved for many states. The OAU during its time of existence produced a number of treaties and protocols on various topics although it was never seen as a very strong organisation.

Parallel to the OAU other efforts at African integration went on, especially in the 1990s. On 3 June 1991 the Treaty Establishing the African Economic Community, the Abuja Treaty, was signed.[151] The Treaty aims to gradually build an economic community in Africa. The creation of such a community shall be made in stages and incorporate existing communities (Article 6 of the Abuja Treaty). The strategy resembles that of the EU with a customs union eventually leading to a common market and a strategy laid out for further integration step by step.[152] Several existing more limited organs of economic and development cooperation should be included in the Community. The existing communities to incorporate include the Economic Community of West African States (ECOWAS)[153] formed in 1975; the Southern African Development Community

148 F. M. Deng, "Africa's Internally Displaced and International Norms" in J.I. Levitt (ed.), *Africa. Mapping New Boundaries in International Law* (Hart Publishing, Oxford/Portland 2010), pp. 65–101, at 78–79.

149 J.P. Pham, "African Constitutionalism: Forging New Models" in J.I. Levitt (ed.), *Africa. Mapping New Boundaries in International Law* (Hart Publishing, Oxford/Portland 2010), pp. 183–203, at 187.

150 T. Maluwa, "The Constitutive Act of the African Union and Institution-building in Postcolonial Africa" in *Leiden Journal of International Law* 16 (2003), pp. 157–170, at 160–161.

151 Www.uneca.org/itca/ariportal/abuja.htm.

152 M. Forere, "Is discussion of the United States of Africa premature? Analysis of ECOWAS and SADC" in *Journal of African Law* 2012 56(1), pp. 29–54, at 36–37.

153 ECOWAS: Benin, Burkina Faso, Cape Verde, Cote d'Ivoire, Gambia, Ghana, Guinea, Guinea Bissau, Liberia, Mali, Mauritania, Niger, Nigeria, Senegal, Sierra Leone, Togo.

(SADC) formed in 1992 and in force in 1993 as successor to the Southern African Development Co-ordination Conference[154]; the Common Market for Eastern and Southern Africa (COMESA)[155]; the Community of Sahel-Saharan States (CEN-SAD)[156]; the Economic Community of Central African States (ECCAS)[157] and the East African Community (EAC).[158] The intended end point of the gradual creation of an economic community is not totally clear from the Treaty; if it should be a customs union or something less far-reaching. The OAU did not always follow the same path as the Abuja Treaty but different integration developments went on in parallel.[159]

The OAU as far as human rights were concerned had a strong emphasis on fighting colonialism, racism and apartheid – the OAU Charter makes no mention of human rights as such. What was in the minds of the drafters were rights against colonial masters but not rights for individuals within states or even rights for groups within the non-colonial African countries (including no right to self-determination as the Biafra case showed). The OAU did not give individuals rights against their own states. Heads of State such as Nyerere in Tanzania and Senghor in Senegal thus took the initiative of the African Charter of Human and Peoples' Rights (also called the Banjul Charter), adopted 1981 and in force 1986, soon ratified by all OAU members.[160]

The OAU Charter did not contain collective security measures. When it came to supporting democracy and condemning what went on in African countries, all OAU did was protest against the apartheid regimes (in Rhodesia and South Africa).[161]

---

154 SADC: Angola, Botswana, Malawi, Mauritius, Mozambique, Namibia, South Africa, Zambia, Zimbabwe, Tanzania, Lesotho, Swaziland.

155 COMESA: Burundi, Comoros, Democratic Republic of Congo, Djibouti, Egypt, Ethiopia, Eritrea, Kenya, Libya, Madagascar, Malawi, Mauritius, Rwanda, Seychelles, Sudan, Swaziland, Uganda, Zambia, Zimbabwe.

156 CEN-SAD: Benin, Burkina Faso, Central African Republic, Chad, Comoros, Cote d'Ivoire, Djibouti, Egypt, Eritrea Gambia, Ghana, Guinea, Guinea Bissau, Libya, Liberia, Kenya, Mali, Mauritania, Morocco, Niger, Nigeria, Senegal, Sierra Leone, Somalia, Sao Tomé and Principe, Sudan, Togo, Tunisia.

157 ECCAS: Angola, Burundi, Cameroon, Central African Republic, Chad, Democratic Republic of Congo, Equatorial Guinea, Gabon, Congo, Rwanda, Sao Tomé and Principe.

158 EAC: Burundi, Kenya, Rwanda, Tanzania, Uganda.

159 Maluwa (2003), pp. 163–164.

160 *Introduction to the International Human Rights Regime,* Manfred Nowak, Martinus Nijhoff Publishers/ The Raoul Wallenberg Institute Human Rights Library Leiden/Boston 2003, pp. 203–214.

161 A. Abass and M. A. Baderin, "Towards effective collective security and human rights protection in Africa: an assessment of the Constitutive Act of the new African Union", pp. 1–38 in *Netherlands International Law Review* Vol. XLIX, Issue 1, 2002, at p. 9. The first steps toward relaxing the understanding of non-interference were seen in connection with the crisis in Chad around 1980. The crisis was several years old by then but not until 1978 did OUA discuss any intervention. Through Resolution 102(XVIII)Rev.1 of the Assembly of Heads of State and Government of the OAU a peace-keeping force was set up to contain and moderate in the crisis in Chad. The next intervention was in the Western Sahara crisis in 1980s which led to Morocco

A process leading up to a Conference on Security, Stability, Development, and Co-operation in Africa (CSSDCA) modelled on the Organisation for Security and Co-operation in Europe (OSCE) was initiated in the late 1980s and early 1990s, as a general response to the end of the Cold War. The culmination of efforts was a 1991 conference in Kampala and an incorporation of CSSDCA principles to the OAU Mechanism for Conflict Prevention, Management and Resolution.[162] In 2000 a CSSDCA Declaration was issued, building upon previous OAU declarations and among other things expressed condemnation of unconstitutional changes of government.[163] This, a serious problem in Africa, was something OAU had tried to take a stand against but it had not managed to prevent military or other coups. The 2000 declaration itself could of course hardly stop coups, although as opposed to more general pronouncements earlier it did include measures to be taken by the organisation in case of unconstitutional taking of power, like condemnation, offering the good offices of the organisation but also concrete measures like visa denials. The importance of gathering all principles on democracy and reaction to unconstitutional changes of government that exist in various documents of African organisations was proclaimed as one aim.[164]

Although integration proceeded apace in Africa, OAU was becoming increasingly irrelevant, when other organs created mechanisms that OAU had not manage to put into effect. This included the 1998–1999 ECOWAS conflict prevention mechanism (see below), which was almost the same as the OAU mechanism. This gave ECOWAS the possibility to authorise enforcement action without the authorisation of OAU or UN and the mechanism of ECOWAS proved more effective than that of the OAU.

II.3.2. ECOWAS

The Economic Community of West African States (ECOWAS) was formed in 1975 (in fact launched in 1972, with the idea having been mooted already 1964, but the Treaty only entered into force in 1975)[165] and is thus among the older of the African regional bodies. ECOWAS from the start had a clear economic

withdrawing from the OAU in 1984. For many years the OAU remained passive and did not intervene in disasters in Congo, Somalia, Rwanda, Burundi, and Ethiopia, Eritrea or others. The last attempt of OAU to play a role was in Liberia when OUA under the leadership of the Ugandan president approached Nigeria to lead a regional force within ECOWAS. *Ibid.*, pp. 9–10.

162 Deng (2010), pp. 86–87.

163 N. Koefele Kole, "Participatory Rights in Africa: A Brief Overview of an Emerging Regional Custom", pp. 233–258 in *Netherlands International Law Review* (2008), pp. 241–242.

164 Declaration AHG 5 (XXXVI), Assembly of the Heads of State or Government, Thirty-sixth ordinary session/Fourth session of African Economic Community, 10–12 July 2000, Lomé, Togo, www.africa-union.org/Special_Programs/CSSDCA/cssdca-solemndeclaration.pdf.

165 Forere (2012), pp. 39–40.

integration aim.[166] ECOWAS originally did not have the competence to deal with peace-keeping or conflict solving missions, but its treaty was amended in 1993 (by the ECOWAS Treaty of Cotonou) after it had found itself faced with situations where a peacekeeping function was required. The revised treaty makes explicit reference to the organisation promoting and consolidating democratic systems of governance.[167] ECOWAS added in 1998 and 1999 a Framework and a Protocol for a binding Mechanism for Conflict Prevention, Management, Resolution, Peacekeeping and Security, providing a role for the organisation in possible intervention in member states in cases where there is a risk of overthrow of a democratically elected government.[168] Among the kind of situations when an intervention can be made are humanitarian disasters, threats to peace in the region but also the overthrow or attempted overthrow of a legitimate government.[169] The 1999 Protocol recognises that peace, security, stability but also democracy and good governance are central for the development of the ECOWAS region. It spells out as a key objective to protect members against overthrow of democratically elected governments and affirms the commitment to promotion and consolidation of democratic government.[170]

In 2001 the role of ECOWAS for democracy protection was made even clearer through the ECOWAS Protocol A/SP1/12/01 on Democracy and Good Governance.[171] This protocol refers to the peace-keeping role of the organisation but especially mentions the need to pay attention to linkages between internal crises, democracy and good governance, the rule of law and human rights. Member states should have mechanisms to protect this and should have democratic processes. Furthermore the ECOWAS court is empowered for cases related to human rights. This protocol is important for the question of democracy protection by regional organisations, as it provides a foundation for promoting and if need be preserving democracy through intervention.[172] The first Article of the Protocol lists constitutional principles shared by all member states, including separation of powers, empowerment and strengthening of parliaments, independence of the judiciary and freedom of members of the bar. In addition, the "zero tolerance for power obtained or maintained by unconstitutional means"[173] is explicitly mentioned as is that accession to power

166 *Ibid.*

167 Article 4 (j). See J.I. Levitt, "Pro-democratic Intervention in Africa" in in J.I. Levitt (ed), *Africa. Mapping New Boundaries in International Law* (Hart Publishing, Oxford/Portland 2010), pp. 103–147 at 112–116.

168 Levitt (2010), pp. 120–124. www.comm.ecowas.int/sec/?id=ap101299&lang=en.

169 Abass & Baderin (2002), pp. 4–6 and Levitt (2010), pp. 116–120.

170 Levitt (2010), pp. 123–124.

171 Www.comm.ecowas.int/sec/en/protocoles/Protocol%20on%20good-governance-and-democracy-rev-5EN.pdf.

172 Levitt (2010), pp. 126–127.

173 Article 1 c. ECOWAS Protocol A/SP1/12/01 on Democracy and Good Governance.

must be through free, fair and transparent elections. Armed forces must be apolitical and under the command of a legally constituted political authority.[174]

Article 45 of the Protocol sets out that in the event that democracy is abruptly brought to an end by whatever means, or where there is a massive violation of human rights, ECOWAS may decide on sanctions. The sanctions may ultimately lead to suspension and in the event of such suspension, ECOWAS monitoring of the status of democracy and human rights in the country continues.[175]

It was possible to adopt such a protocol even if there are important differences between countries, as they at least shared certain basic principles. The protocol contains some detail on elections and social elements of a state, human rights (with a reference to the African Charter) with explicit provisions for intervention to protect its principles. The role of ECOWAS in relation to elections, with monitoring and assistance, highlights the democracy promoting ideals of the Protocol. The fact that the Protocol contains a section on "The role of the armed forces, the police and the security forces in a democracy" (Section IV) illustrates African realities. No new institutions were established by the Protocol, but existing ECOWAS institutions perform the democracy monitoring functions and can decide on sanctions. The Mechanism among its organs counts a Council of Elders consisting of eminent personalities who can use good offices and experience to mediate, thus using a regional cultural element namely the respect for elders. The Council can act also preventively.[176]

II.3.3. SADC

The Southern African Development Community (SADC) was formed in 1992 and entered into force in 1993.[177] It was a successor to the Southern African Development Co-ordination Conference (SADCC), which was an apartheid era organisation (from 1981) with the aim to be a counterweight to South Africa. SADCC only dealt with economic issues, excluding political and security questions. These latter questions were dealt with by the informal anti-apartheid alliance, the Front Line States. After the changes in South Africa, this country became an important member of SADC. A certain apprehension about South African dominance in all areas was behind an initial reluctance to let SADC deal with a more comprehensive range of issues.[178] In contrast with ECOWAS, SADC did not have a clear economic integration aim, but rather a range of aims

174 ECOWAS Protocol A/SP1/12/01 on Democracy and Good Governance www.comm.ecowas.int/sec/en/protocoles/Protocol%20on%20good-governance-and-democracy-rev-5EN.pdf.

175 *Ibid.*

176 Pham (2010), pp. 196–200.

177 Declaration and Treaty of SADC. www.sadc.int.

178 G. Cawthra, "The Role of SADC in Managing Political Crisis and Conflict" (2010), p. 10.

and goals.[179] SADC is generally seen as quite an influential organisation when it does act. It forms part of the African Union's peace and security mechanism. In important cases SADC has, however, been paralysed because of disagreements between members, as the institutional structure is not strong. This has been the case concerning how to deal with Zimbabwe when earlier only fairly weak mediating or observer missions were undertaken. Eventually SADC has been able to play a slightly greater role, by pushing for different rules to be used for elections (in 2008) to ensure some degree of transparency.[180] However, rulings by the SADC Tribunal on the land seizures in Zimbabwe, declaring them illegal,[181] were ignored by the Zimbabwean government that instead questioned the legitimacy of the Tribunal. This in fact led to the suspension of the tribunal in 2010 (only three years after it heard its first complaint) and in August 2012 the suspension was reiterated and the possibility of individual complaints to the Tribunal revoked.[182]

In June of 2011 SADC adopted a strongly worded report condemning the refusal of Zanu-PF party and President Mugabe to accept the power-sharing agreement in good faith.[183] SADC in 2001 adopted a Protocol on Politics, Defence and Security Co-operation – and set up an organ for these matters – which included as a key principle the observance of human rights, democracy and rule of law. Through primarily diplomatic efforts but also if that fails through punitive measures, democratic institutions shall be protected. Even prior to this Protocol SADC could – based on its Treaty – to some extent act in favour of democracy and rule of law, but the extent of possible intervention was not clear.

The possibility and mechanism for SADC to intervene in favour of democracy have thus only been in existence for less than a decade and only partially been tested. The judicial mechanism has not been effective at all, but SADC still continues to exercise some influence in other ways. The earlier intervention in the region (Lesotho in 1998) was an intervention by states (South Africa and Botswana) on the invitation of the Prime Minister, rather than action of the organisation. This crisis nevertheless prompted SADC to strengthen its basis for operations and was what led to the Protocol on Politics, Defence and Security Co-operation and the strategic plan for its implementation, which came into force in 2004. From this time there is a basis for regional peace-keeping and enforcement measures. Like in ECOWAS, the protocol explicitly permits

179 Forene (2012), p. 41.

180 Cawthra (2010), p. 25.

181 SADC (T) Case No. 2/2007 in the matter between M. Campbell and others and the Republic of Zimbabwe, also Case No. 7/2008 in the matter between L.M. Tembani and the Republic of Zimbabwe. www.sadc-tribunal.org/pages/decisions.htm. See also *The Economist* 12 September 2009.

182 Www.opensocietyfoundations.org/voices/end-southern-africas-regional-human-rights-court?utm_source=Open+Society+Institute&utm_campaign=25ea45c3ba-justice-20120823&utm_medium=email (22.10.2012).

183 *The Economist* 25 June 2011.

interventions against threats to legitimate authority of the government in the member states.[184] SADC has intervened in the Democratic Republic of Congo to some extent, together with the UN.[185]

The Protocol stressed principles of international law such as non-intervention and the right to use violence only in self-defence, but also lists situations in which the organisation may take action. This includes if there is a military coup or other threat to the legitimate authority of a state. Methods that may be employed include preventive diplomacy, negotiations, conciliation, mediation, good offices, arbitration as well as adjudication by an international tribunal. As a last resort, enforcement action may also be taken, in line with UN principles for such action.[186]

SADC has organs at both heads of state, ministerial and official level with an Interstate Defence and Security Committee and an Interstate Politics and Diplomacy Committee as decision-making organs.[187]

II.3.4. THE AFRICAN UNION

When Muammar Gaddafi, who was then leader of Libya, launched visions of a united Africa in the 1990s the language was somewhat similar to that of the calls for African unity in the 1960s but neither vision was what eventually emerged in the shape of the African Union (AU). Gaddafi's stated vision included a common government, a common army and no borders between states – thus finally abolishing colonially imposed borders. Between the original 1960s ideas and the envisaged AU of Gaddafi, many different African personalities presented ideas and visions about African unity (although Gaddafi liked to present the AU as his brainchild). The proposals included concrete suggestions for reform of the regional institutions that existed to strengthen them (primarily the OAU) or more far-reaching visions. The 1960s ideas were based on a sophisticated vision but for various reasons did not lead to any specific action at the time.[188] In the 1990s it appeared the time was more right for regional integration, with the example of a strong EU as inspiration. Furthermore, Africa was free of colonialism and independent states had developed over several decades.

The lack of clarity on what integration should lead to and the slow pace of progress, even if there was agreement on the importance of integration, resulted in many different organisations and institutions being created, which

184 J.I. Levitt (2010), pp. 134–138.
185 A. Abass & M.A. Baderin (2002), pp. 4–6.
186 Article 11.2 Protocol on Politics, Defence and Security Cooperation. www.sadc.int.
187 Cawthra (2010), p. 11.
188 T. Maluwa, "Fast-tracking African Unity or making haste slowly? A Note on the Amendment to the Constitutive Act of the African Union" in *NILR* Vol. LI (2004), pp. 195–236, at 200–201. See also Maluwa (2003), pp. 157–170.

exacerbated the lack of clarity. The desire to remedy this contributed to a call being made on 9 September 1999 at an OAU meeting in Sirte to accelerate the process of integration on the Continent.[189] Even if primarily an attempt to make OAU more effective, this eventually led to the creation of a new organisation in the shape of the AU. New positive-sounding concepts for African unity were introduced or strengthened through the AU – like participation of people, democratic principles and human rights – but the organisational structure and implementation mechanisms created were initially rather weak.[190]

Furthermore, the idea of a new Union for the entire Africa was not met only by approval, as some leaders favoured a smaller union such as ECOWAS, which could be more efficient and in which each country might have more say.

The OAU was not immediately abrogated and critics have stressed that the transfer from one organisation to another was not clear. It was not evident if the AU was an entirely new organisation or if it should be seen as a change to the OAU.[191] The preamble to the Constitutive Act of the African Union mentions the Charter of OAU several times as something to be considered without clarifying if it remains or shall be considered as a historical basis. It however appears from the way the new organisation was created as well as from its substance that it was seen as a new organisation and not just as a changed OAU – even if it may build on some of the same basis. Indeed, one of the criticisms against regional integration in Africa is that not only is the OAU-AU relationship less than clear but also other different components of regional integration appear not to fit so well or at least not so clearly together. This concerns for example the human rights system that was set up outside of the OAU and that remains also outside the AU.[192]

Admittedly, this is not different from the European system with the European Convention and Court of Human Rights remaining outside of the EU cooperation.[193] In Europe, through practice (case law) as well as through mention in the EU treaties of the Convention on Human Rights a fairly clear structural relationship between the two systems has been created – such relationship is not yet clear for Africa, although steps have been taken toward clarifying it. In 2004 the African Court on Human and Peoples' Rights came into being through obtaining sufficient ratifications of a 1988 Protocol to that effect, added to the Charter for Human Rights.[194] In 2008 the Court moved to

---

189 As described at the AU web-page, www.africa-union.org (African Union in a nutshell), 21.07.2010.

190 Maluwa (2003), pp. 163–164.

191 Maluwa (2004), pp. 195–236.

192 *Documents of the African Commission on Human and Peoples' Rights*, ed. R. Murray; Malcolm Evans Oxford, Hart 2001.

193 This system changed after the entry into force of the Lisbon Treaty (December 2009) as it stipulates that the EU should join the European Convention on Human Rights, thus creating also a direct link between the systems, but the dual system still remains.

194 Www.african-court.org/en/.

Arusha, Tanzania, and became operational shortly afterwards, harmonising procedures with the previously existing Commission on Human and Peoples' Rights. The Court is listed as an AU organ although it developed separately.

At the 5th extraordinary summit in March 2001 of the Assembly of Heads of State and Government (AHSG) of the OAU representing all 53 member states, the states solemnly and proudly declared the creation of the African Union. The Constitutive Act was adopted by the OAU in Togo, 11 July 2000. Following deposition of the 36th instrument of ratification, meaning two-thirds or members (by Nigeria on 26 April 2001), the Act formally entered into force on 26 May 2001.[195] On 9 July 2002 the formal inauguration took place in Durban in South Africa. OAU transitionally remained operational – the Durban summit was the last formal one immediately followed by inauguration of the AU.[196] Even if some states expressed misgivings about creating a new organisation rather than reforming the OAU, they went on to sign and ratify the Constitutive Act. Only the Democratic Republic of Congo and Madagascar did not ratify it within the first two years. The Act was not just negotiated and agreed in very short time but its acceptance and entry into force was also rapid. Whether this illustrates a shared commitment to enhanced African unity as was proclaimed or if it had to do with more practical considerations is not possible to determine. The Act was amended rather soon after its entry into force, at the first extraordinary Assembly session and at the second ordinary one in February and July 2003 respectively.

The sovereignty of states was the basic principle with a minimalist view regarding joint organs and competences. Discussions on the institutional structure continued after the creation of the Union, leading e.g. to a protocol setting up a Peace and Security Council added only few years after the Act was signed, in 2002 (entered into force in 2003).[197] This Council can recommend AU intervention when for example AU standards of democracy are not met. In February 2004 a Solemn Declaration merging various proposals on non-aggression and common defence, including human security and state security, was adopted.[198] The Peace and Security Council shall be an organ for the collective security of the AU members and an early warning arrangement. The Protocol establishing it also lists the powers of the Council.[199]

195 A. Abass & M.A. Baderin (2002). See the Constitutive Act on www.oau-oua.org/LOME2000/Africa%20Union%20Constitiutive%20Act%20ENG.htm.

196 Maluwa (2003), pp. 157–170.

197 Maluwa (2004), pp. 197–198 and 201.

198 B.Manby, "The African Union, NEPAD and Human Rights: The missing agenda", *Human Rights Quarterly* 26 (2004), pp. 983–1027, at 984–987.

199 A. Abass, "The United Nations, the African Union and the Darfur Crisis: of apology and utopia", *Netherlands International Law Review* (NILR) 2007 Vol. LIV Issue 3, pp. 415–440, at 421.

The issue of interference in what is seen as domestic matters is a sensitive issue in Africa and the interpretation of what is interference (or what is domestic affairs) may mean that cooperation and involvement become extremely difficult even when no threat to national sovereignty can be seen in the regular interpretation of the terms. The non-intervention principle has a long history in OAU agreements and is shown e.g. by provisions that member states should coordinate and harmonise general policies especially in defence and security, but no details of such harmonisation were specified nor any structures created to this end.[200]

A Panel of the Wise was created as a pillar of the Peace and Security Council to assist the Council of the AU, relying on African respect for elders and ensuring that there is a mechanism in place for prevention and mediation.[201] At this time also some amendments were made to the Constitutive Act concerning intervention grounds.[202]

The objectives of the AU as set out in the Constitutive Act include democracy and human rights, explicitly mentioned as opposed to in the OAU. Several objectives like raising living standards, promoting health, supporting and promoting research and technology are seen to require concerted efforts. The Principles Governing Democratic Elections in Africa adopted by the last OAU summit in Durban in 2002 were later taken over by the AU.[203] This document includes principles on rule of law, separation of powers and an independent judiciary. As a declaration it is not binding (unlike resolutions) but it was hoped that it would nevertheless be significant and guide the behaviour of states.[204] The Constitutive Act recognises that sustainable economic development flourishes on a culture of democracy and respect for rights. Article 4 lists such principles as sovereign equality, participation of people in the AU activities, social justice, gender equality as well as condemnation and rejection of unconstitutional changes of government, calling for stability and respect for democratic principles.[205]

Article 30 of the AU Constitutive Act confirms that a government that comes into power unconstitutionally shall not be able to participate in the activities of the Union. Leaders that come to power through coup d'états and undemocratic forms of government shall be ostracized, which should have the effect to discourage such behaviour.[206] Already in 1999 the OAU adopted a decision to

200 Abass & Baderin (2002), p. 9.
201 Pham (2010), at p. 200.
202 Abass (2007), p. 421.
203 Koefele Kole, pp. 241–242.
204 Maluwa (2003), pp. 165–166.
205 K.D. Magliveras & G.J. Naldi, "The African Union – A New Dawn for Africa?", pp. 415–425, *ICLQ* Vol. 51 Part 2 April 2002, especially at pp. 416–417.
206 Abass & Baderin (2002), p. 7.

ban leaders who had taken power through a coup (since the last meeting) from its summits.[207]

The Constitutive Act of the AU has a clear objective of human rights.[208] There is a collective AU institutional obligation – generic and specific – to ensure human rights. Even if the AU system especially as far as its institutional structure is concerned remains less sophisticated than the European system, the aim is that the AU should ensure permeation of human rights into all activities. Political will and commitment could give real importance to this, like it has in Europe, if the AU were to demonstrate through concrete actions the importance of such commitment. This could be done if the AU would monitor and react to human rights violations in the member states, as is prescribed in Article 9(1)(c) and (g) of the Constitutive Act. The Constitutive Act although it contains provisions on non-intervention in the internal affairs of a state (Article 4g) also gives the Union the right to intervene in some circumstances (Article 4h). This Article lists when intervention can happen; it is noteworthy that there is no overt reference to human rights but reference to genocide and other major violations. It is debated whether gross human rights violations can fall under Article 4h as such violations constitute a danger against peace and security.[209] The ability and willingness of the AU to react in the all too common event of coup d'états in Africa and in the regional wars varies greatly between situations.[210] In the OAU so-called Grand Bay declaration in 1999[211] statements were made on the importance of human rights for regional and international peace and security, so the connection has been made in the African context. It is also reflected in Article 58 ACHPR.[212]

The African Union is modelled on the EU even if its competences do not go as far as those of the EU (or even the original European Communities). The Constitutive Act does not state explicitly if the organisation has legal personality – Article 2 just says it is established. It is possible that this omission is because the AU was supposed to replace the OAU (see Article 33 of the Constitutive Act). The OAU had explicit legal personality by a General Convention on the Privileges and Immunities from 1965.[213]

The AU created various organs including a Court of Justice, which, however, was superseded by the decision to create a joint court for justice and human rights, The African Court on Human and Peoples' Rights. There are nine main AU organs. The number of organs appears large, which could be a financial

207 Cawthra (2010), p. 12.
208 Article 3e and h as well as specific rights in Article 4 and the general objectives of the organisation.
209 Abass & Baderin (2002), p. 3, pp. 13–14.
210 Some examples will be discussed in some detail below in section IV.5.
211 Www.achpr.org/english/declarations/declaration_grand_bay_en.html.
212 Abass & Baderin (2002), pp. 27–31.
213 Magliveras & Naldi (2002).

burden as well as make the management of the Union complicated. The supreme organ is the body consisting of Heads of State and Government.[214] The supreme organ, the Assembly, may decide to set up further organs, as set in Article 5 of the Constitutive Act. The Assembly may also decide to incorporate existing organs into the structures of the AU according to Article 33 of the Constitutive Act. Only the Assembly is an OAU organ; all the others are new.

The New Partnership for Africa's Development (NEPAD), created at the OAU summit in 2001, is another example of a programme created independently that later (2010) became part of the AU. NEPAD contains a commitment to democracy, human rights and the rule of law and proclaims that to lift Africa out of poverty there must be democracy, human rights and good governance. But these goals were not visibly integrated into the NEPAD programme for development in the form of concrete obligations. In the initiative, endorsed by the first AU session, there was an amalgamation of different plans for African renaissance, primarily focused on economics (agriculture, science, capital flows etc.), recognising peace, security and good governance only in general words.[215]

The clearest contribution of NEPAD to supporting democracy is a Declaration on Democracy, Political, Economic and Corporate Governance through which African leaders commit to international standards of democracy.[216] The Declaration aimed to make such standards a joint responsibility and to set out clear rules on transparency, accountability and participative governance not just nationally but at the sub-national level as well. The Declaration referred to the AU prohibition on unconstitutional changes of government.[217] A key feature of NEPAD is the African Peer Review Mechanism (APRM) to monitor compliance of the programme objectives (including corporate governance values). African eminent persons conduct peer reviews according to a pre-determined structure and reports may be adopted publicly by NEPAD. A Memorandum of Understanding (MoU) to further develop this mechanism was adopted in March 2003 and only states that accept the MoU are subject to the peer review.[218]

States that join the review system (which is voluntary) must submit to certain reviews regularly and may be subject also to special reviews. The self-assessment of the state e.g. of its democratic system is an important part of the review. NEPAD falls under the AU Assembly and in addition has a Heads of State and Government Implementation Committee, composed of representatives from all AU regions as well as the AU Chair and Chair of the AU Commission that reports to the AU.[219] NEPAD provides a framework for economic and

---

214 Statute Article 6, powers and functions set out in Article 9. See Magliveras & Naldi (2002).
215 Manby (2004), pp. 988–989.
216 Levitt (2010), pp. 139–140.
217 Koefele Kole (2008), pp. 239–240.
218 Manby (2004), pp. 990–992.
219 Pham (2010), pp. 201–202.

other cooperation, although what it means by referring to democracy, good governance and the rule of law is not defined and there is no evidence of any specific measures for enforcement of these values. However, the review process can help to give real meaning to the general principles.[220]

One criticism often made of the AU is that the Constitutive Act is weak as far as institutional issues are concerned. Powers and interrelationship between organs was not clear in the original act. There are a number of institutional/structural weaknesses in the AU institutional set-up. The Assembly's unfettered right to delegate any of its powers and functions to any Union organ potentially can give rise to problems, since it was not the intention of drafters to let lesser organs determine fundamental issues like admission of new member states or establishment of new organs. Provided the Assembly uses the right to delegate wisely this does not have to become a practical problem. Article 6 on the meetings of Heads of State and Government may also lead to complications as decisions by consensus are required. This is traditional in Africa, but such a requirement in an international organisation may well paralyse it. For that reason Article 7 provides another way out, that together with quorum rules in reality means that decisions may be adopted with as little as 23 votes from a membership of 54. Procedural matters including deciding what constitutes a procedural matter need simple majority only, see Article 7. These different provisions make the decision-making process somewhat opaque.[221]

The Executive Council coordinates and monitors policies as provided in Article 10. In Article 13 various technical issues are mentioned but it includes also questions of nationality, residence and immigration. Other more political issues of the AU like promoting peace and security are not within the competence of the Executive Council. The Pan-African Parliament, in Article 17, shall allow for the participation of the people in the governing structures of the AU. The composition and powers of the Parliament shall be defined in a protocol. Magliveras and Naldi feel that the fact that the Constitutive Act itself does not deal with these issues raises questions of the seriousness of the intentions of the founding fathers to allow for real popular participation. The legal relationship between the Constitutive Act and the protocols is not stated, so it is not clear if such protocols become integral parts of the Act, if there will be a need for separate accession to them and other such issues.[222]

The amendments proposed in a series of protocols to the Constitutive Act aim at strengthening the Union in the sphere of human rights or collective security for example, but the way of doing this may not be the most effective. The different proposals are in several protocols that may be but do not have to

220 M. O. Chibundu, "NEPAD and the Rebirth of Development Theory and Praxis" in J.I. Levitt (ed), *Africa. Mapping New Boundaries in International Law* (Hart Publishing, Oxford/Portland 2010), pp. 257–295, at 261–262.

221 Magliveras & Naldi (2002), especially pp. 419–420.

222 *Ibid.*

be ratified *en bloc*, which may lead to different rules applying for different states. This makes the integration and especially the institutional structure complex. Essential issues like development and promotion of common trade, defence and foreign policies as well as the right of intervention are all in protocols.[223]

In 2007 the AU adopted an African Charter on Democracy, Elections and Governance.[224] The document needed 15 ratifications to enter into force, which it did on 15 February 2012.[225] The Charter is a way to make AU principles of democracy more concrete. The Charter has not escaped criticism for being vague and ambiguous but commentators still see in it an important step to consolidate the principle of democracy as an important principle for the AU. The Charter includes a possibility for the AU to play a role to support member states in reaching and maintaining democracy through monitoring and support missions. The Charter explicitly explains what kind of taking or holding on to power that is unconstitutional and unacceptable, such as military coups or the refusal of a democratically elected government to step down after losing an election. The AU Peace and Security Council is to play a role in defining threats to democracy and reacting to them. Sub-regional organs have adopted similar declarations.[226] The Peace and Security Council shall have a role as early warning mechanism, for preventive diplomacy, mediation, peace support and so on. It can authorise the use of force, including for the protection of democracy. Sanctions in case there is an unconstitutional change of government are especially mentioned. This provides the AU with a clear framework for democracy supporting intervention.[227] This is supported also by the ACHPR, which was the first instrument of an international organisation to refer to the Universal Declaration of Human Rights, the first to list "peoples' rights" as collective rights, the first to refer to the right to national and international peace and security and the first to prohibit the use of Member States' territories for terrorist activity.[228] Collective security and human rights have been linked with one another in a manner that in Europe is mostly seen in the context of the OSCE.[229]

The same year 2007 the AU also adopted a declaration to accelerate political integration, the Accra Declaration, even mentioning the words "United States of Africa".[230]

The AU does allow for punitive measures (Article 23 on sanctions) and even suspension (Article 30). Sanctions are listed in an exhaustive fashion. The sanctions are harsh and may be unduly harsh compared with other international

223 Maluwa (2004), pp. 198–199, 202–203, 232.
224 Www.africa-union.org/root/au/Documents/Treaties/text/Charter%20on%20Democracy.pdf.
225 Http://au.int/en/sites/default/files/Charter%20on%20Democracy%20and%20Governance_0.pdf.
226 Koefele Kole (2008), pp. 242–245.
227 Levitt (2010), pp. 143–144.
228 Abass & Baderin (2002), p. 3.
229 *Ibid*. pp. 23–27.
230 Forere (2012), p. 37.

organisations. How to apply Article 30 in practice is rather unclear, e.g. on exactly who determines the possible suspension.[231]

Through history there have been many different attempts to create more integration in Africa, but even with the creation of AU the question on what the nature of the integration is has not been explicitly addressed. Is it supranational or intergovernmental? Is integration a political or an economic phenomenon? If it is economic, what level of interdependence is needed before there can be real talk of integration? Does economic integration imply political integration or does political integration create the space for economic integration to flourish? All these are questions that commentators and occasionally some African leaders discuss, but that are not addressed in the creation of the AU.[232]

From having taken a very restrictive view on when there could be any outside intervention in a state, even to stop serious crises there, the African rules now appear to create a wider possibility to intervene – a novel and debated concept in international law. However, the AU still includes the basic non-interference principle. Looking at the non-interference in the AU and comparing with the principle within the UN Charter, what the AU restricts are other member states intervening in internal affairs of fellow members, not the organisation as such (as is said in the UN Charter Article 2(7) and as was the case for OAU). The AU has an institutional right to intervene in members' conflicts. However, Article 4h of the AU Constitutive Act is couched in terms of a right and not a duty to intervene. The Assembly of Heads of State and Government of the AU will decide on any such intervention and members do not have a right to prevent the intervention if they so decide.

The question how the AU intervention right fits with Article 2(4) of the UN Charter is interesting, especially as there are different views on what it exactly is that Article 2(4) – which includes a reference to the purposes of the UN – prohibits. The UN Charter contains provisions on regional organisations assisting the UN with maintenance of international peace and security. The AU Constitutive Act does not explicitly say it is such an organisation but it fits to fulfil such a role. In any case, there is nothing in international law preventing the setting up of an organisation, freely and voluntarily, which is given rights the states themselves have. If they come together and agree on a legal norm of intervention, for expediency and effectiveness, they can do so rather than agree in every case. The intervention will not be against the UN Charter provided it is properly decided by the organisation and does not violate *jus cogens* rules against the use of force. Questions may arise on the withdrawal of a state from the AU: then it presumably withdraws also its consent to any intervention.[233]

---

231 Magliveras & Naldi (2002), especially p. 423.
232 Maluwa (2003), p. 159.
233 Abass & Baderin (2002), pp. 15–20.

The AU intervention rules are not drafted in the same way as the UN rules. For use of regional organisations as understood in the UN Charter, the Security Council will make a determination under Article 39 of the UN Charter of whether intervention is needed. This first decision remains with the Security Council even when a regional organisation will perform the activities. The AU rules depart from this as the decision on intervention is up to the AU. It will be the AU that decides when to launch its interventionist mechanism; that decides that there is a *casus foederis* for the activation of the machinery. Of course there is always a danger that intervention could be abused for political reasons, but the strict rules on the majority needed for launching the provisions on intervention should take care of this risk. As for the possible conflict with Article 39 of the UN Charter, what Abass and Baderin call a quasi-Article 39 determination by regional organisations, they feel must be seen as a development of international law as there has been no protest from Security Council members or others to the AU mechanism or similar ideas in other regional contexts. The AU does not expect the consent of the UN under Article 54 of the UN Charter as there are no requirements of reporting as set out there. This looks like avoiding the UN Security Council role, which the Council has not been able to fulfil effectively because of the veto of the permanent members or generally because of inefficiency or a lack of balance in dealing with different parts of the world.

It is not the first example of by-passing an ineffective Security Council by use of other parts of the UN Charter. The Uniting for Peace resolution in 1950 shifted responsibility for peace and security to the General Assembly if the Security Council was not able to act effectively. The AU intervention provisions can be seen as an opening for regional bodies acting when the UN as such does not. If the Security Council is not able to perform the tasks conferred on it, it should not have the power to prevent the tasks (maintaining international peace and security in the broad understanding of the term) from being fulfilled by someone else.[234] In practice, so far no such forceful policy of intervention has developed in Africa, but there are examples showing that at the same time, the provisions are not dead letter.

II.4. ASIA AND THE PACIFIC

II.4.1. DEVELOPMENT OF ASIAN REGIONAL INTEGRATION

Asia is a continent without strong regional organisations, although this does not mean that there are no organisations at all. Indeed, one difference to Europe (or increasingly also Africa) with the very dominant EU (or AU respectively) is that in Asia there are several organisations without a very clear dominant one.

---

[234] *Ibid.*

There are many reasons why Asian regional cooperation moves slowly. The market pressure for more integration has not been so strong or has come from outside firms (American, Japanese) rather than from within existing structures. The post-World War II suspicion between former enemy states has not been dealt with in the way that has happened in Europe. In addition, the presence of Communist states (albeit with reformed economic policies) and several authoritarian states means that coherence of political systems (like in Europe and a prerequisite for EU enlargement) is not at hand.

The expression Asia-Pacific is used increasingly to describe the wider region, but there is no consistency in what is meant with this term or what terms are used to describe the regional constellations in this part of the world.

Mattli writes how early integration attempts in the Asia-Pacific region were responses to external events that were perceived as threats to the prosperity of the region, rather than attempts at integration because this was a desired strategy. In this vein, Japan made proposals for a free trade pact in the 1960s. In the 1989 the Malaysian Prime Minister proposed stronger integration as a means to strengthen the position of Asian countries in GATT negotiations.[235]

In June 2008 the then Australian Prime Minister Rudd presented plans for a new Asia-Pacific Community. Mr Rudd hoped to transform the region's diplomatic structure through such a body, which could include countries like the USA, China, India, Indonesia and Japan as well as other states of the broadly defined region. This body could deal with challenges posed by the position of China as an economic giant and as no existing body is up to this task, a new organisation should be created according to Mr Rudd. The community would have security tasks as well. The idea was criticised for being vague both on intended tasks and membership. Mr Rudd mentioned using the EU as a model for the new community, which caused some concern even if the idea for such a degree of cooperation was not intended by Mr Rudd or anyone else.[236] In 2009 the then Japanese Prime Minister Yukio Hatoyama made a similar proposal for a new architecture for Asia-Pacific cooperation that however differed from the Rudd proposal in that no role was foreseen for the US.[237] The role of existing organs such as the Association of South-East Asian Nations (ASEAN), the Asia Pacific Economic Cooperation Forum (APEC) and the East Asia Summit in relation to the new planned body was not made clear although it was mentioned in the Australian draft that such organisations could be used as building blocks for the new organisation. In general, although many commentators remain sceptical about the plans for a new community, many feel that some new

235 Mattli (1999), p. 163.

236 Www.eastasiaforum.org/2011/10/20/china-and-the-enlarged-east-asia-summit-the-makings-of-an-asia-pacific-community/#more-22346.

237 T. Christiansen, E. Kirchner and P. Murray, "Conclusion" in T. Christiansen, E. Kirchner and P. Murray, *The Palgrave Handbook of EU-Asia Relations* (Palgrave Macmillan 2013), pp. 618–642, at 628–629.

regional cooperation mechanisms would be useful as there is no strong forum for regional cooperation and a combination of overlap of roles and lack of a coherent framework.[238]

Australia has at the same time as it launched its general regional integration ideas also set up an international nuclear non-proliferation and disarmament commission, so many commentators see the Australian ideas as different aspects of an Australian desire to become more active globally but especially regionally.[239] This can or cannot be a good reason for initiating regional cooperation. The risk is that it will be interpreted by others as attempts of one state to dominate in the regional organ, but on the other hand it gives an incentive to design the regional cooperation effectively as an effective regional organisation is likely to have much more weight than any country by itself.

In 2008 also Russia put forward ideas of a new security structure for Europe and Asia. The ideas were never much concretised but should be seen more as a reaction against existing bodies such as mainly NATO but also OSCE, seen as not Russia-friendly enough. Russia has through its hostility to OSCE, an organisation of which it is a member, shown that it is not willing to submit to common values protected by an international organisation with some mandate of its own. Russia has occasionally taken the initiative for regional bodies, like the 1996 cooperation with China and some other states (The Shanghai Five), which in 2001 became the Shanghai Cooperation Organisation (SCO).[240] Structurally the design is of an intergovernmental network with sparse and small institutions.[241] The organisation has as its aim to strengthen cooperation and good-neighbourly relations, mentioning politics, trade, culture and many other areas. Media has highlighted statements mentioning promotion of cooperation in the fight against terrorism and against separatism and extremism – tasks that the organisations mainly non-democratic members can easily abuse. The perceived importance of SCO to counterbalance American foreign policy dominance is not hidden. Most commentators do not see SCO as a particularly important body as its members (notably Russia and China) do not agree on strong or close cooperation on most important tasks and in any case are not willing to set up a strong organisational structure that would support independent decisions and bodies.[242]

The Council for Security Cooperation in the Asia-Pacific (CSCAP) and the Council for Asia-Europe Cooperation (CAEC) provide fora for cooperation on security matters, notably non-proliferation in addition to the ASEAN Regional Forum (ARF), the Asia Europe Meeting (ASEM) and ASEAN-EU

---

238 Christiansen, Kirchner, Murray (2013), p. 629.

239 See e.g. *The Economist*, 28 June 2008, 28 March 2009.

240 Www.sectsco.org/EN/.The members are China, Kazakhstan, Kyrgyzstan, Russia, Tajikistan and Uzbekistan; observers India, Iran, Mongolia and Pakistan.

241 T. Renard, "The EU, the SCO and SAARC" in T. Christiansen, E. Kirchner and P. Murray, *The Palgrave Handbook of EU-Asia Relations* (Palgrave Macmillan 2013), pp. 359–373, at 360–361.

242 *The Economist*, 9 August 2008.

Foreign Ministers meetings. On these matters ASEAN countries have shown a desire to work through inter-regional dialogue and cooperation rather than multilaterally.[243]

II.4.2. PACIFIC COMMUNITIES

For very small states, a regional organisation can be the way to get at least the minimum size to be able to participate and have a voice in world affairs. This applies to small Pacific island states that are grouped together in the Pacific Islands Forum. This Forum has, like the AU, taken a stand against unconstitutional means to take power and threatened to suspend Fiji unless the leaders that took power through a coup (in 2006) could show credible plans for elections. The suspension took place in 2009 when no progress had been made. The problem with actions of the Forum is that leaders who face sanctions can select – as did the leader of Fiji – to stay away from Forum meetings and more or less ignore the body. The Forum has so far not acted very strongly. The Forum is not an organisation as such and has almost no institutional structure. It adopted a Political Governance and Security Strategic Plan for the years 2009 to 2011, which includes to strengthen good governance in the region.[244]

Given the regional preference for inter-regional cooperation on security issues, the Pacific Island Forum Secretariat has joined the structures of cooperation such as CSCAP as associate member. It is nominally the Secretariat rather than the organisation as such that is such an associate member.[245]

Apart from the Pacific Islands Forum, the other organisation trying to exert pressure on Fiji through expelling it from its ranks is the Commonwealth that by institutional structure is even weaker.[246] The Commonwealth Heads of Government meetings, which is the highest institutional organ of the body, are informal meetings that do not adopt binding decisions, where notes are exchanged and that may primarily be seen as a chance for leaders to get to know one another.[247]

---

243 S.-J. Yoon and J.-J. Suh, "Nuclear Non-proliferation" (Chapter 25) in T. Christiansen, E. Kirchner and P. Murray, *The Palgrave Handbook of EU-Asia Relations* (Palgrave Macmillan 2013), pp. 406–420, at 410–411.

244 Www.forumsec.org.

245 Yoon & Suh (2013), p. 413.

246 The Commonwealth decided in September 2009 to suspend Fiji, which means that all Commonwealth aid is suspended. *The Economist*, 5 September 2009.

247 Yeo counters criticism of the Asia-Europe Meetings (ASEM) by pointing out that e.g. the Commonwealth has operated on even looser structures than ASEM. L. H. Yeo, "The Asia-Europe Meeting (ASEM)" (Chapter 20) in T. Christiansen, E. Kirchner and P. Murray, *The Palgrave Handbook of EU-Asia Relations* (Palgrave Macmillan 2013), pp. 330–343.

In the region there is also the Pacific Community, founded in 1947 as the South Pacific Commission by colonial governments with colonies in the region. The organisation has later changed to include the various independent states in the area. It deals with specific issues like transport, fisheries etc. but with no integrational powers or ambitions.[248]

II.4.3. ASEAN

The most important of the Asian regional organisations ASEAN lacks strong powers and has mainly been called a discussion forum. In Europe economic cooperation led to more political cooperation, whereas the opposite is true for ASEAN that started as a political and strategic cooperation organisation that only ventured into economic cooperation in the 1990s[249] – interestingly at about the same time as the EU started increasing the political and strategic cooperation. It has been commented that ASEAN has led a largely blameless existence, but this is to a large extent due to the fact that it gently and rather quietly went about its limited tasks, rather than enter into important debates like for example the EU.[250] ASEAN remains committed to enhancing rather than pooling sovereignty, as Möller said in 1998[251] and this has not changed much since – even if there have been some important developments like the adoption in 2007 of a Charter for ASEAN and later on also a human rights regime.[252]

The Charter establishes purposes, principles and decision-making procedures of ASEAN and afford it legal personality.[253] This was a signal that ASEAN was ready to integrate and the Charter contains a commitment to further integration.[254] A more rule-based community with a human rights system are consequences of this commitment to further integration.[255] The first steps toward economic cooperation were taken in 1976 with the Treaty on Amity and

248 Www.spc.int.

249 P.M.C. Koh, "Enhancing Economic Cooperation: A Regional Arbitration Centre for ASEAN" p. 390 *International and Comparative Law Quarterly No. 49* April 2000.

250 *The Economist*, 18 August 2012.

251 K. Möller, "Cambodia and Myanmar: The ASEAN Way ends here" in *Asian Survey* Vol. 38, No. 12 (Dec., 1998), pp. 1087–1104, 1088.

252 ASEAN is also beginning to become more of a factor globally. See M. Cremona, D. Kleinmann, J. Larik, R. Lee, P. Vennesson, *ASEAN's External Agreements* (Cambridge University Press 2015) as well as P. Nguitragool, J. Rüland *ASEAN as an Actor in International Fora* (Cambridge University Press 2015).

253 P. Gillespie, "European and Asian Responses" (Chapter 8) in T. Christiansen, E. Kirchner and P. Murray *The Palgrave Handbook of EU-Asia Relations (*Palgrave Macmillan 2013), pp. 124–142, at 1.

254 M. Cremona *et al.* (2015), p. 25.

255 A. Jetschke, "Regional Integration Support by the EU in Asia: Aims and Prospects" (Chapter 14) in T. Christiansen, E. Kirchner and P. Murray, *The Palgrave Handbook of EU-Asia Relations (*Palgrave Macmillan 2013), pp. 226–243, at 234.

Cooperation and the Declaration of ASEAN Concord.[256] Intra-ASEAN trade is not very large and Preferential Trading Agreements (PTA) are made separately from other cooperation.[257]

There is an ASEAN Regional Forum that includes other states also from outside the region (like the EU, USA and Russia) for discussions on regional issues that have more than just a regional impact. There are also many other constellations with different states, like e.g. the Asia-Pacific Economic Co-operation Forum (APEC) created in 1989, which can only pass non-binding recommendations.

ASEAN was created in 1967 by Indonesia, Malaysia, the Philippines, Singapore and Thailand. In 1984 Brunei joined, in 1995 Vietnam, in 1997 Laos and Myanmar and in 1999 (after a delay because of demands made on the country for entry) Cambodia. As can be seen, the width of the membership increased and the composition changed, with the later members being quite different from the initial ones politically and as far as the economic system is concerned. The Indo-Chinese states are transition economies coming from a Communist background.[258] Their membership of ASEAN coincided with economic reforms (like the Vietnamese "*doi moi* – new way" and the Laotian New Economic Management) and can be seen as the external dimension of these reform programmes. This allowed for a normative convergence between the different ASEAN states. At the same time, neither Vietnam nor Laos intended for the reforms to lead to a total change of system, but rather see them as means to legitimize the Communist regimes and deal with popular unrest.[259]

The difference in political systems but also in economic development and industrialisation contributed to ASEAN not being strong on economic cooperation. The more inward-looking policies of many member states also meant that the cooperation was not a strong feature.[260] The grouping did have economic aims among its stated aims but progress was slow and reluctant. Due to developments in the region, ASEAN started promoting some liberalisation measures in the 1980s and adopting investment and industrialisation strategies. Liberalisation led to growth and as generally there was an opening up of the economies; this in turn led to promotion of further common policies. Foreign investment provided an important push for regional cooperation.[261] In 1992 an agreement was signed on an Asian Free Trade Area (AFTA). The idea was to try

---

256 L. Hong Tan, "Will ASEAN Economic Integration progress beyond a Free Trade Area?" *International and Comparative Law Quarterly* Vol. 53 Oct 2004, pp. 935–967, at 935.

257 Mattli (1999), pp. 165–167.

258 On the Indo-Chinese enlargement, see H.E.S. Nesadurai, "The Indo-Chinese enlargement of ASEAN", pp. 199–215 in B. Fort and D. Webber (eds.), *Regional Integration in East Asia and Europe. Convergence and divergence.* (Routledge 2006).

259 Nesadurai (2006), at pp. 202–203.

260 Koh (2000), pp. 390–391.

261 *Ibid.*

to achieve a borderless area to make the region more attractive, inspired by other integrated regions mainly the EU (then the Single Market of the EC).[262] AFTA was pushed through faster than the initially agreed timetable (2002 instead of 2008), pushed by the financial crisis. There are, however, many exceptions to the free trade and possibilities to make further exceptions for certain products; the area is less far-reaching than other free trade areas. It does not include services and is very limited on labour mobility. At the same time, AFTA was combined with an Asian Investment Area (AIA) as well as an Asian Industrial Cooperation Scheme (AICS).[263] Plans have been made to complement AFTA with an Asian Economic Community (AEC), which according to earlier plans was to be completed in 2020.[264] Later the timetable was shortened and the Community should have been operational in 2015,[265] but this more ambitious timetable is at risk because of recent disagreements between members on (unrelated) issues regarding what attitude to take to China and its various claims in the Asia-Pacific region. General disagreements and inability to reach conclusions according to the accepted consensus mechanism has been seen to be likely to delay also the economic community plans although the formal view in spring 2015 was still that the Community would be created by the end of 2015.[266]As the trade liberalisation does not extend to services, it remains more modest that other free trade areas (such as NAFTA or Mercosur) even if ASEAN as an existing organisation should be able to provide a setting in which such liberalisation could be made, i.e. not starting from scratch but using existing frameworks for cooperation.[267]

In 2009 ASEAN adopted a charter setting out its purposes. Peace, security and stability maintenance and enhancement are among such principles. In practice, the rather modest role of the organisation in regional activities appears to remain, with the inability of ASEAN to play any major role in regional disputes. Without invitation from the states in question and without any powers of enforcement of its own, the organisation can only act decisively if the members explicitly request and accept that.

Hong Tan thinks that the kind of giving up of sovereignty with *supra*-national decision- making that is needed for such a Community is against the ASEAN psyche. Especially the creation of a supranational body was deemed not possible by ASEAN leaders. The regional integration should instead be built

262 *Ibid.*

263 Hong Tan (2004), pp. 940 and 942.

264 Nesadurai (2006), at p. 200 and M. Caballero-Anthony, "Regional institutions and regional crises in East Asia" in B. Fort and D. Webber (eds.), *Regional Integration in East Asia and Europe. Convergence and divergence.* (Routledge 2006), pp. 265–285, at 278.

265 Jetschke (2013), at p. 226.

266 Www.asean.org/communities/asean-economic-community (visited 6 June 2015).

267 D. Webber, "Regional integration in Europe and Asia. A historical perspective" in B. Fort and D. Webber (eds.), *Regional Integration in East Asia and Europe. Convergence and divergence.* (Routledge 2006) pp. 289–310 at 293.

on common norms and consensus, without institutional structures. To show a common identity by supporting one-another in global contexts is another aim of the ASEAN integration, still without any *supra*-national institutions.[268] Chesterman sees in the debate on "Asian values" a knee-jerk reaction to outside criticism rather than somethings inevitably based on cultural differences, as it was often presented.[269] In matters relating to the area of competence of AFTA, ASEAN has somewhat more thorough rules than generally and the institutional mechanisms give a greater role to the organisation within this part of its competence. The traditional model in ASEAN is otherwise one of a minimum of institutional structures and instead the dominance of the principle of non-interference.[270] There is a gradual expansion of matters that should fall within the competence of ASEAN or its related organs. In order to link social issues to the cooperation on economic ones, ASEAN has added plans for a socio-economic community to those of the AEC. The motivation for this is not so much the social viewpoint as such, but rather as socio-economic grievances may weaken the attractiveness for investors of a certain country or region.[271] ASEAN does not have any provisions on free movement of labour, but as there is a lot of (legal and illegal) mobility in the region, some commentators think this would be a logical next step.[272]

Such developments on concrete issues should be seen against the backdrop of ASEAN history. ASEAN was designed as a loose regional association, even avoiding the designation as a regional integration organisation. In its early years all decisions were taken by consensus and generally the association presented and thought of itself as a loose grouping without institutional structure and with the principle of non-interference as a key principle.[273] The less institutionalised approach in ASEAN was a deliberate choice of the member states rather than (as in some organisations) a first step to eventually build up more institutions.[274] Indeed, one of the reasons for ASEAN and for increased interest in it in later years is that a regional organisation can help protect members against such pressures from globalisation that may have a negative effect. A loose regional cooperation will promote the region in global institutions and provide it with a

268 Hong Tan (2004), *op. cit.* identifying that from the beginning of the cooperation the problem of competition rather than complementarity has made cooperation more difficult as has the openness to global economy instead of more inward looking policies. Especially pp. 946 and 948–949.

269 S. Chesterman, *From Community to Compliance? The Evolution of Monitoring Obligations in ASEAN* (Cambridge University Press 2015), p. 43.

270 Nesadurai (2006), at p. 202.

271 Nesadurai (2006), pp. 212 and 214 (n. 3).

272 Nesadurai (2006) p. 211.

273 D.F. Anwar, "Leadership in the history of Southeast Asian integration" in B. Fort and D. Webber (eds.), *Regional Integration in East Asia and Europe. Convergence and divergence.* (Routledge 2006), pp. 59–68, at 60.

274 Higgott (2006), at p. 23.

global voice – while the regional organisation through its own structure protects the idea of non-interference and strongly underlined sovereignty. Regional organisations secure a position globally and then make sure that the sovereign, individual roles of its members are protected.

At the same time, ASEAN covers different types of issues and the organisations has at different times (with or without success) dealt with coordination of foreign policy, so it is not possible to dismiss the regional integration potential of ASEAN just because of its institutional weakness.[275]

One element of the weak institutional structure is the absence of any bodies for dispute resolution in ASEAN.[276] In the 1976 Treaty of Amity and Cooperation some commentators see a beginning of a dispute resolution mechanism. The main mechanism is, however, still informal methods such as discussion and negotiation, rather than judicial or quasi-judicial institutionalised systems. Koh sees this as a reflection of an Asian cultural preference for such informal dispute resolution mechanisms as opposed to Western preference to have "rules of the game" set out beforehand. Koh, however, recognises that regardless of these cultural preferences, for the type of issues the organisation deals with a dispute resolution just based on diplomacy risks being inadequate and threaten the activities of the organisation. Furthermore it is recognised that ASEAN tends to sweep problems under the carpet. Koh sees the existence of a formal dispute resolution mechanism as potentially interesting even only to the extent that if member states attempt to avoid using it (which would be to lose face) this may lead them to undertake further efforts at amicable dispute resolution.[277] Even with a cultural preference for "soft" dispute resolution mechanisms, there needs to be an incentive to actually resolve disputes!

Apparently contradicted by the fact that it is an organisation without strong systems for dealing with disputes, ASEAN was from the start a tool for dealing with regional conflict and has over the years undertaken measures to increase its ability to do this. The creation of the ASEAN Regional Forum (ARF) in 1994 (decision taken in 1993) was such a step. ASEAN's possibilities and mechanisms for conflict avoidance could, through this Forum, be extended to the larger

275 Webber (2006), at p. 293.

276 Chesterman (2015).

277 Koh (2000), esp. at pp. 393–394. The aim of Koh's article is to argue for a regional arbitration centre that would also support private subjects, important in economic relations (like disputes in various trade-related matters, with states and/or private subjects as parties). This would reduce to need for a fully fledged court but may in the view of Koh afford some of the same benefits (of seeing the region as a consistent region in the eyes of investors and similar). See esp. pp. 399–400. With publication of arbitral awards suggested there are some elements in the plans of Koh that have the same potentially beneficial effects as a court would have. Koh, however, recognises eventually a need for an Asean court of justice as the arbitral panel can only fulfil some of the tasks that a court would have and have some of the powers. The arbitral tribunal would for example not provide a link between national and regional legal systems. Koh compares with the Andean Pact and how it was discovered a court was necessary. See p. 411.

Asia-Pacific region and be more suited to face new threats regionally and globally. ARF has 27 members and is thus larger than ASEAN and this means it includes more varied and more distant members, having a different concept of the relevant region.[278] ARF as the principal forum for security cooperation in the region should disseminate rules and norms and through this contribute to trust, peace and prosperity – not solving conflicts (which is difficult without stronger structures) but promoting confidence-building. The principle of non-interference and what Weber calls traditional ASEAN-style diplomacy apply also to ARF. This includes a preference for non-binding, non-legalistic approaches and minimal institutionalisation.[279]

Among measures taken by ASEAN to create a stronger role for itself was the establishment in 2001 of a financial surveillance mechanism to avoid further crises of the 1997–1998 type. In the environmental area, the regional haze problem led to a discussion on the reasons for this and how to avert future re-occurrences, even if this at least implicitly had to include a discussion on domestic policies of member states. Among proposed structures were retreats for discussion of common problems by foreign ministers and an ASEAN Troika (decided 1999 and formally established 2000)[280] for urgent regional situations that could threaten peace and security.[281] The Troika mechanism formalised the *ad hoc* Troika created for Cambodia.[282] These modest steps were means to deal with the lacking institutional structure of ASEAN and the absence of any political will to create such a structure. All these small steps and the important matter of ASEAN actually reacting to internal situations in both Cambodia and Myanmar contributed to a small opening in the idea of non-intervention above all.

Among the initiatives undertaken by ASEAN to strengthen economic cooperation – not least as a guarantee against new such crises as the economic and financial crisis in South-East Asia in the late 1990s – is the *Chiang Mai* initiative for closer monetary integration, dating from May 2000. This initiative was elaborated by ASEAN together with Japan, China and South Korea; a constellation that often came to be called ASEAN+3.[283] It was developed and

278 Caballero-Anthony (2006), at pp. 268–269.

279 K. Weber, "The ASEAN Regional Forum" (Chapter 21) in T. Christiansen, E. Kirchner and P. Murray, *The Palgrave Handbook of EU-Asia Relations* (Palgrave Macmillan 2013), pp. 344–358, at 346. Also Chesterman (2015), *op. cit.*

280 The ASEAN Troika, Terms of Reference Adopted at the 33rd AMM. Bangkok, 24–25 July 2000, www.aseansec.org/3637.htm.

281 J. Haacke, "The development of ASEAN's diplomatic and security culture" in B. Fort and D. Webber (eds.) *Regional Integration in East Asia and Europe. Convergence and divergence.* (Routledge 2006), pp. 150–169, at 151.

282 See e.g. ASEAN Statement on Cambodia 4 September 1998, www.aseansec.org/16284.htm.

283 On the Chiang Mai initiative, see N. Hamilton-Hart "The Chiang Mai Initiative and the prospects for closer monetary integration in East Asia" in B. Fort and D. Webber (eds.), *Regional Integration in East Asia and Europe. Convergence and divergence.* (Routledge 2006) p. 109. Although not including the latest development, it still gives a good picture of the background and aims of the initiative.

multilateralised in 2010.[284] ASEAN+3, which was first created in December 1997, gained a lot of attention in the early 2000s.[285] The Japanese Prime Minister Koizumi in 2002 suggested that ASEAN+3 should be built upon to create an East Asian institution. However, the body did not progress to create a codified institution or otherwise to formalise the vision of cooperation that was behind its creation.[286]

In an Indonesian proposal for an ASEAN Political and Security Community (ASC) in 2003 (adopted by the member states in October 2003), the word democracy was mentioned by ASEAN for the first time as a political objective. ASEAN leaders agreed to establish the ASEAN political, security and socio-cultural communities until 2015 to examine innovative ways to strengthen regional security, given that the countries in the region are closely linked with one-another. This would include norm-setting, conflict prevention, possible conflict-resolution as well as post-conflict peace building. The ASC has not amounted to much, but this mention may still be seen as a small, hesitant step to establishing certain goals that the regional integration organisation should promote. The Indonesian proposal for ASC included various issues such as a centre for combating terrorism, a peace keeping training centre and a maritime surveillance centre, all to be placed in the ASEAN framework. Caballero-Anthony sees the fact that such initiative was made within the ASEAN framework as a reflection of how the organisation responds to new challenges and is becoming more proactive.[287] The fact that the initiative did not amount to much in practice may counteract this claim. Caballero-Anthony stresses that ASEAN has not been entirely ineffective in dealing with security challenges and the greatest obstacles for further success are to be found in the weak domestic capabilities of the members.[288] The plans for ASC had to be seen in the usual ASEAN framework of non-interference and quiet diplomacy, and the proposal was through various twists and turns watered down to be little more than a reaffirmation of what could already be seen to be there.[289] It was an unprecedented move in Asia towards regional integration, but many commentators dismiss it as rhetoric, while at the same time agreeing that these initiatives did lead to some notable changes like the Asia Free Trade Area project and the charter of ASEAN.[290]

---

284 Gillespie (2013), p. 135.

285 See e.g. Webber (2006), especially pp. 303–305.

286 S. Tang, "Leadership in institution building. The case of ASEAN+3" in B. Fort and D. Webber (eds.), *Regional Integration in East Asia and Europe. Convergence and divergence.* (Routledge 2006), pp. 69–82, at 69 and T. Terada, "The birth and growth of ASEAN+3", pp. 218–235 in Fort & Webber (2006), at pp. 218–219.

287 M. Caballero-Anthony (2006), p. 266.

288 Caballero-Anthony (2006), pp. 266–267.

289 Haacke (2006), pp. 158–160; Caballero-Anthony (2006), p. 278.

290 M-G Manea, "The Institutional Dimension of the EU/ASEAN Plus Three Inter-regional Relations" (Chapter 19) in T. Christiansen, E. Kirchner and P. Murray, *The Palgrave Handbook of EU-Asia Relations* (Palgrave Macmillan 2013), pp. 313–329, at 323–324.

A key term in ASEAN has been the principle of non-interference. This has traditionally been interpreted to be quite far-reaching, going further than the UN principle of non-interference in internal affairs or at least using the most extensive interpretation of this international law principle. In the past decades there have been some attempts to give ASEAN more strength and in these attempts, the need to fit a more active role for the organisation within the framework of non-interference has been a major challenge. Against the backdrop of the Cambodia crisis in 1997, the Malaysian leader launched an idea of "constructive intervention", allowing certain ideas of support and intervention in the political situation of a country.[291] In June 1998 at the time of the severe economic and financial crisis in the region and in the midst of a controversy regarding Burmese membership, the then Thai foreign minister launched the idea of "flexible engagement" as a term encapsulating the idea that ASEAN members should be able to discuss domestic policies of others if these had or might have a regional impact. Not only should discussion be possible but also public comment. It thus had to be reconciled not just with non-interference but also with traditional quiet diplomacy. The discussion should be by governments of ASEAN members, as the organisation more or less lacks an institutional structure that would be able to deal with such matters. Still, it was seen by some as a challenge to the idea that ASEAN should not get involved in bilateral or intra-ASEAN disputes, if even by just commenting. Despite attempts by the initiator of the idea to fit it within the existing ASEAN notions, the opposition to the idea meant that it at the time did not lead to any concrete measures. At the same time, it may have been a starting point for the development of a somewhat more active role for ASEAN. If flexible engagement was not all right, "enhanced interaction" was. The difference was not just semantic but also that in this latter concept, it was clearer that it was a possibility for member states to act and react and not for ASEAN as such. Even this proved to be too much and the idea was more or less abandoned quite soon in favour of the traditional emphasis on non-intervention and nothing else.[292] Even so, just having the discussion may have opened up the idea of a stronger ASEAN and some other actions have shown that this idea has not been abandoned.

In 2009 ASEAN Members through the Cha-am Hua Hin Declaration created an Intergovernmental Commission on Human Rights to implement the human rights commitment of the 2007 ASEAN Charter of Association of Southeast Asian Nations (Article 14).[293] The commitment to human rights shall continue

---

291 On this, see more below. Also, Caballero-Anthony (2006), at p. 277 and fn. 12.

292 J. Haacke (2006), especially at pp. 150–151. See also A. Acharya, "Europe and Asia. Reflections on a tale of two regionalisms", pp. 312–321 in Fort & Webber (2006), at p. 315.

293 T. Hsien-Li, "Persistent engagement and insistent persuasion: the role of the working group for an ASEAN Human Rights Mechanism in institutionalizing human rights in the region", pp. 127–143 in H. Nasu & B. Saul (eds.), *Human Rights in the Asia-Pacific Region* (Routledge 2011); www.aseansec.org/22769.htm.

to evolve and the Terms of Reference for the Commission shall be reviewed every 5 years. In November 2012 an ASEAN Human Rights Declaration was elaborated.[294] ASEAN is thus a newcomer to regional human rights protection and the relationship between such protection and the extensive interpretation of the non-intervention principle remains to be seen.

The Commission is based on the Charter. Various instruments like Terms of Reference on the parameters and structure of the body, declarations on the aspirations of it and blueprints on human rights objectives give further detail on intended work and responsibilities.[295]

II.4.4. THE ARAB WORLD

In 2010 momentous developments started in the Arab world leading to what became generally known as the Arab Spring.[296] Though it is still early to predict the wider outcome of the movements for democracy in many Arab states there have been several negative developments after the early euphoria – the bloody and prolonged civil wars in Syria and Libya and the unrest in Egypt are prominent examples. Tunisia, the origin of the Arab Spring, has been a more positive example with a new constitution adopted in early 2014 and democratic elections held for presidency and parliament, but also there developments have not only been stable. Although the revolutionary movements spread from one state to another, there has not been much organised regional cooperation and so far no regional integration systems have played any role in the situation. The Arab League[297] has generally been seen as an ineffective body and efforts at integration in the Arab region have floundered. The Arab Spring meant some small changes to this, but the body fell far short of taking on a leading role.

The Economist in 2009 aptly described the Arab League as doing little more than organising bad-tempered summits, fending off Western criticism of human rights abuses and denouncing Israel[298] and in 2010 it adds to its description that none of the members are stable and fully fledged democracies.[299] Mallat introduces the Arab League as the most telling example of failed attempts at Arab integration.[300] This situation changed somewhat in connection with the Arab Spring, when the Arab League started playing a more active role. For example, its members agreed to invite the UN Security Council to intervene

294 Www.asean.org/news/asean-statement-communiques/item/asean-human-rights-declaration.

295 Hsien-Li (2011), pp. 128–129.

296 G. Joffé, "The Arab Spring in North Africa: Origins and Prospects", *The Journal of North African Studies* Vol. 16 No. 4 December 2011, pp. 507–532, esp. at 509–511.

297 Www.arableagueonline.org/.

298 *The Economist* 25 July 2009.

299 *The Economist* 17 July 2010.

300 C. Mallat, *Introduction to Middle Eastern Law* (Oxford University Press 2007), p. 151.

in Libya in 2011[301], which led to the UN Security Council Resolution 1973.[302] However, the momentum was not kept up and even if the League is still more visible than it was before the Arab Spring, it did not assume a leading role in the regional developments. The Arab League was founded in 1945 through a Treaty[303] signed initially by Egypt, Iraq, Jordan, Lebanon, Saudi Arabia and Syria. It is a loose confederation and decision-making is by consensus. The aim was generally to protect common interests and achieve better cooperation between Arab countries. The League has played some role as a counterpart to other regional integration organisations like the EU and as mediator in conflicts, primarily through its Secretary-General. The Secretary-General implements decisions of the representative organ of the member states, the Council, which meets irregularly and at different levels. The Arab League created a number of specialised treaties on matters from postal cooperation to tourism, most of which have been ineffective. The most prominent activity is in relation to the boycott of Israel but also here common implementing bodies or structures are lacking.[304]

Not until in 2004 did the Arab League adopt a regional human rights instrument,[305] the Arab Charter on Human Rights, which entered into force in 2008.[306]The Organisation of Islamic Cooperation in 1990 passed the Cairo Declaration on Human Rights in Islam.[307] This document stipulates that it is to be a document of guidance on human rights. It is not enforceable or institutionalised. The aim was rather to counterbalance what was felt to be a Western dominance in the global human rights debate that did not take Islamic views into consideration.

In addition to the Arab League there are some more limited (geographically) integration efforts in the Arab region, such as the Gulf Cooperation Council. Other earlier attempts have failed, like the Arab Cooperation Council, which lasted only one year (1989–1990).

The Gulf Cooperation Council (GCC) is a regional integration body that has also political integration aims. The GCC was created in 1981. Its members are Bahrain, Kuwait, Oman, Qatar, Saudi Arabia and the United Arab Emirates.[308]

---

301 T. Tudoroiu, "The Arab Spring: Last Episode of the Cold War", *Contemporary Politics* 2013 19:3, pp. 304–320, at 308. Also Vidmar (2013), p. 36.

302 S/RES/1973 (2011) Libya, www.un.org/en/sc/documents/resolutions/2011.shtml.

303 Founding Charter of the Arab League, Jami'at al-duwal al-'arabiyya. 22 March 1945.

304 Mallat (2007), pp. 151–152.

305 The Arab Charter on Human Rights was initially adopted by the Arab League in 1994, but at that time none of the member states ratified it so an amended version was adopted in 2004.

306 B. Saul, J. Mowbray & I. Baghoomians, "Resistance to regional human rights cooperation in the Asia-Pacific: demythologizing regional exceptionalism by learning from the Americas, Europe and Africa", pp. 107–126 in H. Nasu & B. Saul (eds.), *Human Rights in the Asia-Pacific Region* (Routledge 2011), p. 107.

307 Www.oic-oci.org/english/article/human.htm.

308 Www.gcc-sg.org/eng.

The body was created as a reaction to the Iran-Iraq war and it was another war – the Iraqi invasion of Kuwait in 1990 – that highlighted the ineffectiveness of the organisation and led to scepticism about its potential. Institutions like a Supreme Council, a Ministerial Council and a secretariat do exist.[309] The GCC has a customs union and harmonisation of policies as its aims but the external common customs tariff has not been implemented. As far as the political goals are concerned, these have not been very vigorously pursued and politically the states are quite different. The Council in the spring of 2011 declared that it would accept Jordan and Morocco as members, despite the fact that Morocco had never asked to join and the application status of Jordan was also not clear.[310] Apart from this bemusing reaction to developments in the Arab World, the Council has not played any major political role and cannot be seen to have any integrating effect. It appears more as a well-established but not politically very active cooperation body for states of similar, and in the global context rare, organisational structure and wealth.

Quite aside from the activities formally undertaken in the framework of the GCC, its member states have to some extent coordinated their activities for example as regards embarking on a quest to reduce their reliance on oil to position themselves in other areas like finance or the media. The most known example of the latter is the creation by the Qatari regime of the Al Jazeera television channel in 1995. Although this channel has undoubtedly put Qatar and the region on the global map for broadcast news as well as led to improvement in the available media picture in the region, apart from some discussions broadly in the GCC framework, the regional body has not been involved formally in these initiatives.[311]

The Arab Maghreb Union (AMU) was founded in 1989 and includes Algeria, Libya, Mauritania, Morocco and Tunisia. The aim of encouraging free trade has not been reached (with such trade still very limited) and the organisation has not held any summits since 1994 although meetings of specialised ministers or officials are held.[312] However, formal institutions have been created, with a Presidential Council, a Council of Foreign Ministers, a Consultative Council of Parliamentarians and a committee of judges.[313]

---

309 Mallat (2007), p. 149.

310 *The Economist*, 21 May 2011.

311 N. Sultan, "Al Jazeera: Reflections on the Arab Spring", pp. 249–264 in *Journal of Arabian Studies 3.2*, December 2013, at p. 249.

312 Www.maghrebarabe.org.

313 Mallat (2007), p. 148.

III. HOW DO REGIONAL INTEGRATION INSTITUTIONS IMPOSE THEIR WILL UPON MEMBER STATES?

III.1. LEGITIMACY

Legitimacy is a way to express the link between the ruler and those being ruled. Legitimacy expresses acceptability and something more than just conforming to rules – legality.[314] It is of historic importance as the question of why someone can rule over someone else is a very old philosophical question. The answer to it has varied through history, but interestingly the basic content of the question remains similar. The right to rule is either given from some abstract, superior power (such as God) or it is created. If the direct link to religion does not play a significant part in modern legal philosophy, the question of where human rights come from and if a ruler can rule in any way or has to abide by some universal human rights is still current and in many ways is just another way to look at the same thing: is the legitimacy of the ruler and the way he/she rules something created or something that exists in any case?

Mather identifies legitimacy as a prerequisite for successful political government and divides legitimacy – linkage between the ruler and the ruled – into a shared conviction, an artificially created device, an accepted system and something invested in a particular person or government. She discusses the many definitions of legitimacy such as the ruler's right to rule and trust or allegiance (interpersonal or institutional). Legitimacy may contain a normative element as there must be a means of securing it, expectations must be met.[315] Mather summarises a legitimate regime as having a normative element (rule bound and justifiable); having demonstrable popular consent; enabling citizens to identify with it; is authoritative; and meets popular expectations. To this should be added that legitimacy does not need to be absolute, but may be partial or conditional.[316]

As can be seen, these criteria per se can also fit a regional integration system, not just a state. In a globalised world with trans-border problems that individual

314 Focarelli (2012), p. 245.

315 J. Mather, *Legitimizing the European Union. Aspirations, inputs and performance.* (Palgrave 2006), at p. 10.

316 Mather (2006), at pp. 12–13.

states can only partially deal with[317], the legitimacy criteria may even fit other units than states better, especially as far as meeting expectations is concerned.

At the same time, the state has a historically established structure where the constitutional order is protected and respected, because of its link with a politically legitimate authority that can make itself obeyed by those to whom it issues rules and orders. This exact same type of legitimacy cannot easily be transferred to the international arena.[318]

Contrary to states, a regional integration organisation does not in general draw its legitimacy from people's emotions or feelings of patriotism and identity, of belonging to a certain group or of attachment to a certain territory. Such feelings will enhance the legitimacy of a state and for states that for various purposes have problems with national unity, the solution is found in enhancing the feelings of belonging of all groups. Most people accept the legitimacy of states. Those (minorities for example) that may challenge the state most often do not challenge the state as such, but its borders or government. The problem of lack of belonging may also apply to the territory, if the attachment is to a group but this group does not have control over its territory or does not even live on its historic territory. In both cases, the state that wants to strengthen its legitimacy has a known framework in which to operate: building on the belonging to a people or a territory and underlining the common features, reducing the importance of the divisive ones.

The question of expectations is important for legitimacy of a regional integration system. As the international system is built up around nation states (although in historical terms only since quite recently), just like there is often presupposed to be an inherent legitimacy in states, there is presumed to be an expectation about what a state can and should do. If the expectations are not met, there may be a challenge to legitimacy. If and to what extent it matters depends on other factors, primarily the reason for the failure and whether such reason is external to the state or internal. States that are only partially recognised such as Kosovo may serve as an example. The state cannot perform all the functions that would be expected from a state, but as long as a majority of the population see this as a result of external factors, the state does not necessarily lose its legitimacy.

A regional integration system may similarly be subject to various expectations and different factors will determine if these can be met. However, if the expectations on a certain body such as a regional integration system are low or diffuse, it may well be able to meet these expectations but only because they are set at a very low level. If the expectations are turned up (for example that the

[317] Discussed by Mather (2006), at p. 178, suggesting the EU should be the focus for legitimacy in Europe and the source from which member states derive legitimacy, rather than the other way around. She also mentions the creation of the EC in the mid-20th century as a first step away from a Peace of Westphalia idea of militarily efficient states, defined by their ability to engage in conflict with one-another. P. 29.

[318] C. Focarelli (2012), p. 125.

regional integration system can guarantee democracy) without the means being given to it to undertake any real measures, the legitimacy suffers. Legitimacy being created by the very process it is created for may look like an unsolvable chicken-and-egg question,[319] but rather than taking this view, it should be seen as a series of factors, including expectations, that compose a web. For a state there are certain given factors that form the main part of this web, whereas for a regional integration system the components of the web are less clearly defined.

In the discussion on influence of regional integration organisations for democratisation a preliminary question is the status of such organisations *vis-à-vis* the member states. The further the integration progresses, the more it is shown that an organisation is not just the sum of its parts but can be more than that. This is shown by the EU as the furthest reaching organisation of regional integration, which shows that it can do more than the states in it could do without the organisation. Bieber mentions as examples that no single state could impose fines on companies outside its borders or fix customs tariffs for other states. More generally, being able to provide for security and welfare of citizens within the confines of one state is also increasingly unlikely. This is especially so for smaller states but not just for these.[320] What the issues are that states can only deal with effectively if they do it jointly is a question of interpretation. It also affects the view on subjects of international law and whether it is still adequate to regard only states as proper subjects or if this is an outdated view. Commentators studying the EU point to a need to revise the state-centred view somewhat but at the same time, the discussions around the treaty changes of the EU (leading up to the Lisbon Treaty entering into force in December 2009) instead underline the traditional view. The ruling of the German Constitutional Court in June 2009 on the legality of the Lisbon Treaty is based on the understanding that democracy, self-determination and citizenship derive from the sovereign state.[321] Such a state must have a people and as long as there is not one united people in the regional integration organisation (in this case the EU), such an organisation cannot replace the state and thus does not need meet the same demands as a state regarding democracy.[322] Bieber is critical of this view of the Constitutional Court as it, in his opinion, is not consistent neither with theories of democracy and transnational governance, nor with the realities and intentions of the EU.[323]

319 Mather (2006), at pp. 173–174, discusses the same chicken-and-egg question regarding the European Parliament, which cannot be given too big powers as it lacks proper legitimacy and which does not attract the required attention in the form of participation in the vote, etc., to make it worthy of greater powers. She interprets this as a misguided attempt to just insert liberal representative democracy on the EU system without it necessarily fitting it.

320 R. Bieber, "The Lissabon-Urteil: An Association of Sovereign States", *European Journal of Constitutional Law* 5(2009), pp. 397–398.

321 Bundesverfassungsgericht (Germany) 30 June 2009, available (also in English) at www.bundesverfassungsgericht.de/entscheidungen/es20090630_2bve000208en.html.

322 Bieber (2009), pp. 396–397.

323 *Ibid.*

However, the widely quoted ruling has been influential for how both academics and political leaders talk about EU and its relationship with its member states.

There are many different levels on which a regional integration system can be legitimized. Mather discusses these in relation to the most advanced system, the EU. There is the technocratic, rule based, EU; a state-centric one; a multi-level polity one or a Federal Europe. Different components work together and elements of all these different types of cooperation and integration may work together. Good, useful rules can legitimate the EU as can a new form of representation that is not just centred on the nation-state and its majority populations.[324]

Schütze discusses if the people, the constituency, have to precede a polity or if it can be the result of it. It is not only for regional integration organisations that the question arises, as there are also many examples of multi-national states where the people of the state is a political and constitutional creation rather than based on ethnic or historic circumstances. In such cases as in the EU, notions of what Schütze calls dual citizenship (albeit in a different meaning than the regular one for this term – citizenship of more than one country) have been created: being citizen of several layers of a constitutional or other creation, like the EU citizenship.[325] One legitimacy does not exclude another as long as they are not incompatible by content.

The conceptual issues regarding legitimacy that have been seen during the history of the concept and the legal philosophy that underpins it are similar for different subjects in the modern discussion on legitimacy for other bodies than states. One such issue can be stated simply as the question of who decided what issues fall into the competence of what body.[326] If there is a clear basic unit of the system, this unit has powers that it can use itself or give away. If the unit is the state, all legitimacy of organs consisting of states comes from the basic legitimacy of the state. Today this is the way international organisation including the EU are construed – their competence is derived – but it is theoretically not the only possible source of legitimacy. It is not utopic at least in a more distant future to see another basis for legitimacy of regional integration.[327]

One basic element for legitimizing regional integration in the minds of people (leaders as well as populations) is that the region is seen as a real concept. There needs to be a shared interest in issues and other factors that bind states together.[328] In Asia, there are vast inter-Asian differences so an Asian attitude

---

324 Mather (2006), pp. 170–173.

325 R. Schütze, *From Dual to Cooperative Federalism. The Changing Structure of European Law* (Oxford University Press 2009), p. 64.

326 Mather discusses this problem in relation to the division between secular and divine power. See Mather (2006), pp. 16–17.

327 K. Nyman Metcalf, "Regional Integration and Sovereignty; The Sum is More than its Parts?" in P. Sevastik (ed.), *Aspects of Sovereignty* (Martinus Nijhoff 2013), pp. 83–100, especially at 93–97.

328 The lack of this as a factor hindering closer cooperation in Asia in the ASEAN+3 framework is discussed by Terada, see especially pp. 218–221 in Terada (2006). The Asian financial crisis of

to international relations is harder to determine than a European such attitude. Also, when Europe has seen integration and cooperation as a way to get more power on the world stage, in Asia strategic alliances with great powers have been favoured. Multilateralism in Asia has often been seen as a way to preserve state sovereignty rather than transcend it.[329] In Africa there may be a common identity through a similar history (like in the post-Colonial struggle) but with time, regional rather than pan-African groupings may be more likely to rely on such a common identity. A large part of the Americas share a common language and also some common history and there are some signs this may belatedly lead to integration although it has so far not had much of this effect. The need for at least a certain level of similarity in political systems for deeper integration can be seen in all different regions.

Clearly the mind-set of States (if such a thing can be imagined) plays a role for the success of integration, together with practical matters such as how well institutions function and similar. One example can be taken from ASEAN+3, an attempt to bring big powers like China, Japan and Korea closer to the rest of the region – the members of ASEAN. Mental barriers may hinder cooperation, but as is suggested by Tang,[330] may also favour it, if the big powers are unable to overcome mutual suspicion, but may learn to cooperate through a multilateral framework in a way that would not be possible bilaterally.

III.1.1. CONSTRUCTING LEGITIMACY: ORGANS AND INSTRUMENTS

Based on the analysis above, it can be said that a regional integration organisation has to construct its legitimacy. It cannot obtain this legitimacy automatically from anywhere but it will be created as a direct consequence of the institutional structure as well as credibility and influence of the work of the organisation. Method and effect are part and parcel of the same processes. This means that the legal instruments setting up the regional integration organisation as well as the institutional structures supporting the functioning of it, will help to create the legitimacy that after a certain time will be able to fulfil a role to actually support these same institutions.

Regional integration structures are created through international law and the instruments and methods available in this legal system. What is created may, however, be something that is somewhat outside of regular international law, a *sui generis* structure. De Witte points out how international law is very free as

the late 1990s made countries aware of their interdependence and the common interests that they in fact had. This prompted regional leaders to ask why Asia alone among the three poles of the world economy should not have a regional bloc to speak for it. Terada (2006), at p. 227.

329 Acharya (2006), at pp. 317–318.

330 Tang (2006), at p. 81.

to the form it allows for states to agree on things and mentions as one difference of EU law as compared to public international law that the EU does not allow this freedom of form. One element of the *sui generis* character of EU law is that member states have bound themselves to act within the system, also when it comes to e.g. changes to the treaties.[331] This legal construction is important for the strength of the regional integration system, to afford it a sense of permanence.

Mattli calls organs like the Court of Justice and the Commission in the EU "commitment institutions". These provide for monitoring and enforcement in a manner that is out of the hands of the member states directly. Such institutions are prerequisites for a successful regional integration system, in Mattli's view together with market pressures and a regional leader or hegemon.[332]

In *Regional Integration and Courts of Justice*[333] the importance of courts for the enhancement of legitimacy was shown. Courts and a legalistic interpretation of tasks of the organisation give the regional integration its contours; they help show in a functional manner the potential of an organisation. This strengthens the organisation as the functional success may lead to a legitimacy that reaches outside of the actual functions carried out. If an organisation was successful in creating a common market for coal and steel (CECA) it may be successful in creating a common policy on asylum (EU), as the basic organisational structures and the way the Court of Justice protected these worked so well.

Courts of Justice have a very important role in the institutional structure of a regional integration.[334] Courts can strengthen the rest of the institutional structure and determine the division of competence between the organisation and its member states. This constitutional role of the court will make the organisation different from international organisations with a more limited mandate, where there is no independent organ to determine division of competence but this will always be done by the members themselves.

The significance of courts is evident, but courts cannot be the only strong institution. Legitimacy needs more than just the court. There is no question at the present time that national governments have a higher degree of legitimacy than regional integration organisations with the possible exception of the EU. For such organisations it is thus necessary to prove the legitimacy in a different way than that which applies to state decisions. It is in this context that the importance of the institutional structure of the body is very clearly shown.

The principle of legal accessibility is a component of a rule of law state. This principle means that a legal order has an organisation of some kind that can help individual subjects to realise law and to thus enjoy the rights that a legal system may give them. Legal accessibility is more than just the existence

---

331 B. De Witte, "International Law as a tool for the European Union", *European Constitutional Law* 5(2009), pp. 265–283, especially at 269.

332 W. Mattli (1999), especially at pp. 13–15. See also Webber (2006), at p. 302 and fn. 8.

333 Nyman-Metcalf & Papageorgiou (2005).

334 As has been further elaborated in *Regional Integration and Court of Justice*.

of courts or other organs as it includes also a real possibility to get access to justice. The importance of legal accessibility is seen for example in the number of cases in the European Court on Human Rights concerning violation of Article 6 of the ECHR, the Article dealing with fair trials and access to legal remedies. Among requirements for real legal accessibility are demands that processes be not overly complicated or time-consuming and that there be practical as well as formal guarantees for an actual access to courts or other legal bodies.[335]

The principle of legal accessibility is not only relevant for states, but if there is a legal system that includes other actors than states that may influence the rights of individual subjects, there must be legal accessibility also in relation to such organs. This can mean that organs have courts of their own or that the decisions taken by the organs can be tried in national courts (or a combination of the two). In the most advanced regional integration system, the EU, the existence and powers of the European Court of Justice as well as the supremacy of EU law to be applied by national courts contribute to legal accessibility in the sphere of EU law to the same extent as in the sphere of national law. The references in the EU treaties to the ECHR including Article 6 underline this understanding.

For enforcement of decisions in a rule of law state, there must be corresponding access to justice or legal accessibility. If a regional integration system is created without such guarantees, it could rightly be seen as a weakening of the rule of law. This would be the case also if the system made access to justice more complicated, even if it did not make it impossible. For a positive impact of a regional integration system on rule of law and democracy, the effective enforcement combined with guarantees of legal accessibility (including appealing decisions to a judicial organ) are a necessary prerequisite.

The institutional structure needs to be determined in the founding documents of the organisation or otherwise the way in which such structure will be created (through a constituent assembly) needs to be established. The structure must be clear enough to be effective but at the same time flexible enough to allow the organisation to grow with its tasks. The credibility and success of an organisation are strengthened if details concerning its activities can be established by the organisation's organs themselves. Static organisations where any changes to their role and functions need to go back to the member states for decision have less of a long-term chance of success or at least of taking on an independent role. Member states must be willing to give the organisation the possibility to lead some life of its own if it is to influence the region in which it operates, rather than just carry out clearly delimited operational tasks given to it by the member states.

Bieber finds that the EU model of not subordinating systems of governance to one-another in a more classical hierarchical structure is an example of successful

335 A. Frändberg, "Legal Accessibility" in *Festskrift till Anders Fogelklou* (Iustus, Uppsala 2008), pp. 33–47.

sophistication, where different interests will be balanced against one another in an ongoing dynamic that obliges continuous adjustment of all the parts. This can lead to an increased sense of responsibility and an understanding of common interest. It does not necessarily lead to, nor should it lead to, identical solutions but to different solutions in a common framework. Democracy as a concept is the example brought by Bieber of a notion that is wide enough to be filled with different content, but where a common understanding exists. In such a case there is a benefit for the concept as such of the process of learning and adjustment.[336]

The EU appears to have strong legitimacy as seen through the acceptance of its decisions, but even so the question arises if this is legitimacy or just law-abidingness? There are many debates on the exact limits of competence between the EU and its member states, both on what is suitable *de lege ferenda* and what it in reality is *de lege lata*. However, there are few serious commentators that would question the legitimacy of the EU as such. The legitimacy has been built up through the powers given by member states to the organisations so like the powers of it, the legitimacy is derivative. This derivative nature of the EU is made clearer in the Lisbon Treaty.

The EU shows examples of indirect increasing of legitimacy (if you accept the decisions on something of one organisation because they are usually good, you will accept the decision also on other things by the same organisation – which is why even something as technical as competition law helps to increase the overall legitimacy of the EU).

As Terada puts it, the habit of cooperating can be conductive to strengthening shared beliefs and promoting further cooperation and consensus. Through cooperation not only will there be a useful exchange of information, but the nations can learn solidarity and understanding of social and cultural differences, which will help increased cooperation.[337]

III.1.2. CULTURAL DIVERSITY AND LEGITIMACY OF REGIONAL INTEGRATION

It is possible to see the principle of cultural diversity as restricting regional integration. This is proposed by Von Bogdandy[338] but he himself immediately states that the argument is not convincing as cultural diversity is a recent concern of international law and one that does not have sufficient support in state practice. The idea of cultural diversity as common heritage of mankind

336 Bieber (2009), p. 403.

337 Terada (2006), at p. 233.

338 A. Von Bogdandy, "The European Union as Situation, Executive and Promoter of the International Law of Cultural Diversity – Elements of a Beautiful Friendship", pp. 241–275, *European Journal of International Law* Vol. 19 No. 2 (2008), at p. 252.

that UNESCO has suggested[339] would, however, point in the direction of an aspiration that cultural diversity will become a concept with a role in international law that must be taken into consideration in various contexts – including creation of regional integration organisations. It could be a breach of international law for a state to do something that might endanger the cultural diversity – like sign a treaty of regional integration that has this effect. Von Bogdandy also says it would be a novelty if general international law posed any restrictions on the integration of states, decided by the free will of such states. For the argument to be valid in the first place, the regional integration system should be some kind of threat to cultural diversity. This is far from evident, indeed the furthest reaching regional integration system – the EU – contains an explicit ban on harmonisation in the sphere of culture.[340]

Von Bogdandy finds that international law poses a requirement to respect human rights including cultural pluralism, which has to be taken into consideration when creating an organisation for integration – like the EU. This obligation is primarily found in Article 27 ICCPR, which also has a bearing on minority rights. Von Bogdandy speculates about an EU people becoming a minority in the framework of the EU but finds that this is not the case, as there is no majority culture as such.[341]

The EU like also other regional integration systems (of which the EU is by far the strongest and furthest reaching) have integration as their core task. This means that although the integration system may well allow for and even promote cultural diversity, convergence and standardisation are more likely results of the integration with the ensuing possible risks for cultural diversity.[342] The aspect of the EU as a potential threat to diversity has been reflected in different ways at different times in recent EU history[343] and has also influenced the EU treaties (like with the introduction of the subsidiarity principle). EU law as it stands

339 UNESCO Declaration on Cultural Diversity, adopted 2 November 2001. http://unesdoc.unesco.org/images/0012/001271/127162e.pdf.

340 Von Bogdandy (2008), p. 252. His references are to *India – Quantitative Restrictions on Imports of Agricultural, Textile and Industrial Products*, Panel Report WT/DS90/R of 6 April 1999 and Appellate Body Report WT/DS90/AB/R of 23 August 1999 such limits of regional integration were discussed in the light of the WTO; see in detail von Bogdandy and Makatsch, "Collision, Co-existence or Co-operation? Prospects for the Relationship between WTO Law and European Union Law" in G. de Búrca and J. Scott (eds), *The EU and the WTO* (2001), at pp. 131–150.

341 Von Bogdandy (2008), pp. 254–255.

342 *Ibid.* p. 248.

343 See case law on potential threats from the creation of the single market to national cultures: Cases 60 and 61/84, *Cinéthèque SA v Fédérationnationale des cinémas français* [1985] ECR 2605; Case C-154/89, *Commission v. France (Tourist guides)* [1991] ECR I–659; Case C-148/91, *Vereniging Veronica Omroep Organisatie v Commissariaat voor de Media* [1993] ECR I–487; Case C-379/87, *Groener v Minister for Education and the City of Dublin Vocational Educational Committee* [1989] ECR I – 3967; Cases C-338/04, C-359/04, and C-360/04, *Criminal proceedings against Massimiliano Placanica (C–338/04),Christian Palazzese (C–359/04) and Angelo Sorricchio (C–360/04)* [2007] ECR I–1891.

does not pose a threat to cultural diversity but instead EU policies act to protect cultural diversity as well as safeguard the European position in the world, itself bulwark against global uniformity.

III.1.3. GLOBALISATION AND LEGITIMACY

The stated ambition of the studied regional integration bodies differs as does their impact and role in practice. For successful integration, the aim of the organisation should be réalistic, which means that it needs to be limited or at least gradual. Deepening integration has to be an organic, gradual process. As for widening integration – taking in more subject matters and/or more states – this can be achieved through changes to the constitutional instruments of the organisation or other political decisions. Deepening integration can evidently also be written into the constitutional instruments, but would most likely not be achieved through this alone, as the legitimacy of such deeper integration needs to be achieved in parallel. In modern political science, regional integration systems are often criticised for being too far from the people and to lead to alienation of populations from decision-making.

The state is usually regarded as having inherent legitimacy and ability to act autonomously by being the main element of the international system and the centre of power over individuals. The sovereignty of states and their possibility to decide over their own matters is, however, challenged by globalisation, which means that in many cases a state cannot determine various issues independently even if it formally and in international law has sovereign power. Schneiderman says that economic globalisation has disrupted state functions and relocated its authority upwards, downwards or nowhere at all. For economic globalisation there is both regulation and deregulation, changes within and without national legal systems.[344] Although this is true to a large extent in economic relations (which is what Schneiderman writes about) when it comes to democracy and democracy support, the state retains its powers, although even here that power may be circumscribed by networks of international relations. The kind of developments Schneiderman discusses may raise issues of legitimacy as the traditional features upon which the role of states are built (the social contract) do not present themselves, but there needs to be some new reason to support transnational legitimacy.[345]

Legitimacy of a new, foreign-backed regime and of an organisation backing such a regime are closely linked and mean that the legitimacy of an organisation can have a spill-over effect on international efforts to create stable governments

344 Schneiderman (2006), p. 390.

345 *Ibid.*, pp. 390–392. One main point of Schneiderman's article is a criticism of Hard and Nedri's theories on the obsolescence of the state in the globalised system.

in failed or post-conflict states. If the body that supports an international regime (as what has been used to greater or lesser degree in Bosnia-Herzegovina, Kosovo, Afghanistan and other countries in recent decades) has strong legitimacy itself (like the EU), the regime may be able to gain legitimacy even if the "normal" legitimacy for a governing structure created and elected by the people is not there.[346]

Schneiderman's main message is the continued necessity of the state, the local level, within the globalised systems. It is not convincing in his arguments that a transnational system cannot have its own legitimacy if this is built up over time and rests on solid foundations, as he does not convincingly answer why a state that holds legitimacy could not transfer this to a different institutional structure. If the way this is done and the guarantees built into this structure are sufficient, there is no reason why the legitimacy should disappear along the way. Today the only way to achieve transnational legitimacy is that states create this, as states are the building blocks of today's system. It is important that transnational rules are followed and implemented, for which in the current international system states are necessary.[347] Even in the EU, the by far furthest reaching regional integration system, the states are responsible for implementing and enforcing EU law. However, the system includes sufficient guarantees and mechanisms to ensure that such implementation takes place – in some ways making states the tools for the common policy. Schneiderman finds states essential in structuration of transnational legality, in limiting some of the effects of the economic decisions because of social consideration.[348]

There is a general acceptance in the discussion that the EU influences the view on regional integration, as a model and an example of what is possible. The EU experience can be a strong precedent when it comes to giving up sovereignty or at least the rights that form part of the notion of sovereignty. It may be discussed if the EU can be a model in its specifics or if it is rather an example of what is possible as an idea.[349]

The most extensive literature on legitimacy of regional organisations concerns the EU. As this is by far the organisation with the furthest reaching powers, it is understandable that its legitimacy is the subject of much discussion. This is particularly so as the institutions of the EU can act with a great deal of autonomy from member states, which poses the question of their legitimacy as something clearly separated from the legitimacy to states. The Treaties establishing the EU – at least till the challenge of the negative referenda concerning the Constitutional

346 For a discussion on similar issues linked to nation-building, see A. Ghani and C. Lockhart, *Fixing Failed States: A Framework for Rebuilding a Fractured World* (Oxford University Press, Oxford 2008).

347 Schneiderman (2006), especially p. 394.

348 *Ibid.*, p. 404.

349 C. Hall, "Constitutionalism as Liberal-Juridical Consciousness: Echoes from international law's past" in *Leiden Journal of International Law* 22 (2009), pp. 251–287, at 276–277.

Treaty and the Lisbon Treaty[350] – have a high degree of constitutional legitimacy thanks to the way they have been adopted by member states. This is an important aspect of any regional integration organisation as it ensures that the organisation is properly set up as a tool for member states to exercise their sovereignty in the manner they wish.

The character of a particular state may be more or less contested but the idea that states are the fundamental elements of the global organisation and the main construction units of organisation of mankind is not questioned in any serious way. A particular state may have to struggle to establish its legitimacy but the framework for this is well established.[351] The struggle will typically be to include different ethnic groups or a particular part of the territory or to counteract claims from other states to territory (or even to people, as the Russian aggression against Georgia in 2008 and Ukraine in 2014 with the stated aim to protect Russian citizens showed). The struggle will not be to gain acceptance for the idea of a state – only for the idea of that particular state. The regional integration body has to start several steps back and establish that the body as such can have any legitimacy at all, that a body like a regional integration organisation can participate in the global system.

Every now and then in the debate, there are suggestions to get rid of one or other international organisation that is seen to be inefficient. However, if organisations were indeed got rid of there would be a need to replace them with something and unless the core issues underlying problems in international organisations could be solved, the same problems may arise in the new organisation: how to ensure maximum representation while at the same time allowing for efficiency? It is more difficult to imagine starting from scratch now with so many existing organisations and creating something entirely new, devoting time and resources to it both in the inception and later in the functioning of the organisation does not look as an efficient solution.

A regional integration organisation in most cases does not *per se* have emotional legitimacy elements to build upon. There may be exceptional cases where such elements do exist, if the division into states in a certain region is the anomaly and historic and emotional ties instead link people across state borders, or the emotional ties can come after a while. As an example of the first situation, the African continent can be mentioned, where the ruler-straight national borders show the drawing skills of someone at a desk in London or Paris rather than ethnic or historical realities, but as so much time has passed since the borders were drawn and as states accepted the *uti possidetis* principle of borders not changing when they

350 Although the reasons for these referenda were different and, on occasions, opposing, it remains that they have shaken the fundaments of popular legitimacy of the EU, which is, generally, blamed for such diverging issues as globalisation, unemployment, immigration etc. The consequences of such a situation will not be discussed in the present book, which excludes the EU from its scope – they nonetheless will influence on the conclusions and the impact on the legitimacy debate for other regional organisations.

351 Nyman Metcalf (2013), pp. 83–87.

achieved their independence from the 1950s onwards, even here the potential for emotional attachment to regional bodies is not very likely in reality. As an example of the second situation can be mentioned that the European Union does evoke feelings of emotional attachment, but this is only after many years of existence and for most people this emotional attachment will still be complementary (and often secondary) to their emotional attachment to their country – just like the EU citizenship is complementary to national citizenship.[352] Emotional attachment to regional integration is weak in Europe and almost non-existent elsewhere. Europe as well as other regional integration organisations are creations of the mind. There is emotional response to the EU but more pronounced in the negative sense.

Lake argues that the assumption that regional integration systems like the international system in general are anarchic as there is no higher legal power than the state, is not necessarily correct or at least not the full truth. Such a view is based on a formal-legal conception of authority whereas states may have an informal hierarchy, which is based on relative authority and which creates regional hierarchies.[353] That it is clear that the global system is anarchic in that it lacks an authority above its members does not translate into all sub-systems consisting of states being equally anarchic. Authority is fundamentally a social contract also between states, where certain states have a duty to comply with orders of another state – which has the legitimate right to issue orders. The formal-legal conception of authority (and that which is used in legal studies) is that authority is given by prior lawful institutions.[354] In regional integration systems formally such institutions must be created by the states that form part of the system as there is no other authority to do this. Lake looks at the fundamental philosophy of why social orders of authority are created and sees how this translates to the relationship between states. Certain states may accept the authority of others or more usually of one dominant state if they get something in return for such acceptance. The acceptance of a legitimate right of a state to decide over another may cover certain issues rather than being total – a state will accept commands and will follow these only for certain issues.[355]

Focarelli points out that authority may relate to persons or to norms and refers to the classical Weberian interpretation that authority exists when commands can be expected to be followed. Even if there may be many levels and many reasons why this happens, the current international system is still construed around states and the state authority as the ultimate reason why commands are obeyed – whether they are commands from private bodies or state-created bodies.[356] Focarelli does not deal specifically with regional

352 Article 17 Treaty of the European Community.
353 D. A. Lake "Regional hierarchy: authority and local international order", pp. 35–58, *Review of International Studies* 2009 (British International Studies Association), at p. 36.
354 Lake (2009), p. 37.
355 *Ibid.*, pp. 38–39.
356 Focarelli (2012), pp. 144–145.

integration systems and for such systems the additional question is if the authority that the state possess at some point may actually move to another organ of which the state is a part.

Often in regional integration systems such hierarchy between states is set out in practice rather than by the legal documents for the organisation as it is very rare that states will formally accept hierarchy of states where they are not all equal. In practice, if there are perceived benefits of such a system it is possible that state do accept it. Possible examples may be found in monetary issues (accepting the currency of another state, so-called dollarization but not just restricted to the dollar[357]), trade relations where a state may allow another state to decide conditions also for its relations with third countries, but most clearly the hierarchy and acceptance of decisions of another state can be seen in defence-related cooperation (exchanging sovereignty for protection).

Lake explains how the relationships between states where certain (weaker) states accept to be subordinate to a strong state are formed in regional systems as the fact that many states in a region have a similar kind of relationship may increase the attractiveness of the system as such: The stronger state will deal with issues between the weaker ones as they all have a similar hierarchical relationship to the stronger one. A separate issue is how to ensure that all relevant players take part and some states do not try to be free riders of the benefits of a system without any of the burdens of accepting a certain subjugation – they want to know a powerful state will protect them but they do not accept that this powerful state is hierarchically above them. Lake takes the US involvement in Europe and especially its support for the creation of a democratic West Germany as an example. In this context the regional organisations created such as NATO and the clause on mutual guarantees in the NATO treaty should ensure that states do not have to accept the orders of one country – the US – as such but the positive effects of one dominant country over others (especially the occupied West Germany) can still be achieved and without free riders.[358]

In practice what often happens is that one dominant country conducts operations and gets acceptance of these by a regional integration organisation, sometimes after the event. Lake takes as examples the OAS supporting US intervention in the Dominican Republic in 1965 and later taking over this intervention by an Inter-American Peace Force. In 1983 the invasion of Grenada was similarly accepted by the Organisation of Eastern Caribbean States.[359]

The argument of Lake is interesting in that it illustrates that real power and hierarchies created not based on formal legal instruments but rather on dominance in reality by one state may be conductive to certain behaviour of states, such as supporting democracy, and the regional integration organisation is of lesser

357 Lake (2009), pp. 46–47.
358 *Ibid.* pp. 40–42.
359 *Ibid.*, p. 44.

importance or secondary to the dominant state. It may be more important as supporting the actions of the dominant state and perhaps making them more sustainable rather than as the trigger for the action. This of course depends on the strength relatively of the organisations and dominant countries. It is interesting to note that for many, one factor in support of the EU is that the organisation shall become a counterbalancing force to US dominance. Lake mentions ASEAN as an organisation created to withstand dominance by any one state.[360] As for Europe, Lake takes the EU as an example of how a regional organisation can replace the dominance of one state, in Europe the dominance of the EU, and how through greater institutionalisation an alternative system and an emergent European identity can be created. Lake, however, feels that instead of institutions, a measure of international hierarchy and authority is needed to protect, constrain and discipline member states.[361] This is an interesting argument and although one can agree on the need to have constraints, in the international system the equality and sovereignty of states can be protected if such constraints are created and given to the system rather than held by one state that is powerful enough to dominate others.

Bieber[362] states that individual self-determination in any society will entail a multitude of different loyalties and cannot be expressed just as nationality of a state. States can expand the scope of democratic choice as well as the possibilities for democratic control if it pools and delegates competences. For the individual democracy with all its components can thus increase through regional integration. Bieber brings the European Convention and Court of Human Rights and rights deriving from EU law as examples.[363] He states "Establishing a constitutional setting which combines the exercise of power at national with supranational level may increase the inclusiveness of the exercise of power, the respect for minority rights and its efficiency, because it may be a more genuine reflection of the interest of the peoples."[364]

Williams on the other hand stresses the failure of EU to establish strong democratic structures as something that serves to diminish conceptions of liberty in the EU. Early on in the history of the EU, the ECJ did not pay much attention to enforcing democracy. Williams feels this left the EU a bit outside of the idea of supporting an ideological notion of democracy. In his view, the latter attempts to inscribe democracy as a value that the EU supports in provisions on citizenship or transparency for example are "vaguely desperate". He also sees ambivalence regarding the rule of law.[365] Williams puts down these weaknesses to an absence of a philosophy of law for the EU. However, for other systems of

---

360 *Ibid.*, pp. 54–55.
361 *Ibid.*, p. 56.
362 Bieber (2009), p. 400.
363 *Ibid.*, p. 400.
364 *Ibid.*
365 A. Williams, "Philosophy of EU law", *Oxford Journal of Legal Studies* Vol. 29 Autumn 2009, pp. 549–577, at 568.

regional integration that are practically far behind the EU, it may be premature to think of a philosophy. Or, it may be so that the philosophy that the regional integration structure supports should be there at an early stage rather than somewhat as an afterthought grafted onto a structure created by compromise.

Williams' ideas are linked to the debate on whether there is a European demos, a people through which the demands for democracy can be raised. The German Constitutional Court in 2009 pronounced that there is no such demos.[366] The development of the EU does show how a practical and functional cooperation can lead on to more ideological cooperation and to notions of shared values. Williams is one of many authors who see the process of values and practical tasks to enforce these values as a bit backward, with cooperation on a wide range of issues first and then when such cooperation shows it is essential to have and protect common values, such values are found or created. In Williams' view the paramount consideration when it comes to EU protection of values is still to protect the integrity of the EU legal system.[367] The much noted Kadi case[368] where the ECJ stated that public international law (in the form of UN resolutions) cannot be applied if it conflicts with EU fundamental principles thus is also mainly an attempt to save the system, not so much certain specific rights.

The Example of the EU

Many organs of regional integration include democracy as a requirement in their constitutive documents. This trend is rather new, which is illustrated by the fact that the AU is among the many organisations that have done this but the older OAU did not. The OAS protocol of Washington 14 December 1992 included democracy as a requirement for American states and Mercosur makes such a demand as well. The Treaty of Amsterdam from 1999 was the first time that the EU spelled out the possibility of suspension of membership rights because of a failure to uphold e.g. principles of democracy. The Commonwealth Action Programme on the Harare Declaration established a mechanism to deal with unconstitutional overthrow of democratically elected governments.[369]

Even if the EU does not form part of the main study objects of this book, it is still relevant to compare with the EU when determining possibilities for regional integration organisations having impact on democratisation and related reforms in the member states, as the EU is by far the most influential regional integration organisation. Because of this there is also a multitude of literature on the EU influence.

366 Bundesverfassungsgericht (Germany) 30 June 2009, available (also in English) at www.bundesverfassungsgericht.de/entscheidungen/es20090630_2bve000208en.html.

367 Williams (2009), especially pp. 570–571 and 575–576.

368 Case C-402/05P, *Kadi* (2008).

369 K.D. Magliveras & G.J. Naldi (2002), especially pp. 417–418.

The general conclusions drawn from EU influence can in many respects be transferred to any regional organisation, only provided that such an organisation has the possibility to exert real influence (which in itself is another very important question, but one which for the theoretical discussion on tools of influence can for now be left to one side). If the regional integration organisation makes concrete demands that are directly relevant for the conditionality of certain assistance, application of policies (free trade, customs or currency union, etc.) the likelihood of the success of these demands is greater than if the demands are diffuse and even contradictory. The latter will be the case if the regional integration system itself does not have any clear rules and preferences but builds its proposals on divergent solutions in its members. If the policy that the organisation promotes is clear and consistent, the chance that it will be successfully absorbed by the target state is high. In addition to the clarity of the policy, the importance of it for the regional integration system plays a part. If democracy is a key concept for the system and it is clear what is meant by it, the regional integration system is likely to be able to exert considerable influence on its members to adhere to principles of democracy. If on the other hand there are no clear benchmarks and the policy does not appear to be very significant for the operations of the regional integration system, even a stated aim to promote democracy is likely not to have any real impact.[370] Even for the EU, the fact that it is a multinational body means that through the necessity for trans-governmental coalition formation and a tendency to avoid strategic decision-making, according to Grabbe reduces its possible impact or at least increases unpredictability if compared to that of a single state.[371] To this must be contrasted the greater impact a regional integration body (especially one as powerful as the EU) has as opposed to that of a state, which within the framework of international law cannot do anything else than suggest and encourage reforms in other countries.

Indeed, because of the nature of the EU and the great interest of states to join, the applicant countries tended to meet whatever criteria the EU set up. When they were uncertain of what was required they often instead of challenging the criteria actually asked for more detailed demands to be able to ensure that their actions met the requirements.[372] Such a strong pull-factor cannot be created easily. In the case of the East and Central European enlargement of the early 2000's, it was also combined with the internal situation in the countries in question. Having recently emerged from the destructive Communist system, there was a need to reform the entire economic and administrative structures of the states. The policy-makers lacked relevant experience and there was also a high degree of financial and practical help from the EU and its members. Thus,

370 In the EU system this is well described in H. Grabbe, *The EU's Transformational Power. Europeanization through Conditionality.* (Palgrave 2006), especially at pp. 186–208.

371 Grabbe (2006), at p. 190.

372 *Ibid.*, especially at pp. 192 and 195.

a strong impact of a powerful regional integration system was implanted on barren land, very receptive to an implant. The success of the process can be seen according to Grabbe[373] when the EU policies are no longer described as such, but just become the policies of the states concerned themselves.[374]

The requirements for membership, which put a strong emphasis on the rule of law and democracy, are essential. Other regional organs such as ASEAN do not make such demand on potential members. In the EU the situation is such that compliance generally varies dependent on many factors but it is in many instances better at the regional (EU) level than for both national and international law rules. The EU has a higher level of legalisation and effective monitoring mechanisms and sanctions. Globalisation and especially for Europe, Europeanisation, has led to ever more intensive legalisation on the transnational level. Examples can be seen in areas of state aid control, foodstuffs and redistribution how the EU level is the most effective.[375]

The legitimacy of the EU can even be used to support states that fail to function properly. This is seen in Bosnia Herzegovina where the position of EU Special Representative added legitimacy to the High Representative set up through the peace agreement. But also in an EU Member, Bulgaria, have there been suggestions by certain politicians and given a lot of attention in the media (in 2009) that the EU should be given power to intervene in Bulgaria in order to help the country come to grips with the problems of corruption that have led to some EU funds to the country being suspended. Advisers to the prime minister suggested giving the Commission and other EU Members powers to intervene when there are weaknesses that can be regarded as structural and persistent and that cannot be solved by the Bulgarian government alone. EU officials and diplomats would monitor implementation of laws, manage funds and supervise courts. Especially in cases of corruption and organised crime where the Bulgarian authorities have been slow or unable to react, European officials should have the possibility to act. The system would be managed by Bulgaria and the EU together. However, such an extraordinary handing over of the functions of a state to the EU has not been met with much enthusiasm from the EU or other member states. It is not suitable to establish parallel structures in a country and the system might also weaken the normal possibilities for the EU to react (especially strong for Bulgaria that was admitted to the EU with special conditions). Among the population the plan might well be popular as a very high percentage of the population trusted the EU (75%) at the time of joining and an equally high proportion did not trust the government, parliament and courts (80%).[376] However, the current EU system – or any

---

373 *Ibid.*, p. 205.

374 *Ibid.*, pp. 195–199 and 205.

375 M. Zürn & C. Joerges (2005).

376 *The Economist*, 21 March 2009.

other regional integration system – construed around states being Members and giving certain powers and functions to the organisation does not appear suitable for the organisation to take over duties if a state fails. Rather the idea is that the organisation gets powers in certain areas and carries them out based on the transfer.

III.2. DEMOCRACY

III.2.1. THEORIES OF DEMOCRACY

This book does not intend to analyse theories of democracy in depth, but the discussion on these theories is limited to such aspects that are relevant for the evaluation of how regional integration systems can support democracy.

As stated in the introduction and as shown by the analysis of different regional integration systems we do not by the term democracy refer just to the holding of free elections and a (parliamentary) system based on such elections. In addition, respect for human rights; the landscape enabling free elections including media and other communications; the absence of fraud; and the principle of legality are included.

It is a very basic tenet of democracy that it includes the right for people to decide their own political order – Agné says it goes without saying.[377] Most authors stress that the concept of democracy has to be seen as evolving, even if its roots are found far back in history.[378] One important change is that in modern theory, democracy presumes a participation of (almost) the whole population in voting, which was not a feature of early democratic systems in which a carefully selected group had the right to vote.[379] However, also the content of the democratic doctrine has changed. Schumpeter in the 1940s proposed a definition that challenged the normative doctrine of democracy and instead meant that the key concept of democracy was the competitive process or struggle for the people's vote and not the end result.[380] A completely just liberal democracy is generally seen as utopic,[381] so thinkers concentrate on how to achieve as many of the positive aspects of democracy to as great an extent as possible.

377 H. Agné, "Democratic Founding: We the people and the others", *International Journal of Constitutional Law* (2012) Vol. 10 No. 3, pp. 836–861, at 861.

378 Altman (2013), p. 615; J. Vidmar, *Democratic Statehood in International Law* (Hart, 2013), pp. 15–19.

379 D.M. Loades, *Politics and the Nation 1450–1660* (Fontana/Collins 1974), p. 445.

380 J. Schumpeter, *Capitalism, Socialism, and Democracy*, 3rd ed. (Harper and Brother Publishers, 1950).

381 J. Rawls, *A Theory of Justice* (Harvard University Press, 1999). Also P. Weithman, "John Rawls and the Task of Political Philosophy", *The Review of Politics* 71(2009), pp. 113–125, at 114.

In the more recent academic and political debate the international aspects of democracy get increasing attention.[382] It includes the possibility that it may be legitimate that external actors push for the creation of a democratic state.[383] This aspect of democratisation is especially important for this study. The fact that in the last quarter of a century many states all over the world, with many examples in Eastern and Central Europe or in Asia, have moved toward democracy means that there has been theoretical as well as practical re-evaluation of what is meant by a democratic transition. Many initial theories on 'transition' designating a certain route to democracy, the rule of law and market economy[384] have been shown to be in need of modification. The recognition has grown of the fact that the initial conditions for democratisation are of such complexity and disparity that it is not possible or useful to designate any standard route that would be globally applicable.[385] This led to a debate between "preconditionists" and "universalists" on whether a state must be ready for democracy before it starts reforms to implement it or whether such support is always possible as any state can become democratic.[386]

Despite some claims to the contrary,[387] it is not possible to find (liberal) democracy as the victorious and perhaps even only viable political model.[388] The idea of democratic entitlement with democracy as a legitimate expectation or a principle of international law is contested.[389] Nodia points out that the problems with introducing liberal democracy are likely to lead to one of two attitudes: that democracy is not suitable for a certain society so attempts to achieve it are pointless or that even if there are impediments, it is still the ultimate goal (even if people have no experience of it).[390] Collins finds that it has been shown that values such as commitment to democracy cannot be vindicated in their own rights and imposed due to a presumption of cultural superiority.[391] Democracy

382 D.J. Galbreath, "Securitizing Democracy and Democratic Security: A Reflection on Democratization Studies", *Democracy and Security* 2012, 8, pp. 28–42, at 29.

383 Agné (2012). For example, Agné raises the point that the determination of who are the people who should take part in democratic decisions for the people is in itself a decision to be made, so it cannot per se be illegitimate that a wider range of people take part in decisions. *Op. cit.*, pp. 840–841.

384 T. Carothers, "The end of the transition paradigm", *Journal of Democracy* Vol. 13, No. 1, January 2002, pp. 5–21.

385 J.J. Linz & A. Stepan, "Toward Consolidated Democracies", *Journal of Democracy*. 7.2 1996, pp. 14–33.

386 S. Berman, "Lessons from Europe", *Journal of Democracy* Vol. 18, No. 1, January 2007, pp. 28–41. The details of this debate fall outside of the scope of this book as the regional integration systems studied have not engaged to any major extent in democracy assistance, in the way the EU for example has done (or non-regional organisations such as the World Bank).

387 F. Fukuyama, *The End of History and the Last Man* (Avon 1992).

388 Collins (2009), p. 277.

389 Franck (1992).

390 G. Nodia, "The Democratic Path", *Journal of Democracy* Vol. 13, No. 3, July 2002, pp. 13–19, at 17–18.

391 Collins (2009), p. 278.

like other values has to be shown to be the most suitable system of governance in a specific setting, thus being shaped to suit this setting.

Despite the many theories and contested issues, it is possible to make a list of attributes of democratic states, as long as it is made clear that such a list is not static and probably cannot be comprehensive at any point in time. The attributes include elections for key positions of society, with near universal voting rights; fair and correct elections, the results of which are respected; recognition and protection of civil liberties and human rights.[392] Discontent with a political regime in a democracy should be expressed through electoral voices and political debate, leading to formally correct changes of government. Legality and especially constitutional legality, i.e. respect for formal constitutional rules, is a main element of democracy. For a democracy to be consolidated there should not be any morally or political viable alternatives to following the rules set out in the constitution.

Even for the recognition of a state, adherence to certain principles and basic values has become a precondition.[393] This means that for new states, the requirements to even be seen as states and thus as participants in the global order are stricter than for existing states. There is no suggestion that established states would cease to be recognised as states if they regress in matters of democracy. At the same time, the notion of a legitimate concern about the basic values of new states gives support to the idea that the international community should react to violations of democracy within existing state.

As criteria of democracy, the existence of a debate is crucial. It is relevant in its own right and a prerequisite for other aspects of democracy, notably the possibility for people to make use of their right of choice in elections. Habermas regarded media as a crucial factor in the transition to liberal democracy, as media created the public sphere in which individuals could discuss in a way that led to accountability and democracy. For media to have this role it must report on issues of government and similar: it must be able to do this and be interested in doing so.[394] Media provides the information from which a public debate can arise.[395]

Absence of corruption is important for democracy, as presence of corruption can distort the democratic nature of a state. Montinola and Jackman[396] argue that the relationship between political competitiveness and corruption is nonlinear: Corruption is more frequent in countries with intermediate levels of political competition, *i.e.* transition countries, than in their authoritarian counterparts.

392 Altman (2013), p. 616.

393 Agné (2012), p. 861.

394 J. Habermas, *The Structural Transformation of the Public Sphere. An Inquiry into a category of bourgeois society* (The MIT Press 1991 paperback ed.).

395 J. Harrisson & L. Woods, *European Broadcasting Law and Policy* (Cambridge University Press 2007), p. 31.

396 G. R. Montinola & R.W. Jackman "Sources of Corruption. A Cross-Country Study", *British Journal of Political Science* Vol. 32, Issue 1, January 2002, pp. 147–170.

But in countries with a stable a complete democracy, corruption is a much lower level. Treisman[397] writes that "[T]he fact that a country is democratic today makes just about no difference to how corrupt it is perceived to be. What matters is whether or not it has been democratic for decades."

Another way to describe the process of democratisation is to focus on institutions that safeguard the democratic system. This is the angle employed in much legal research where the ability of the legal system to protect democracy is the key element. Constitutional courts and judicial review as well as mechanisms for protection of human rights are elements of such an analysis. Although it is possible to have constitutional courts and various review mechanisms for rights also in non-democratic states, the nature of these legal instruments is such that they fit with the democratic system or at least with aspirations of democratisation. In practice this is seen by the way constitutional courts have emerged during different waves of democratisations.[398] Early constitutional courts were introduced after the Second World War in Germany, Italy, and Austria; in the 1970s in Spain, Portugal and Greece after the fall of the authoritarian regimes there; in the 1990s in East and Central Europe and Central Asia. In the rest of the world some such courts have emerged over the past few decades, linked to a general democratisation process.

III.2.2. FEDERALISM

There can be ideological attachment to regional integration through the ideology of federalism.[399] Federalism is the ideology of the political movement supporting European political unification rather than the official ideology for European regional integration.[400] The examples of regional integration organisations that exist today explicitly do not base themselves on a federal ideology – rather such ideology lies behind a number of states (like the United State of America, Germany or Austria) and the regional organisations on the contrary often point out that they are not construed according to the federal model.

The one continent where federalism may be said to be the strongest is the American continent. In the Americas federalism as an ideology has strong support, not just in the form of federal states (like the USA) but also as principles of the Bolivarian ideology. All the same, this remains a theoretical attachment

397 D. Treisman, "The causes of corruption: A cross-national study", *Journal of Public Economics* 76 (2000), pp. 399–457, at 438–439.

398 S. Huntington, *The Third Wave* (University of Oklahoma Press 1990).

399 Burgess (2006).

400 R. Castaldi, "A Federalist Framework Theory of European Integration" (Centre for Studies on Federalism, Turin 2005), p. 1.

and approach rather than one that would influence the actual policies of states or of any of the regional integration bodies.[401]

Federalism as an ideology[402] includes that power shall be distributed to different levels: higher or lower than those in a centralised state. The decision-making shall be effective as well as close to the people, which puts an emphasis on division of powers and on the representative organs and which interests they most particularly represent. Federalism can be seen as an ideology which seeks to separate the governing structures from the unitary state idea as well as from the confederation idea – the cooperation without transfer of powers.

After a certain point, increased autonomy of the regional integration organisation presupposes federalism. A simple example can illustrate this: The United States of America would never accept for example Nevada to become an undemocratic state. As there are no effective mechanisms at the international level to definitely prevent such possible changes of government, a body that reaches a certain level of integration needs to have some element also of federalism. The big question is when such level has been reached – even for the furthest reaching regional integration body, the EU, there is far from consensus on whether and what extent of federalism that is needed.[403]

Federalism presupposes some basic principles, even if it can and does look in different ways in the different states where it is implemented. In some troubled regions of the world, some of the basic concepts of it may not fit. This is the view of Mallat[404], who examines it for the Middle East and points to the need to have a territorial model, whereas what the Arab world shows evidence of is rather corrective representation of communities. These are difficult to define, they are not regionally based and where they exist, they are more or less mixed and interwoven with other groups. Mallat means that the Middle Eastern citizen has dual allegiances but not to a state and a region, but to a state and a religious/sectarian group.[405] In the federalist structure, the people's interest should be represented in the governing structures and thus need to be identified in a manner which permits this.

Federalism remains essential as the ideology of unification through regional integration. At the same time, until today it has been instrumental in creation of unitary states from different component states, but for regional integration of different independent states that are not ready to become one (traditional) state, it remains a political ideology for a specific political movement rather than the predominant ideology behind integration.

401 K. Nyman-Metcalf & I.F. Papageorgiou (2005), p. 14.

402 As mentioned in the Introduction, this book does not purport to discuss various ideologies for integration as such, but rather concentrates on the analysis of application of integration. Thus the short mention here of various ideologies is only to set the stage for the particular analysis.

403 Castaldi (2005).

404 Mallat (2007), pp. 177–178.

405 *Ibid.*

III.2.3. HUMAN RIGHTS

The enforcement by regional organisations of human rights is an interesting illustration to the possibility of an organisation to impose its will. If a regional integration structure is able to involve itself actively in the protection of human rights of the citizens of its member states, such an organisation will have an independent relationship with citizens and can thus contribute to integration of peoples, rather than just of states. The international, regional enforcement of rights also means that a standard of human rights is established that is wider than the national interpretation. Again, it is Europe that is the most advanced with the European Convention on Human Rights and the Court to implement it. However, in the area of human rights also other parts of the world have established systems.

The Council of Europe that administers the European Convention on Human Rights and the elaborate enforcement system set up for that Convention does have the possibility as an ultimate reaction to the failure of a state to meet human rights requirements to suspend such a state. There has never been full use of this possibility although it was close to being used in 1970 against Greece, where there was then a military dictatorship, which had stated that it did not respect the rights of the Convention. Eventually, Greece withdrew from the Convention before they could be expelled.[406] With a larger membership and a more diverse one with states such as Russia and Azerbaijan that are not democratic one could imagine more instances of use of the suspension possibility although this has not been the case in practice.

Other continents have similar but less elaborate special systems for regional human rights enforcement. The Asian and American systems are rather weak as far as individual complaints and active enforcement mechanisms are concerned. The situation in Africa appears to aim more towards a system similar to the European one but is still far from it in practice. In Africa the monitoring system is far less innovative than the substantive rights, which indicates the scepticism that African leaders feel against "interference" in internal affairs. The African Commission on Human and Peoples Rights was vested with many competences but monitoring procedures, reporting requirements, inter-state and individual complaints procedures were not well developed or efficient.[407] Views on the African human rights system set up through the Banjul Charter vary between it being an expression of taking rights seriously to doubts about any effectiveness of the system. States can join without any questions asked about their previous human rights record.[408] The African Court on Human and People's rights that

---

406 C. Ovey and R.C.A. White, *Jacobs & White The European Convention on Human Rights* 4th edition (Oxford University Press 2006), p. 504.

407 *Introduction to the International Human Rights Regime,* (2003), pp. 203–214.

408 A.K. Wing, "Women's Rights and Africa's Evolving Landscape: The Women's Protocol of the Banjul Charter" in J.I. Levitt (ed), *Africa. Mapping New Boundaries in International Law* (Hart Publishing, Oxford/Portland 2010), pp. 13–33, at 25–26.

became partly operational in 2008 with the first ruling delivered in 2009 and rules of the court adopted in 2010 has finalised 23 cases until May 2015.[409] The Court is an improvement to the human rights system of the African continent and may yet prove to be very important. It is still early to say much about its role and influence.

Also its predecessor, the Commission had rather comprehensive jurisdiction. It could issue advisory opinions, rule on issues of interpretation as well as deal with complaint from state parties and even individuals, groups and NGOs. In theory the human rights monitoring system was a genuine *actio popularis* in that also those not directly concerned could complain about a violation, but in practice there were many restrictions: The Commission had to be unanimous, the issue had to be part of a systematic pattern of gross human rights violations and in any case there were no effective enforcement mechanisms.[410]

The creation of a Court in 2005 and the incorporation of the Commission as part of this Court gave rise to optimism.[411] It was hoped that the Court would improve the situation for individual complaints. One of the few notable cases before the African Commission on Human and Peoples' Rights deals with enforcing democracy. This is the case *Dawada Jawara v. The Gambia*[412], brought by an ousted Head of State. The complainant won the case, which was brought using the ACHPR or Banjul Charter. The ousted Gambian Head of State referred to Articles in the Banjul Charter on democracy as a background to bring a case before the African Commission on Human and Peoples' Rights. He argued that following the military coup of July 1994, that overthrew his government, there was blatant abuse of power by the military junta, which among other things by a military decree abolished the country's Bill of Rights contained in the 1970 Constitution and banned political parties. The Commission ruled in favour of the complainant (affirming its previously stated view) that the banning of political parties was a violation of the complainant's rights to freedom of association guaranteed under Article 10(1) of the Banjul Charter. Any limitations to rights in the charter should be made in accordance with the possibilities for such limitations as set out there. The Commission examined the way the government had come to power. While it was true, the Commission noted, 'that the military regime came to power by force, albeit, peacefully. This was not through the will of the people who have known only the ballot box since independence, as a means of choosing their political leaders.'[413] The military coup was therefore a grave violation of the right of Gambian people to freely choose their government as provided for in Article 20(1) of the Banjul Charter.

409 Www.african-court.org/en/index.php/about-the-court/brief-history.

410 *Introduction to the International Human Rights Regime* (2003), pp. 203–214.

411 *Ibid.*

412 See *Dawda Jawara* v. *The Gambia*, African Commission on Human and Peoples' Rights, Comm. Nos. 147/95 and 149/96 (2000) and Koefele Kole (2008), p. 248.

413 *Ibid.*

Dawda Jawara v. *The Gambia* is one of very few cases on political rights such as the freedom of association to come before the African human rights system. The decision supports the right to constitutional democratic governance and democratic participation.[414] The Commission has in several statements supported free and fair elections.

The AU is not the only regional integration organ in Africa that has a court. ECOWAS also has a court of justice whose rulings are binding. This court has shown a potential for having a positive effect on human rights in Africa and on ensuring that constitutional guarantees for rights are indeed respected. In October 2008 the ECOWAS court issued a landmark ruling on slavery.[415] A woman from Niger, born into slavery and later sold to be raped and abused, took a case to a local tribunal after being charged with bigamy for running away and marrying a man of her own choice. The ECOWAS Court has jurisdiction over alleged abuses of human rights in its member states under a supplementary protocol from 2005 to the original 1991 protocol on jurisdiction.[416] The ECOWAS court found that slavery is illegal under international law, through special conventions and the African Charter on Human and People's Rights. These instruments do not allow for exceptions and the provisions on illegality are also included in the constitutions of many states (like Niger). The case relevant here was complicated by many factors, such as the master of the woman in question releasing her when threatened with prosecution under the anti-slavery rules but instead using Niger customary law to reclaim her as his wife. She managed to get a local tribunal to rule that she was not legally married to the man but that ruling was changed when she later married and was accused of bigamy. It was only the ECOWAS court that came out strongly in defence of her rights also in practice, stating that the rules on slavery prohibition must have a real meaning. The implementation of the ruling is another matter however.[417]

Regional systems for the protection of human rights exist in most parts of the world and as many of them have been created or amended in order to be strengthened and brought closer to the people, it can be said to be a trend to recognise regional interest in enforcing human rights. This has the potential to be a key to the way regional integration systems can influence democratisation in their region including within the member states, for the state's own citizens. At the same time, against this positive interpretation must be seen the often rather weak implementation mechanisms, which underlines that the establishment of a human rights system is only the first step.

---

414 Koefele Kole (2008), p. 248.

415 *Mme Hadijatou Mani Koraou v The Republic of Niger*, 27 October 2008, ECW/CCJ/JUD/06/08.

416 Supplementary Protocol A/SP.1/01/05 of 19 January 2005 amending Protocol A/P.1/7/91 of 6 July 1991. H. Duffy, "Hadijatou Mani Korua v. Niger: Slavery unveiled by the ECOWAS Court", *Human Rights Law Review* 2008, pp. 1–20, at 6.

417 Duffy (2008), pp. 2–5; *The Economist*, 1 November 2008.

III.2.4. NATIONAL CONSTITUTIONS

A first prerequisite for enforceability of decisions of a regional integration system is that national constitutions allow decisions of international organisations to be implemented and enforced in the country. For a regional integration system to be able to act independently the member states must give away a certain amount of sovereignty to the body. The amount and the method to transfer sovereign decision-making powers to the organisation can vary. National constitutions may through the description of such possible relinquishing of sovereignty promote or prevent effective regional integration. The political will in the country is the key to the question of handing over sovereignty but this political will needs to be reflected in legal instruments for sustainability. National constitutions must allow the pre-eminence of the regional integration system. The domestic legal status of international treaties and decisions of international organisations determines the effects of integration. Such status may vary, as is seen in the EU context related to judicial and quasi-judicial decisions as well as to the differences between what used to be referred to as pillars.[418]

It is unavoidable that any regional integration just like any international organisation must be acceptable under the national constitutions. This may entail constitutional amendments to join international bodies – which is not a problem if there is a political will – but also an oversight by constitutional organs in states. One example of attempts to deal with pressing and difficult issues through regional bodies that ran into constitutional problems is the example of the UN International Commission against Impunity in Guatemala (CICIG) that was set up to investigate the many murders in the country after the end of the war there. The Constitutional Court of Guatemala rejected the organ as a violation of sovereignty. The organ exists but its mandate is not very strong. The body was ratified by the Congress of Guatemala but the court still had its objections. The idea of such a body is good and might be used as a model in other war-torn countries.[419] At the same time, constitutional oversight is a good idea. The problem is when two good ideas have opposing results.

Given the extensive powers of the EU and the direct effect of EU law, which may appear to challenge notions of national sovereignty and law-making prerogatives of national parliaments in parliamentary democracies, different European states have used different methods to fit the new supranational legal system into their constitutional systems. The voluntary adherence to the EU and the decision in accordance with the national constitution to accept EU law is important and can have varying ideological bases. The will of the people is expressed to delegate certain state powers to an international organisation

418 N. Lauranos, *Legal interaction between decisions of international organisations and European Law* (European Law Publishing, Groningen 2004).
419 *The Economist*, 22 March 2008.

and thus the sovereignty of the people's will is not violated, just exercised in a different manner. Jakab calls it a temporary self-limitation with the remaining possibility of revoking it with sovereignty itself not affected but the way it is exercised. Jakab sees a certain kind of self-deception, as if nothing has changed when in reality is has. Sovereignty tends to be a politicised word and especially in East- and Central European states where sovereignty was only recently regained after decades of Soviet dominance, it is sensitive to talk of giving it up.[420]

Schütze explains the concept of supranationalism as arising from the absence of a theory of federalism beyond the nation state. This was what led the creators of the EU to pronounce it *sui generis* and to invent supranationalism as a theory. Schütze also sees this as the start of dark ages for European constitutional theory as he sees *sui generis* as an anti-theory rather than a theory.[421]

Jakab suggests different models like shared sovereignty according to the United States model and reminds that the US was seen as sui generis when created, just like the EU today. He acknowledges that the concept of explicitly shared sovereignty will not be politically acceptable for the emotional attachments to the notion as mentioned. This emotional and political nature of the concept means that most solutions on how to distribute sovereignty between member states and the EU are not feasible, as most such solutions would mean for member states to actually accept that sovereignty is divided. Alternatively one remains in the fiction that nothing is actually given away in which case the powers of the EU are not properly recognised. The only solution may be a redefinition of sovereignty or Maduro's contrapunctual law, according to which (like in music) different tunes can be played at the same time but still achieve a harmony.[422]

However this may be – and the Maduro theory is indeed attractive – the national constitutions must allow for real powers of an integration system. In the EU this is the case, although the exact extent of it as well as the sources for it are debated, but in other integration systems the constitutions may not be well equipped to allow real powers of an organisation.

---

420 A. Jakab, "Neutralizing the Sovereignty Question: A new compromise formula", *European Constitutional Law Review* 2(2006), pp. 375–397, especially at 387–389 and 390–391.

421 Schütze (2009), p. 3. The cooperative federalism Schütze advocates is that of the United States of America, with states within, as part of the Union rather than states and the Union more or less side by side. This latter construction is how he feels much of European law operates today, even if as organs there are examples also in the EU of cooperation.

422 Jakab (2006), pp. 392–396.

IV. DEGREE OF ACHIEVEMENT: CASE STUDIES

In recent years there have been several examples of regional integration organisations intervening in different ways in conflicts and against illegal changes of government. As already mentioned in the beginning of the book there are several examples of the different kind of effect that actions by regional integration organs can have to support democratically elected organs. The picture is not consistent, as both the situations addressed and the means to do it vary considerably. Furthermore, in almost all cases of political turmoil it is very hard to establish clear cause and effect chains.

However, as the primary objective of the book is to examine how regional integration organisms prevent or frustrate attempts of unconstitutional take-over of power in its member states, the study of cases is the obvious way to set the theory into a practical setting. There are many examples to select from, as situations of unconstitutional take-over of power have arisen frequently during the last couple of decades, since the end of the cold war. It is obvious that the process of regional integration organs exercising influence on member states is a long and complex process and in any event, social science is not an exact science. However, the trend is there and can be analysed through a selection of cases from different parts of the world. There are no perfect and exact examples as the process is long and complex. At the same time, the very different situations from very different regional integration organs allows to draw conclusions on effects, successes and obstacles to regional integration influence, as analysed in the last part of this book. It is not desirable to try to obtain a regional balance of cases, as different parts of the world present a very different amount of eligible case studies, with Africa dominating. Thus, this section contains many African cases against a smaller selection of others, but sufficient to help analyse global trends.

IV.1. THE AMERICAS

The Americas present the somewhat contradictory picture of on the one hand, strong apparent indicators for regional integration (common language for many countries, a largely common history, and ideological – albeit theoretical

– adherence to federalism[423] while on the other hand the regional integration organisations are not very strong. The picture is made more complex still by some organisations, especially SICA, having quite a strong institutional structure but in reality not being very active or having much influence. In recent years there has been a strengthening of different organisations as well as creation of new ones. The few examples of situations in which regional integration organisations have reacted in cases of undemocratic assumption of powers in the Americas, however, show a weak reaction without making full use of potential means of using regional integration as a lever of influence.

IV.1.1. HONDURAS

In the Americas the 2009 events in Honduras present an example of a situation where a regional integration organisation potentially should be able to influence domestic political events. The UN General Assembly adopted a resolution[424] calling for a restoration of the elected government and condemning the coup, while the regional system was more careful, even if it possesses clearer tools for such a situation. For the UN, there is no explicit legal instrument demanding democracy as a universal norm so the mentioned resolution was adopted based on general principles.[425]

Honduras is a member of SICA, the furthest reaching integration organisation in the Americas with various elements of supranationality. The 1991 Tegucigalpa Protocol[426] explicitly mentions the integration of Central America as a region of peace, freedom, democracy and development. Such objectives shall be attained by consolidating democracy and strengthening the institutions of SICA on the basis of the existence of Governments elected by universal and free suffrage with secret ballot, and of unrestricted respect for human rights in the member states, listing fundamental principles that the member states shall follow.[427] However, the Protocol does not include any specific mechanism for sanctioning or expelling violating members.[428]

This supports the impression that internal democracy is not at the forefront of the objectives of SICA members which instead concern economic integration. In this setting, it is not a coincidence that the SICA remained on the side-lines during and after the June 2009 coup. The Tegucigalpa Protocol provisions were not even invoked by other members. Although the Meeting of the Presidents condemned the military takeover and froze trade and political relations with

---

423 Nyman-Metcalf & Papageorgiou (2005), p. 14.
424 UN Doc A/RES/61/301 (1 July 2009).
425 Vidmar (2013), p. 33.
426 See details above, in section II.1.2.
427 Articles 3 and 4 of the Tegucigalpa Protocol I 1991. See section II.1.2 above.
428 Articles 5 and 6 of the Tegucigalpa Protocol I 1991.

the de facto government, SICA played only a minor role in the ensuing political and diplomatic initiatives. Mainly this was handled by the OAS. The SICA Court of Justice is competent to rule on conflicts between the constitutional organs of the SICA's member states and could have acted in the case.[429] This could have happened at an earlier stage in the conflict when the escalation before the coup between President José Zelaya and the Congress of the Republic could have been brought before the Court and resolved there. In the event there was no such proposal or even discussion on this.[430]

The Honduran crisis brought to the forefront an important problem of regional integration and obstacle to real effect on democratisation. Even if the fundamental principles including democracy are stipulated in constitutive documents, what is lacking in the integration legal texts is any reference to some form of sanctions against a member state that violates the democratic principles. Thus, it is no coincidence that the Meeting of the Presidents that met in Managua to discuss the coup in Honduras on 28 June 2009 could only use Article 2 of the Framework Treaty on Democratic Security, which stated, generally, that the 'Central American model is governed by the rule of law which includes the supremacy of law, legal security and effective exercise of citizens' rights, as well as the subordination of armed forces … to civilian authorities',[431] in order to condemn the coup. Even after the normalization of the situation in Honduras, no regional or national debate arose as to the possibility of amending the integration treaties in order explicitly to affirm the obligation of member states to remain democratic.[432]

The role of SICA in relation to the coup in Honduras thus shows how even when there are some provisions that could be used to react in support of democratic principles in a member state and there is even an institutional structure potentially able to support such reaction, in the absence of a clear political will – at least while the institutional and regulatory structure is still weak – the potential is not fulfilled.

IV.1.2. PARAGUAY

On 21 and 22 June 2012, President Fernando Lugo of Paraguay was impeached by the Paraguayan Congress. Fernando Lugo was elected President of Paraguay

429 Article 20(f) of the Court's Statute points out that the Court is competent 'to examine and rule, at the request of the affected party, on conflicts that may arise between the fundamental Organs or Powers of the State, as well as when judicial rulings are not respected in fact'. The Statute has been ratified by Honduras.

430 I.F. Papageorgiou, "Central American Integration System" (Chapter 23) in L. Levi, G. Finizio, N. Vallinoto, *The Democratization of International Institutions* (Routledge 2014), pp. 299–315, at 309.

431 Special Declaration of the Council of Ministers of Foreign Affairs on the situation of Honduras.

432 Papageorgiou (2014), p. 309.

in 2008, head of a coalition of several opposition parties, beating for the first time the ruling Colorado Party. His presidency was marred with social and political controversies as he lacked a solid majority in Congress. On 15 June 2012, police and landless peasants clashed in eastern Paraguay, resulting in 17 deaths. In response to the incident, Lugo dismissed the head of the police and replaced the interior minister, member of the Liberal Party, with a controversial member from the Colorado party. As a result, the liberals withdrew from the coalition and accused the President of incompetence. On 21 June, the Chamber of Deputies formulated and approved, by 76 votes to 1, an accusation against the President for `bad performance of his functions.'[433]The following day, the impeachment went to the Senate. Lugo and his defense had less than 24 hours to examine the indictment and prepare the case. The trial in the Senate was also immediate and Lugo's impeachment was approved on the same day by 39 votes to 4.[434] The Vice-President and leader of the Radical Party, Federico Franco, took office immediately after. The entire process took only 48 hours but was conducted respecting the letter of the relevant constitutional provisions; it was also considered legal some days later by the Supreme Court of Paraguay and the Electoral Authority of the country.[435]

Fernando Lugo was seen as a left-leaning personality, his impeachment and replacement was thus considered by most leftist governments of the region to be a "camouflaged coup" organized by the ruling elite of the country, an allegation he himself sustained, claiming that the entire process was unconstitutional as he was deprived of the right of due process.[436] These developments led to a reaction both from Unasur and from Mercosur.

On 29 June 2012, the Mercosur Heads of State met in Mendoza (Argentina) without Paraguay's presence[437] and decided on the basis of the provisions of the

---

433 Article 225 of the 1992 Constitution of Paraguay provides that "The President of the Republic ... shall only be impeached for bad performance of his duties, for crimes committed in the exercise of his functions or for common crimes".

434 The trial coincided with the Rio+20 summit on Sustainable Growth in Rio do Janeiro. The heads of State of Unasur present there hurriedly sent a delegation of the organization's foreign ministers to Paraguay. They met with Lugo and expressed their support for him, calling the process a "rupture of the democratic order by not respecting due process." They also attended the trial in the Senate. See Mercopress 21.6.2012 in http://en.mercopress.com/2012/06/21/unasur-delegation-travels-to-paraguay-to-ensure-democratic-system-integrity and "UNASUR Applies "Democracy Clause" On Paraguay" in Opeal (Observatorio de Politica y Estrategia en America Latina) 11.09.2012 www.opeal.net/index.php?option=com_k2&view=item&id=12202:unasur-applies-"democracy-clause"-on-paraguay.

435 A detailed analysis of the process of suspension of Paraguay from Mercosur can be found in G. Vidigal, "Enforcing Democracy at the Regional Level: Paraguay's Suspension before the Mercosur Court", *Cambridge Journal of International and Comparative Law* (2)2: 337–349 (2013).

436 See La Nacion 23.6.2012 in www.lanacion.com.ar/1484248-lugo-se-juega-su-mandato-en-un-sorpresivo-y-veloz-juicio-politicov.

437 Some days earlier, on 24 June 2012, the meeting of Foreign Ministers of the remaining member states of Mercosur as well as associate members adopted the "Declaración de los

Ushuaia Protocol to apply sanctions and suspend the country's membership in Mercosur.[438] The final common communiqué of the Presidents stated that "5. [They] Reiterated their condemnation of the breach of democratic order produced in [...] Paraguay, stressed that the restoration of democratic institutions is essential to the development of the integration process and decided to suspend, under the Protocol of Ushuaia [...], the right of that country to participate in the organs of MERCOSUR". The communiqué insisted that "the application of this measure" should not "cause injury to the Paraguayan people" and confirmed that suspension "shall cease when, according to the provisions of Article 7 of the Protocol of Ushuaia, the full restoration of democratic order in the party concerned is verified".[439]

Unasur was in a more complicated situation. Although the organisation had adopted a "democratic clause" Protocol, the 'Additional Protocol to the constitutive Treaty of Unasur on Democratic Commitment' adopted, on November 2010 in Georgetown (Guyana), which included sanctions in case of a breach of the democratic order, the Protocol, albeit ratified by Paraguay, was not yet in force.[440] The Constitutive treaty of Unasur did not provide for the suspension of a member. Nevertheless, on 24 June Unasur foreign ministers – with the exception of Paraguay's – met in Lima to discuss the Paraguayan situation, described the events in Paraguay as "a rupture of democratic order" and announced the suspension of Paraguay's membership on the grounds that Paraguay should hold democratic and transparent elections before joining again the group.[441]

The decisions of Mercosur – and even more those of Unasur – were clearly politically motivated and legally problematic. The Ushuaia Protocol provided in Article 3 that in case of "any breach in the democratic order in one of the States Parties to this Protocol" the first steps to be taken should be "consultations between the State affected and the others" and only in case such consultations fail to produce results, further measures should be envisaged. This has not taken place, as the decision to suspend Paraguay was taken almost immediately. It is clear that the impeachment and trial of President Lugo was a party political move, done on the margins of legality and that due process was definitely not

Estados Partes del Mercosur y Estados Asociados sobre ruptura del orden democrático en Paraguay" whereby they condemned the breach of the constitutional order in Paraguay and decided, in accordance with the Ushuaia Protocol to suspend Paraguay from the right to participate in the 43rd Meeting of the Common Market Council and the Summit of Presidents of Mercosur, as well as from all other preparatory meetings that would take place in Mendoza, between 25 and 29 June 2012". It also established that the Mercosur summit would adopt further measures.

438 "DECISIÓN SOBRE LA SUSPENSIÓN DEL PARAGUAY EN EL MERCOSUR EN APLICACIÓN DEL PROTOCOLO DE USHUAIA SOBRE COMPROMISO DEMOCRÁTICO". In www.puntofocal.gov.ar/doc/comunicado_conjunto_presidentes_ep.pdf.

439 *Ibid.*

440 It only entered in force in 2014.

441 "UNASUR Applies "Democracy Clause" On Paraguay" in Opeal... *op. cit.*

applied in his case; it remains that the nature of the measures taken by the other Mercosur member states were disproportionate, in particular as one of the first acts of the new president was to call for new elections. It appears that the issue was an attempt by the remaining Mercosur member states to bypass Paraguay's blocking of the accession of Venezuela to the organization. Venezuela was an associate member since 1998 and had applied for full membership status in 2005. Accession negotiations started almost immediately[442] and were concluded quickly; the Accession Protocol was signed in 2006. However, Paraguay's Senate stalled the ratification procedures on the grounds that the government of Venezuela did not fulfil the democratic conditions set in the Ushuaia Protocol in terms of respect of human rights. The suspension of Paraguay allowed to overcome this obstacle. Indeed, in the same meeting in Mendoza, the three presidents decided to seize the opportunity and allow the entry of Venezuela to Mercosur and "called a meeting for the purpose of the official admission of Venezuela to Mercosur on July 31, 2012", in Rio de Janeiro. Such decision was clearly in breach of the principles of the Treaty of Asuncion; Paraguay was only suspended rather that excluded from the organization and the treaty provided clearly that accession needed the ratification of all states parties. In fact, Paraguay challenged the matter before the Permanent Review Court (TPR).[443] Interestingly, the Court did not refuse to examine the case in principle, stating among others that it considered it competent to rule on such matters, but dismissed the case because Paraguay had not undertaken negotiations with the other parties on the settlement of the issue before appealing to the TPR. It would have been interesting to know how it would have looked at the case, but even the fact that the matter was taken up demonstrates that the TPR has an itch to act as a supranational court of Mercosur.

The suspension led to another interesting issue, namely whether the suspension could affect the Mercosur Parliament and the Paraguayan members in it. Paraguay was, in fact, the only Mercosur member that had proceeded to the direct election of its members to the Parliament. The Ushuaia Protocol referred to countries rather than to individuals. The impossibility to resolve the issue led to the neutralization of the Parliament for more than a year.

Eventually, Paraguay was admitted again in Mercosur, after the newly elected President, Horacio Cartes, was sworn in, in August 2013,[444] and, despite its initial refusal to accept Venezuela's membership, the new Congress of Paraguay ratified Venezuela's accession to Mercosur in December 2013.[445]

---

442 Decision 29/2005 of the CMC.

443 Vidigal (2013), pp. 339–340.

444 The decision to cease the suspension was taken in Montevideo on 13 July 2013. See "DECISIÓN SOBRE EL CESE DE LA SUSPENSIÓN DEL PARAGUAY EN EL MERCOSUR EN APLICACIÓN DEL PROTOCOLO DE USHUAIA SOBRE COMPROMISO DEMOCRÁTICO" in www.mercosur.int/t_generic.jsp?contentid=4506&site=1&channel=secretaria&seccion=3.

445 See www.telam.com.ar/notas/201312/45200-el-congreso-paraguayo-aprobo-el-ingreso-de-venezuela-al-mercosur.html.

Unasur also lifted the suspension in August 2013, following the election of President Cartes. Although, Unasur's Peru, which held at that time the rotating (*pro tempore*) presidency announced that "on August the Council of Heads of State of Unasur adopted the Decision to lift the suspension of Paraguay's participation to the organs and instances of the Union" with effect from 15 August 2013.[446] President Cartes was present in the VII ordinary meeting of the Heads of State and Government that took place in August 30, 2013 in Pernambuco (Surinam).[447]

Although clearly politically motivated and widely considered of doubtful legality, the case of Paraguay raises interesting questions as to the use of a democracy clause by a regional organisation to condemn a violation of democratic rules in a member state. It is not clear whether the same process would be followed under other circumstances: electoral irregularities in Venezuela's 2013 elections were not considered as raising democracy issues. As Vidigal rightly puts it, the most problematic element in Paraguay's suspension has to do with the "inconsistency in the formulation and application of the so-called `democratic clause' provided by the Ushuaia Protocol", which "fails to address situations of `democracy erosion' by charismatic leaders and domination of other branches of government by the executive".[448] A genuine 'democracy clause' could benefit from a more ideologically neutral application.

IV.2. AFRICA

Africa is a continent prone to military take-overs and although these still occur there, the condemning attitude taken by African regional integration organs may at least eventually influence the situation as coups will not be seen as a regular and normal occurrence. There is no reason to believe that military and other irregular taking over of power are regarded by African citizens and the elite as legitimate and action by regional organs to prevent, condemn and reverse coups is as a consequence seen as illegitimate. It is only after 1999 that first the OAU and later the AU has promoted the principle that illegitimate governments should not be seen as representatives of the population, that not any regime should be accepted as representing a country.[449] There is no shortage in Africa of tests of the policy not to condone regimes that have come to power through irregular means. More and more, the continent also provides examples

---

446 *El Clarin*. 11.8.2013 in www.clarin.com/mundo/Unasur-anuncio-levanta-suspension-Paraguay_0_972502838.html.

447 Www.mre.gov.py/v1/Noticias/922-vii-reunin-ordinaria-del-consejo-de-jefes-y-jefas-de-estado-y-de-gobierno-de-la-unasur.aspx.

448 Vidigal (2013). p. 349.

449 G. Lynch and C. Crawford, "Democratization in Africa 1990–2010: an assessment" in *Democratization* 18:2 (2011), pp. 275–310, at 278.

of action by regional integration bodies, although the multitude of bodies as well as the fact that there are still also many examples of intervention by states alone or jointly means that the overview of cause and effect is not clear. In the AU or other bodies, new acts are adopted to give clearer and greater powers for intervention to preserve values of the organisations but the lack of consistence especially in implementation remains a problem.[450]

Some positive examples of action by organisations can be observed, like the ECOWAS interventions that managed to reverse the coup in Sierra Leone in 1998 or helped to end the civil war in Guinea Bissau in 1998–1999. Thus, there is a foundation for the belief that the right kind of regional integration framework might well act to prevent unconstitutional changes of government in Africa.

The first ECOWAS intervention was the cease-fire monitoring group ECOMOG created by the ECOWAS Standing Mediation Committee in 1990 to intervene in the Liberian crisis to stop killings and destruction of property and to create conditions for free and fair elections. Later on the situation was handled by the UN under Security Council Resolutions (as a threat to peace in the region) with a role for ECOWAS as the regional enforcer of UN decisions, in accordance with the UN Charter. The ECOWAS action was important to launch the intervention and the organisation also later had an important role as regional enforcement is presumed to be more effective for fulfilling UN decisions.[451] The example from Sierra Leone some years later shows ECOWAS action even more clearly. After a 1997 military coup in Sierra Leone, the democratically elected president requested assistance from Nigeria and ECOWAS. There were separate interventions (in 1997–1998), by Nigeria and by ECOWAS, both sanctioned afterwards by the UN.[452] There were elements of humanitarian intervention as well as intervention to protect democracy, as the democratically elected president requested the intervention. At the time, Levitt says that the possible right to intervene to protect democracy was not well developed but in this situation, statements were made e.g. by the UN Secretary General to indicate that coups against elected governments should not be tolerated and it must be possible to take action to restore the democratic order.[453] Indeed, Levitt calls the Sierra Leone case the first clear case of a shift in the law toward recognising a right to pro-democratic intervention.[454] The OAU also unequivocally condemned and rejected the unconstitutional change of government in Sierra Leone.[455]

---

450 Manby (2004), pp. 984–98.

451 Levitt (2010), p. 114.

452 Vidmar (2013), p. 33.

453 *Ibid.*, p. 149.

454 Levitt (2010), pp. 116–120.

455 As referred to in Declaration AHG 5 (XXXVI), Assembly of the Heads of State or Government, Thirty-sixth ordinary session/Fourth session of African Economic Community, 10–12 July 2000, Lomé, Togo, www.africa-union.org/Special_Programs/CSSDCA/cssdca-solemndeclaration.pdf.

ECOWAS reacted to the situation by in 1998 adopting the Mechanism for Conflict Prevention, Management, Resolution, Peacekeeping and Security (as mentioned above), allowing for intervention in case of overthrow or attempted overthrow of a democratically elected government.[456] The Mechanism was needed. In Guinea-Bissau in 1998 the democratically elected government asked for outside help, first from neighbouring countries and then also from ECOWAS in the form of ECOMOG intervention, to protect its power. Eventually the intervention was transformed into a mission to maintain security at the border, but also here one can see that the main reason for it was to protect the democratically elected government. Levitt sees it as another example of how an intervention to preserve democracy can be lawful and legitimate.[457]

Also the AU has been faced with a number of situations on non-constitutional changes of government. Sao Tome and Principe was the first situation in which the AU mechanisms for supporting democracy were tested. In 2002 there was an attempted coup in the country, which, however, was reversed rather quickly following pressure by the AU as well as several countries.[458] There was no intervention as such and it is difficult to see to what extent the pressure from the AU or that from certain powerful states in the region led to the result. However, it is still interesting to observe this example as it was probably one factor contributing to the AU developing its mechanisms for possible interventions, leading to the adoption in 2003 of the Protocol establishing the Peace and Security Council of the African Union.

In August 2008 the AU membership of Mauretania was suspended because of the coup there. The dictatorial regime of the country was ousted by the military in 2005 and the military kept their promise to arrange elections, taking place in 2007. However, the restoration of democracy was not as complete or clean as it was made out to be, but the military rulers stayed close to power. In fact, the election can be seen as a way to consolidate the power of the military.[459] There was a difference in the reaction of two regional integration organisations concerned, the AU and the Arab League. The AU suspended the country although its envoy was still rather conciliatory whereas the Arab League claimed to have been reassured that democracy would again be restored so there was no cause for action.[460] The Arab League is generally regarded as ineffective in both political and economic or specialised cooperation[461] so this difference in reaction should not be surprising. Also Guinea was suspended from the AU in 2008 following a military coup as was Guinea Bissau in 2012. The AU knows

456 Abass & Baderin (2002), pp. 4–6 and Levitt (2010), pp. 116–120.

457 Levitt (2010), pp. 121–123. Also this intervention was welcomed afterwards by the UN.

458 Levitt (2010), pp. 141–143.

459 Lynch and Crawford (2011), p. 278.

460 *The Economist*, 16 August 2008.

461 Mallat (2007), p. 151.

its own credibility may suffer if it is not seen to react against coups and similar unconstitutional behaviour.[462]

In addition to ECOWAS and the AU, SADC also plays a role for African regional implementation of democratic values. ECOWAS as well as SADC handle the role of actual implementer for the AU (or the UN). SADC has played quite a decisive role in its area of competence. However, the weak way of handling Zimbabwe shows that this organisation may not be able to act decisively in favour of democracy or at least not consistently.[463]

That countries threatened with sanctions and with exclusion or suspension from ECOWAS and the AU complied is regarded by Koefele Kole as a sign that the sanctions threat is efficient.[464]

In Togo, both ECOWAS and the AU reacted to attempts backed by the military to engineer a non-constitutional transfer of power after the death of the long-serving president Gnassingbe Eyadema in 2005 by imposing sanctions. The ECOWAS sanctions came first and the organisation also suspended Togo from membership. The AU through its Peace and Security Council authorised further sanctions and supported the ones imposed by ECOWAS. The sanctions had effect in that the unconstitutional president (the son of the previous one) stepped down and elections were organised – as it was, won by the same man. Still, the intervention by the regional organisations can be seen as successful as the situation was handled in a constitutional manner. Levitt shows this as an example of how an unconstitutional transition of power is successfully reversed by a regional organisation. Levitt feels it was successful because there was domestic pressure as well but also as the intervention was from regional, African organisations rather than Westerners.[465] While the example of Togo as well as that of Liberia earlier point to the importance of regional organisations for imposing democratic values, in the Central African Republic in 1997 a similar action was taken by an ad hoc grouping of states in the region.[466] The action as well as the effect was similar, which could infer that the organisation and its structures are less important. At the same time, the absence of an organisation and institutional structures makes the possibility and possible outcome of an intervention less secure and transparent.

The Darfur crisis in Sudan was the first time the AU militarily intervened in a conflict. The intervention was in the form of a peacekeeping mission but had some aspects of humanitarian intervention as well. Although the general issue of humanitarian intervention is controversial in international law, a certain

---

462 *The Economist*, 16 August 2008, 7 February 2009; http://allafrica.com/view/group/main/main/id/00016477.html.

463 See among others Cawthra (2010).

464 Koefele Kole (2008), pp. 258–259.

465 Levitt (2010), pp. 127–129.

466 *Ibid.* pp. 132–133.

such possibility has been created under the AU. In 2004 the AU initiated inter-Sudanese peace talks and the search for a diplomatic resolution of the Darfur conflict. These continued in seven phases and culminated with the Darfur Peace Agreement (DPA) in May 2006. The DPA is quite an elaborate agreement, containing more than thirty articles and attempting to create a legal framework to redress imbalances between the government and the population as well as relations between Darfurians themselves. It is not just a straight-forward peace agreement in the sense of ending of a conflict but includes provisions on power and wealth sharing, participation in political processes, a transitional Darfur regional authority, creation of a federal system of government and provisions on human rights and fundamental freedoms, displaced persons as well as judicial responsibility. The DPA includes previous agreements made on some of these issues. International support for the DPA was swift and strong. In June 2004 AU started its military intervention in Darfur, under a mandate from the AU Peace and Security Council.[467]

The legal basis of the military intervention is found in Article 4 of the AU Constitutive Act (the right to intervene), see Article 4h, which can include use of force to really ensure democracy.[468] In July 2007 a hybrid UN/AU mission was created for Darfur, UNAMID, based on the UN Security Council Resolution 1769.[469] One issue concerning the mission in the difficult context it operates in is the debate around the desired African character of the mission. Some commentators feel it is almost a mantra that there must be African solutions to African problems and this should not be used to make the mission less effective. The international system (both the UN system as such and the more recent International Criminal Court) foresee local – and thus in this case African – solutions under the complementarity principle as prescribed in the ICC statute. The use of such local solutions, however, presumes that there are laws and systems in place for such procedures and that they can be effective. The "local solution" should not be a way to avoid any solution at all to a conflict or other situation.[470]

A somewhat different approach to enforcing democracy was taken in the case *Dawada Jawara v. The Gambia*[471] using the ACHPR or Banjul Charter.[472] Here an ousted Head of State from Gambia referred to articles in the Banjul Charter on democracy and brought a case before the African Commission on Human and Peoples' Rights, which he also won.

In the following some African examples will be treated in some more detail.

---

467 Abass (2007), pp. 418–420.

468 Levitt (2010), p. 139.

469 S/Res/1769 (2007). See also www.un.org/en/peacekeeping/missions/unamid/.

470 Abass (2007), p. 435.

471 See *Dawda Jawara* v. *The Gambia*, African Commission on Human and Peoples' Rights, Comm. Nos. 147/95 and 149/96 (2000) and Koefele Kole (2008), p. 248.

472 See above, section III.2.2.

IV.2.1. COTE D'IVOIRE

One example of regional integration influence was the work of ECOWAS and the AU to push for the respect for the democratic regime in Cote d'Ivoire in relation to the troubles there in 2000–2002. The example is interesting also as it illustrates how incomplete the abilities of regional integration organisations still are, as the intervention of the former colonial power France probably had much more effect on the actual developments in the country that the actions of ECOWAS and AU.

Cote d'Ivoire had in many respects been seen as an African success story, until a coup in 1999 and civil war starting in 2002. The background to the war was a coup in 1999, which was followed by elections as well as referendum on a constitutional change in 2000. The idea of the referendum called by the military coup leader and effective ruler of the country was largely to make sure that a popular candidate (the then Prime Minister Ouattara) would not be eligible to be elected, due to changed nationality requirements. Following the elections, the incumbent – the coup leader – refused to recognise the results or the legitimacy of other candidates, but after some violence the winner of the elections, Laurent Gbagbo was sworn in, however, maintaining the policy of disqualifying Ouattara, which led to a rebellion from the North of the country – Ouattara's region and area of strong support.[473] Regional organisation, mainly ECOWAS reacted by condemnation but the most noticeable intervention was in fact a French one: French intervention in Cote d'Ivoire in 2002 – which was in fact a peace-imposing intervention – was supported by ECOWAS.

Before the country could recover politically and economically from that war, the consequences of elections in 2009 and 2010 led to political turmoil and unconstitutional actions, which also led to widespread violence. Both ECOWAS and the AU suspended the country from membership in December of 2010 due to the failure of the sitting president to resign after losing the elections. Travel bans and other sanctions were also applied on the regime that refused to step down after losing elections.

The AU used Article 30 AU, which allows it to suspend states with governments that come to power by unconstitutional means from AU activities. Such a possibility also existed in OAU (since 1997), which means that similar measures could be applied at events taking place at different points in time but the impact still varies, depending on how important it is to be in a regional integration organisation. From this viewpoint, the AU can exercise more pressure than the OAU, even with the same tool, as the membership of AU – and perhaps even more of ECOWAS – is more important for the member states.

---

473 B.E. Withaker, "Citizens and Foreigners: Democratization and the Policy of Exclusion in Africa", *African Studies Review*, Vol. 48 No. 1 (April 2005), pp. 109–126, at 114.

In March 2003 pressure from regional organisations led to a power-sharing arrangement.[474] This was important to end the conflict but regrettably did not lead to a sustainable solution. At the same time, the arrangement may well have prevented even worse bloodshed. As mentioned, it did not prevent that new political turmoil erupted in 2009–2010.

IV.2.2. MADAGASCAR

Madagascar in March 2009 presented an example of an army-backed but somewhat unusual coup, which brought a former mayor, Andry Rajoelina, to power and ousted president Ravalomanana.[475] The unusual features included that the process of the coup was not as evident as in more traditional military take-overs (like e.g. in the Comoro Islands in 2008 when the AU sent a military force to restore order after a "classical" military coup). In Madagascar the president "voluntarily" stepped down and handed power to a military directorate, which later handed power to Mr Rajoelina in order to restore democracy with elections to be held within two years. Mr Rajoelina and his supporters claimed that they had not done anything wrong or even staged a coup at all. According to them, there had been rioting and protests against rising food prices as well as the autocratic behaviour of the President and Mr Rajoelina took control to prevent more serious rioting and violence, preventing a military take-over of power. The "coup-makers" claim to act in defence of the constitution, against a regime that had violated it at different occasions. Security forces as well as other institutions came out in support of the new powers.[476] Mr Rajoelina indeed asked the President to step down or to face impeachment by the Constitutional Court, thus using elements of the Constitution. How exactly the president was made to step down is not well known. The Constitutional Court quickly came out in support of the new leader Mr Rajoelina and said he had the powers outlined in the Constitution for the president albeit for no more than 24 months within which period he must hold elections. Regional organisations and other countries in the region as well as elsewhere have been confused about how to act. The then chairman of the AU, the Libyan leader Qaddafi said to the new leader that his power would be recognised but regardless of this, the AU suspended Madagascar from the Union. The AU decided to give six month for restoration of constitutional order or otherwise the country would be subject to sanctions. As this did not happen, Madagascar remains suspended from the AU and the EU has suspended its aid to the country. SADC through

---

474 *Ibid.* (2005), p. 115.

475 The coming to power of Mr Ravalomanana in 2002 was not without controversy, with the OAU – just then becoming the AU – holding off recognition to his government for a while and even after the Supreme Court had endorsed Mr Ravalomanana. Cawtrha (2010), p. 13.

476 Cawthra (2010), p. 17.

its security sub-committee also strongly condemned the coup and stated that it was against the SADC treaty and the AU charter. Also SADC mentioned the possibility of sanctions if the county was not returned to constitutional rule and the organisation opened up the possibility to use all relevant resources to restore order if necessary, thus alluding to a possibility of use of force to restore constitutional order.[477] In November 2010 there was an attempt by the military to take over power, but this more traditional coup was quickly put down.[478]

During the years since the 2009 change of power, there have been various attempts by international organisations to mediate in the conflict in Madagascar and achieve democratic elections, which keep being postponed. The most important part has been played by SADC that sponsored a roadmap for ending the crisis, issued in September of 2011. Elections to be held according to this roadmap were delayed, although the government repeatedly promised elections as soon as possible. The first round of the presidential elections were held in October 2013 and the second in December 2013 while local elections were held in July 2015. Meanwhile a range of transitional institutions have been established.[479] The AU imposed targeted sanctions on Mr Rajoelina and members of his administration in early 2010 and the EU suspended its aid in the same year. The fact that such actions have not persuaded the government to agree to hold elections or to implement the different plans for power sharing that have been sponsored by the international community could be seen as a failure of external actors, including regional integration systems, to support democracy. However, the situation is not as negative as this, as the on-going attempts to find a solution indicate that the government cannot afford to ignore the suggestions. The pressure on it and the efforts of SADC have concretely pointed the country in the direction it needs to take if to return to the international community.

At some point in 2009 there was even a discussion of military intervention, using the forces available for SADC for such intervention (SADCBRIG), and although this was not a serious option, it gave rise to a lot of anxiety and protest among the people of Madagascar – exploited by Mr Raojoelina.[480]

In the case of Madagascar, the absence of an organisation (preferably a strong regional organisation) to take a leading role in the international efforts to influence the country to get back on the constitutional track, meant that the international efforts were less coherent and effective than they might otherwise have been. Although there was some coordination in an international contact

---

477 *The Economist*, e.g. 7 February 2009, 21 March 2009, 28 March 2009. Madagascar joined SADC only in 2005, being outside of the core region of this community.

478 As an unusual parenthesis, it may be mentioned that a former judge of the International Court of Justice was charged with having arranged this coup. http://jurist.org/paperchase/2012/03/former-icj-judge-on-trial-for-madagascar-coup-plot.php (of Tuesday 20 March 2012).

479 For a country profile and facts, see www.state.gov/r/pa/ei/bgn/5460.htm#political. Also Cawthra (2010), pp. 14–15.

480 Cawthra (2010), p. 20.

group of different organisations, the mediation even led to some tension between organisations (like the AU and SADC) regarding who should play the leading role.[481] Such disagreements between organisations are swiftly exploited by those who look to discredit international or regional pressure.

Something else to which Madagascar can serve as an illustration is the need not to overplay the hand of the regional organisation and take too heavy-handed action against the unconstitutionally created governing structures, with the risk of otherwise causing widespread negative feelings among the population and perhaps increasing support for the unconstitutional leaders.[482]

Madagascar also appears to indicate (it is too soon to speak with certainty of the matter, as the issues is on-going) that the use of sanctions, like cutting of aid, is more effective than exclusion from a regional integration organisation or other measures taken by such an organisation.[483] This evidently depends on the state in question (Madagascar is very aid-dependent) as well as the strength of the regional integration organisation (exclusion from SADC or AU has fewer practical consequences that exclusion from the EU for example). Also, in the case of Madagascar, commentators find that the organisations that acted strongly against the unconstitutionality – the AU and SADC – as Cawthra says[484], painted themselves into a corner, by taking such a strong principled position, but not ensuring that all (many) international players involved were singing from the same song sheet. In this respect, the Madagascar issue can serve as an illustration to the fact that a well-organised and strong regional integration system will have totally different possibilities to influence than one where the course of action is created more or less *ad hoc*. This may appear evident but does not lead to the organisations necessarily drawing the relevant conclusions or at least not acting upon them. Even if SADC since the mid-2000s has possibilities to take action against unconstitutional changes of power, it does not possess a clear mechanism or strategy for this. Cawthra quotes[485] the lack of capacity of SADC to support the mediation and other processes it insisted upon, with the lack of professional capacity as well as of proper civil society involvement – as well as the doubt about whether its position was principled or more based on personal sympathies or a fear of contagion with popular uprisings – as factors weakening the impact of this particular regional organisation. In Cawthra's view, a professional secretariat would have had a positive impact on the organisation's (SADC or AU) abilities to affect the outcome of the political situation in the country.

481 *Ibid.* p. 15.

482 *Ibid.* p. 20. In Madagascar, there was no military intervention but the fact that this was discussed (SADCBRIG intervention) entailed protest and fear among the population – exploited by the coup-makers. *Ibid.*

483 Cawthra (2010), p. 21.

484 *Ibid.*

485 *Ibid.*, p. 22.

Another interesting matter brought up by Cawthra[486] in relation to Madagascar and that the current authors would like to stress, is the possible role of regional integration organisations after a conflict (in the form of a military coup or some other form of unconstitutional taking of power) has been averted. If the regional integration organisation has the capacity to assist in the building up of the post-conflict system through election monitoring, concrete assistance to the government or any other positive measures, it gets a better position through this from which to play a proper and effective role in preventing unconstitutional changes of government in the future.

IV.2.3. MALI

Mali experienced rapid growth and a promising future until in 2012 radical Islamist increasingly gained control of the north of the country and in addition, an inconclusive coup weakened the state power further. The coup (in March 2012) led to suspension of the country from the AU according to Article 30 AU. The suspension was lifted in October 2012, as the AU considered that the legitimate government had regained sufficient control over the country.

Mali in 2012 presents a clear example of how regional integration organisations have an important role to play in strengthening democracy, as support to democratically elected governments – but sadly, without necessarily having the tools to perform such a role effectively. What is interesting in Mali is that the government has been calling for help to ensure order in the whole country, amidst fears that the northern part of Mali will fall completely in the hands of radical Islamist. Both ECOWAS and the AU are supporting the Mali government as well as calling on the rest of the international community to prevent the spreading or prolongation of the crisis.[487]

The National Movement for the Liberation of Azawad (MNLA) has been calling for independence of northern Mali. In a Declaration on 6 April 2012 the ECOWAS Commission made a Declaration on this call for independence for part of the country. The Commission stated that it had learnt from the international media of the so-called Declaration of Independence by MNLA. The ECOWAS Commission denounced the declaration and considers it null and void, and of no effect, reminding all the armed groups in the North of Mali that Mali is one and indivisible entity and that ECOWAS would take all necessary measures, including the use of force, to ensure the territorial integrity of the country. The declaration clearly reaffirms the ECOWAS commitment

486 *Ibid.*

487 See various news reports from an international, inter-governmental meeting held in Bamako on 22 October 2012, e.g. www.bernama.com/bernama/v6/newsworld.php?id=703832 (25 October 2012).

to the unity and territorial integrity of Mali and says that "it wishes to put all on guard against any temptation to proclaim any part of Mali as a sovereign state, as it will never recognize any such state".[488] This is a strongly worded statement and designed to discourage the MNLA to approach ECOWAS for any legitimisation.

Ahead of the ECOWAS summit of 2013, representatives of the organisation expressed that ECOWAS wants to provide a supportive framework for rebuilding constitutional rule in Mali and ensuring that not just elections are held but that problems of different communities in the country are addressed.[489]

The examples are too few and disparate to draw clear conclusions on whether there is a trend to be observed or not, but it is not too daring to see a step-by-step increase in the idea of possible intervention by regional integration organisations.

IV.3. ASIA, THE ARAB WORLD AND THE PACIFIC

Outside of the Americas, Africa and Europe, the more mixed collection of regional integration organisations also offers a more mixed bag of examples of how integration systems can influence states. The absence of any one important and powerful organisation (for each region) means that the effect of exclusion or sanctions may be less important.

ASEAN was created to some extent to withstand external influence and dominance over the region. It was created at the time of the US wars in Vietnam and is in the words of Lake the only regional body without any dominance of any state and outside a regional hierarchy.[490] ASEAN, even if weak as an organisation, did manage to play some role in connection with regional conflicts (Malaysia – Indonesia, Malaysia the Philippines) by providing a framework and a diplomatic device for such conflict solution or at least defusing conflicts. The tools consisted of formal agreements as well as informal mechanisms, the latter – called the ASEAN way – being the most important.[491] As far as organisational structures or adopted norms of democracy as requirements for membership, ASEAN has almost nothing to show. Its influence has thus been of an ad hoc character and even if there are now some examples to point to, there is a lack of legal certainty of what would happen in any analogue situation in the future. Other regional bodies in the wide area included in this section are even less structured.

488 ECOWAS Commission Declaration following the Declaration of Independence of Northern Mail by the MNLA. www.ecowas.int/publications/en/statement/mali06042012.pdf.

489 Www.dw.de/ecowas-summit-focuses-on-mali-guinea-bissau/a-16959010.

490 Lake (2009), pp. 55–57.

491 Caballero-Anthony (2006), at p. 268.

IV.3.1. FIJI

Fiji shows an example of a small country that was expelled from two regional systems following an unconstitutional taking of power: Fiji was suspended in 2009 from the Pacific Island Forum as well as the Commonwealth. However, this did not lead to the country taking steps to restore democracy but rather meant that it went on following only its own timetable for restoration of democracy. The leader of the country, who came to power unconstitutionally, claimed that the election laws favoured racism and thus contributed to a culture of coups, so it would make more sense to amend such laws rather than hold early elections. The coup of December 2006 was justified with the aim of safeguarding the constitution. This was the second coup in a short time, with one having taken place in 2000 (and also one in 1987). The constitution (from 1997) survived that first coup.[492] The 2000 coup and the intention of the military government that assumed power after it (having been handed power by the coup maker Mr. Speight, described as a business man and adventurer) to draft a new constitution was found unconstitutional by the constitutional court of Fiji and the attempts abandoned after that – until the next coup a few years later, this time by the military commander at the time and with the aim to protect the constitution.[493] The promises made to regional bodies of elections not later than 2009 were not met and even if exclusion from regional bodies followed, this was not seen to be serious enough to warrant a change in behaviour. Actions by powerful states in the region (Australia and New Zealand) like imposing or lifting travel bans appear to have more importance for the state than the regional organisations. In September of 2014 elections were finally held, with a strong showing for the party of the incumbent prime minister. Following these elections the suspension of Fiji from both the regional fora was lifted.

IV.3.2. MYANMAR

In September 1988 military rule was proclaimed in what was then called Burma under the State Law and Order Restoration Council, crushing the civilian governing structures and the democratic movement. The country was officially renamed Myanmar in 1989. Despite severe repressions, in elections organised in 1990, the National League for Democracy, which united the main opposition groups under the leadership of Aung San Su Kyi won 392 of 485 seats. However, the Parliament was never allowed to convene. Several countries instituted

[492] Y. Ghai and J. Cottrell, "A Tale of Three Constitutions: Ethnicity and Politics in Fiji", *International Journal of Constitutional Law* (2007) 5(4), pp. 639–669, at 640.

[493] *Ibid.*, pp. 664–665.

sanctions against the Burmese regime to pressure it to respect democracy and human rights.[494]

ASEAN at first was not able to agree on a common stance regarding these events in its region. Different states had different relations with the country and for several, trade with Myanmar increased at this time and there was little appetite for sanctions or other measure that could disturb such relations. Thailand suggested in the early 1990s to invite Myanmar as an observer to ASEAN (although the country itself was not very positive to ASEAN) and also some other suggestions of multilateral discussions were made. In 1994 Myanmar voiced an interest in attending an ASEAN meeting and was duly invited by the Thai hosts, including attending the first Asian Regional Forum. Myanmar was seen as an interesting market and furthermore ASEAN members wanted to act against what they saw as a growing Chinese influence. Some comments were made about positive developments in Myanmar politics, even if at the same time several countries were still quite concerned about the political situation. Thailand that generally supported accession by Myanmar or at least closer relations with ASEAN was important in pushing for some political developments, like the release from house arrest in 1995 of Aung San Su Kyi, which gave a possibility to let Myanmar sign the ASEAN Treaty of Amity and Cooperation and to apply for full membership of the organisation.[495] The membership was initially intended to be granted in 2000 but during the Malaysian chairmanship in 1996, this was accelerated to 1997. Renewed severe repressions by the military regime in 1996 appeared to jeopardize the early accession, but again ASEAN was out of sync with other powers like the USA and the EU that initiated sanctions[496] against Myanmar because of these repressions. ASEAN could not agree on a common standpoint, but did make some contacts in order to warn the country that it may lose its chance of early ASEAN accession.[497]

What was seen as a fairly mild statement by many observers was a big step for ASEAN, when the organisation following severe violence in Myanmar in May 2003 condemned this violence and made some calls on the government of the country to deal with the situation. The main importance of the reaction of ASEAN is that it is seen by many commentators as a starting-point for the acceptance that the organisation can take a standpoint regarding internal developments in Member Countries, if these threaten the region. For ASEAN, what they said about Myanmar in 2003 was the most far-reaching effort of the organisation to influence domestic politics of a Member State.[498] More active

494 Möller (1998), p. 1088.
495 *Ibid.* pp. 1089–1090.
496 The effectiveness of which have been questioned, Focarelli (2012), p. 452. The EU increasingly applies so called smart sanctions, meaning more targeted ones that are not supposed to harm the general population. *Ibid.* p. 484.
497 Möller (1998), p. 1091.
498 Haacke (2006), p. 157.

measures such as invoking the Troika regime (of ASEAN foreign ministers, a mechanism established in 1999 to address urgent situations with a potential to threaten peace and security) were not agreed upon and the main regional response was not fashioned within the ASEAN structure, but rather bilaterally (by Thailand) and resulting in an ad hoc multilateral forum.[499]

Given the importance of the widely interpreted principle of non-interference as the major basis for ASEAN, the fact that the organisation did react to what was happening in Myanmar is interesting. However, even if Myanmar also later than 2003 provided many circumstances in which international sanctions would be warranted, there was no clear line of action from ASEAN. The idea with the statements and actions of ASEAN was to encourage Myanmar to adopt democracy (to some extent at least) but while making these statements, the principle of non-interference was stressed to show that what ASEAN did was not to get involved in internal matters.[500] Reacting to one specific situation did not necessarily mean that other violations would trigger a reaction, as there was no clear framework or established organisational mechanism to react to situations.

A weak measure as such does not necessarily mean that it will be ineffective. If the country at the receiving end of serious criticism is in need of good relations with the sender of the criticism, even just a warning can be important enough. The ASEAN censure of Myanmar has not reached such level of importance, both as there is a lot of uncertainty and ambiguity about what ASEAN really can and should do, and because the actual role of ASEAN as a major regional factor (as opposed to various bilateral agreements, other multilateral agreements and others) is less than clear. The importance of ASEAN for the current democratisation process in Myanmar is difficult to establish, but it may well have been a contributing factor, as one trigger for change appears to be a desire to end international isolation.

At the same time, it cannot be overlooked that there was a lot of external pressure on ASEAN[501] to take some kind of stance regarding Myanmar, so the efforts to give the organisation some role in supporting democracy and peaceful developments may not have been very whole-heartedly approved – or at least not initiated – by the organisations own Members. There was a fear that the collective standing of the organisation would suffer if it did nothing in the face of international expectations to undertake real measures. In July 2003 the (then outgoing) Malaysian leader even mentioned a possibility of expulsion as a sanction against Myanmar – something other leaders quickly distanced themselves from.[502] ASEAN is not the only body that has hesitated on what measures to take against Myanmar, with reference to the issue of internal affairs.

499 See e.g. Haacke (2006), pp. 152–154 and Caballero-Anthony (2006), pp. 276–277.
500 Haacke (2006), p. 156.
501 *Ibid.* p. 161.
502 *Ibid.* p. 163.

Not unusually, China and Russia vetoed UN Security Council measures against Myanmar with this justification.[503] The recent opening up and democratisation of Myanmar has allowed some ASEAN leaders to feel vindicated – that progress happens at its own pace.

In the 2012 elections in Myanmar ASEAN had a limited role in election monitoring, which is significant as it is one of the few democracy related monitoring activities undertaken by ASEAN as an organisation.[504]

IV.3.3. CAMBODIA

For Cambodia, the first effect of regional integration systems demanding certain standards came in relation to its application to join ASEAN.[505] In 1997 (the year of its 30th anniversary) ASEAN admitted – or rather planned to admit – new members: Cambodia, Laos and Myanmar.[506] None of these states were democracies and also economically they were different from earlier members. The membership can be seen as a desire by the organisation to include the entire region, sacrificing commonness of systems and ideals. But even with this said, the coup staged in Cambodia at the time (against a background of tumultuous development since independence)[507] meant that the organisation suspended the accession of Cambodia for a bit over one year and the admission happened in April 1999.[508] Second Prime Minister Hun Sen ousted the First Prime Minister Prince Noordom Ranariddh through a violet coup in July 1997. ASEAN made contradictory and unclear statements about what kind of action through mediation or other measures the organisation might offer and how this fitted with the principle of non-intervention. Umbach states this as an example of the inability of the old elite coming to terms with new challenges of the 21st century and its globalisation trends.[509] Despite the all-important principle of non-intervention, interpreted in a wide manner and the absence of any requirement

---

503 Like in 2007, see Focarelli (2012), p. 372.

504 Chesterman (2015), p. 47.

505 K.Hauerstein, "Aspects of Administrative Law and its Reform in Cambodia" in K. Hauerstein & J. Menzel (eds.), *The Development of Cambodian Administrative Law* (Konrad Adenauer Stiftung, Cambodia 2014), pp. 29 and 33.

506 Möller (1998), p. 1087.

507 J. Menzel, "Cambodia: From Civil War to a Constitution to Constitutionalism?" in C. Hill and J. Menzel (eds), *Constitutionalism in Southeast Asia*, Konrad Adenauer Stiftung 2008, at pp. 42–46.

508 Statement by the Secretary-General of ASEAN Welcoming the Kingdom of Cambodia as the Tenth Member State of ASEAN 30 April 1999, ASEAN Secretariat www.aseansec.org/3338.htm (22 October 2012). See also *The Economist*, 12 February 2011.

509 F. Umbrach, "ASEAN and Major Powers: Japan and China – A Changing Balance of Power" in J. Dosch and M. Mols (eds.), *International Relations in the Asia-Pacific* (St. Martin's Press, New York 2000), pp. 171–213, at 172.

of democracy or other norms of state behaviour for membership, unlike the EU, ASEAN did take quite a tough stance by postponing Cambodian accession.[510]

In and after the Indochinese war of 1979–1991 ASEAN and its members had played a role by facilitating talks, providing assistance to find solutions and in other ways supporting (without direct intervention) the finding of a sustainable solution.[511] When violence broke out again in Cambodia in 1997 the Malaysian leader Anwar Ibrahim made a proposal for what was called constructive intervention using ASEAN. This would include various measures, such as direct assistance to the electoral process, increased commitment to legal and administrative reform, development of human capital and strengthening of civil society and the rule of law. The full programme was not adopted under this name, neither was a similar proposal by the Thai foreign minister fully adopted, nor his call for more flexible engagement between member states.[512] At the same time, ASEAN support and the actions and interventions of the member states in a bilateral fashion were in practice not very different from possible organisational sanctions[513] and the facilitation measures undertaken under an ASEAN heading are seen to have had some effect.[514] Internal divisions between ASEAN members as well as lack of support from the rest of the international community took the edge of the attempts to influence the situation in a more robust fashion. The Cambodian response was to protest about interference in internal affairs. At the same time, the country was still interested in ASEAN membership and kept up its contact with the organisation, while denying that it had any legitimate reason to have views on the political events in the country. This gave ASEAN the possibility to keep up pressure on the country to organise the elections that had been planned for 1998 and that ASEAN had offered some help with.[515]

One difference compared with the EU and its demands on new Members is that the EU links the demands it makes on states with a programme to support them. ASEAN generally had not had these kind of demands, nor the aid to help the states meet the demands.[516] The pressure on Cambodia was thus a new situation for the organisation.

---

510 Nesadurai (2006), at p. 201 and Umbrach (2000), p. 172.

511 Möller (1998), p. 1094.

512 Umbrach (2000), p. 172.

513 Caballero-Anthony (2006), p. 277 and fn. 12.

514 "ASEAN – though the ASEAN Troika on Cambodia – has been engaged in efforts to assist in the restoration of political stability in Government. It maintained open and regular dialogues with His Majesty King Sihanouk, Second Prime Minister Hun Sen, HRH Prince Norodom Ranariddh and other leading political personalities and high officials of countries, and in particular the "Friends of Cambodia", with the objective of facilitating the holding of free and fair elections and fostering national unity. The election that took place on 26 July 1998 was a major step in restoring political normalcy in Cambodia." ASEAN Statement on Cambodia, 4 September 1998, www.aseansec.org/16284.htm.

515 Möller (1998), p. 1097.

516 Acharya (2006), fn. 2 at p. 320.

By treating Myanmar and Cambodia differently, ASEAN opened itself up to criticism for inconsistency. Not making demands on Myanmar has by many been seen as a sign of weakness of ASEAN, embarrassing the organisation. At the same time, it is still interesting that the organisation despite its strict adherence to and wide interpretation of non-interference used pressure on states to change their domestic policies. ASEAN deferred membership of Cambodia because of the coup there but admitted Myanmar despite its dismal human rights record. Cambodia had to meet some specific demands like holding free and fair elections and establish a Senate. Later on again ASEAN failed to react against human rights abuses and violation of democratic principles when it did not act regarding East Timor in 1999. This crisis was seen as an important regional crisis and many commentators were disappointed at the lack of action from ASEAN. The organisation referred to its traditional non-interference principle and to the UN as the only body that legitimately could act in a situation like the one in East Timor.[517]

At the same time as describing the weak or even absent reactions of ASEAN (as well as the ARF) to regional crises, Caballero-Anthony underlines that at least the organisation(s) did react even if in an ad hoc manner. The organisations help create confidence-building measures and if the members want the organisations to be strong and effective, they may be so. However, the absence of institutional structures and formalised procedures means that the organisations (ASEAN and by extension ARF) are as strong and as effective as their members want them to be in a given situation regarding a given conflict.[518] This actually does not mean they cannot be strong and effective, only that it is a decision of states as states rather than of a regional integration system that determines this strength and effectiveness. The only influence of the organisation is that it may make the states come together and discuss and take action – but this can be a role that is not without importance.

Organisations that in some way deal with human rights have a possibility to exert a positive influence on democratisation of states in the broad sense. The more far-reaching procedures that exist (through individual complaint mechanisms for example) the more direct such an influence can be, as the European Convention and Court on Human Rights illustrate. But even a weaker system can have some influence, as it provides people with a place to bring complaints and this may elevate issues to the public debate.[519] This is why the ASEAN Intergovernmental Commission for Human Rights may be important not least for Cambodia, even if it is a body without much teeth.

---

517 Caballero-Anthony (2006), at pp. 269–272 and Acharya (2006), fn. 2 at p. 320. The more recently created and wider Asia Regional Forum did not take any action either.

518 Caballero-Anthony (2006), at pp. 274–275.

519 S. Anstis, "Using Law to impair the Rights and Freedoms of Human Right Defenders: A case study of Cambodia", *Journal of Human Rights Practice*, 2012, pp. 1–22, DOI:10.1093/jhuman/hus017 at p. 18.

Haacke finds[520] that although there is a precedent of sorts for ASEAN, this does not mean that predictions can be made for future cases. This can be concurred with. In international relations all cases tend to be very different, but even more importantly, there is no formal structure or system in ASEAN to deal with situations. If there is such a system, even widely diverging cases will be handled similarly and precedents can be used as inspiration, but in ASEAN the actions have been ad hoc and at most may have laid a foundation for the very general notion that ASEAN can (and perhaps even that it should?) react against some abuses in internal politics of its Members.

The *ad hoc* Troika mechanism used with some success *vis-à-vis* Cambodia in 1997 and later formalised has not been invoked again by ASEAN. The operationalisation and modalities of the Troika were agreed upon, only for progress to be stalled for political purposes a bit later.[521] Foreign ministers were to have a retreat for discussion of common problems, an ASEAN Troika (established 1999) should address urgent regional situations that could threaten peace and security and the High Council of ASEAN adopted rules of procedure (in 2001).[522]

IV.4. REGIONAL INTEGRATION AS AN OBSTACLE TO POSITIVE DEVELOPMENTS

To underline that the idea of regional integration exerting a positive influence on democratisation and respect for human rights is not necessarily the full truth, a counter example is presented of how regional integration can support anti-democratic measures. A regional organisation can hinder international involvement in human rights, if the organisation itself is not supportive of such rights. Then the organisation by being stronger than any one Member State and often also stronger than the sum of its members would be without an organised forum, can use its strength to block other international bodies such as the UN and its human rights system from investigating members. The Organisation of Islamic Cooperation (until 2011 the Organisation of the Islamic Conference) supported by a number of African States (in addition to its members) has played that role in the UN Human Rights Council to stop the Council from examining human rights in Muslim or African countries.[523]

The impact of regional integration on democracy can also be seen in the reverse as the regional system supporting non-democratic systems and lessening

520 Haacke (2006), p. 166.
521 Caballero-Anthony (2006), p. 280.
522 Haacke (2006), at p. 151.
523 See e.g. Human Rights Watch, www.hrw.org/news/2006/11/03/how-put-un-rights-council-back-track.

the desire for state to promote reforms. In the absence of an institutional system, there are no formalised ways to challenge this but states are prey to the strongest in the region, who can use loose groupings to impose their views. Within the framework of the Arab League, the Council of Arab ministers of information in February 2008 adopted a Broadcasting Charter on principles of regulating satellite radio and TV transmission in the Arab region.[524] The document was signed by all members except for Qatar and Lebanon. The charter requires satellite broadcasting to conform to religious and ethical values of Arab society and mentions the protection of Arab identity from the harmful effects of globalization. It bans broadcasting with negative influence on social peace, national unity or public order and decency or such broadcasting that harms the supreme interests of Arab states, defames Arab leaders or national and religious symbols. Specific mention is made on banning encouragement of sexual activity and alcohol consumption. Satellite channels need to show responsibility for the sake of protecting Arab countries' interests. The document stressed the right of each Arab state to pass the necessary laws and regulations for preserving its national sovereignty. The Article on respecting Arab societies' ethics and values could give governments room to control the materials aired by satellite channels. The terminology used is general enough to allow different interpretations depending on the different understandings in different countries.

Supporters of the document stress that it is a way to give effect to media ethics, supported by a commission and various committees within the framework of the Arab League to implement the principles. Human rights organisations have criticised the document for its ambiguous content and for the way it was adopted, not being properly ratified by the member states. The critics see statements on protection of various interests as means to limit freedom of expression even if the document itself proclaims to protect it.[525] The nature of the document is unclear as it is called a statement of principles but at the same time includes concrete sanctions like confiscation of equipment and cancellation of licences.

Critics of the document feel that since its adoption several countries have stepped up action against satellite broadcasts. Egypt that initiated the charter has since its adoption asked state-run Nilesat to stop the transmission of several foreign-based programmes and confiscated property of a company that provided satellite transmission and equipment to several television networks.

Advocates argue that the implementation of the principles proposed by the document would improve the Arab media. It was approved to guide the performance of satellite channels so as to overcome the current chaotic situation. Article 3 of the document stress the freedom of expression, which is

524 Www.arabmediasociety.com/?article=648 See also www.al-bab.com/media/charter.htm.

525 M. Price "A Charter of Contradictions", *Arab Media and Society* 2008, at www.arabmediasociety.com/?article=648.

indispensable for the progress of Arab media and the document emphasises the importance of responsibility in the field of media for the sake of protecting interests of Arab countries.[526]

Mechanisms regulating satellite transmission already exists in many parts of the world including the US and the EU. On the whole, however, the governments can do little to influence a large segment of the broadcasts that reach their people. In addition to transmitting information that governments may wish to suppress, satellite broadcasting in the Arab world is reshaping popular perceptions of the public sphere. Political talk shows allow ordinary citizens to call in and express themselves, even seemingly apolitical programming can encourage democratic norms through voting in contests. Although the charter is non-binding on *governments*, it recommends that the signatories render it binding on broadcasters under their jurisdiction, append its provisions automatically to all existing broadcasting agreements (including those of stations in so-called "free media zones"), and punish violators with confiscation of assets and withdrawal of licenses.

526 Price (2008).

V. TRENDS OF DEMOCRATISATION IN REGIONAL INTEGRATION

The mixed bag of examples from different parts of the word on the effect of regional integration on democratisation needs to be examined through the prism of the various stages and elements of real or potential effect, before conclusions can be drawn. These stages are partly consecutive, partly hierarchical but may occur in a different manner or in different order – but at least in some respect they need to be included for regional integration organisations to be able to play a role.

In this context, legitimacy of the regional integration system is essential: this facilitates prevention, allows reaction and justifies intervention. In that sense, the higher the degree of legitimacy of an institution – the bigger its credentials will be when exerting pressure in favour of democracy. As discussed above, no regional integration system has reached a degree of legitimacy that is similar to that of national states. This is due to several reasons: the shorter periods of existence of these systems as compared to the traditional nation states; the absence of emotional ties within the society (the absences of a *civitas* – no imagined community); the structure of the international legal system and of international relations. These are all relevant to explain this. For these reasons, legitimacy for international institutions is acquired by the commonality of interests, a generalised sense of respect of decisions and fairness in treating similar situations in the same way.

V.1. PREVENTION

The first step in influencing behaviour is through prevention of undemocratic behaviour by the activities of a regional integration system. It is an uphill battle: the example of the recent mistrust in EU decisions concerning the Eurozone debt crisis is an obvious example of problems even in the most advanced regional integration system. In order to achieve the objectives of reaching the highest possible degree of legitimacy, regional organisations have to apply rigorously within themselves the principles stipulated in their charters such as rule of law and democracy and to maintain the course set out in their constitutional documents. In this sense, being objective is of paramount importance. If an organisation treats similar situations in the same way, it creates legal certainty and legitimate expectations not only on the specific matter but in the expectation of other – perhaps totally different – cases. This can have a preventive effect *vis-à-vis* potential unconstitutional behaviour by a Member State even in the absence of any specific action (or threat of action) by the organisation. Legitimate expectations make it very hard to deviate from the rights that subjects expect.

Even in the limited area of its competences, a constant positioning of the regional integration organisation enhances the legitimacy of its actions. Furthermore, the creation of the legitimate expectations – showing that the organisation would not hesitate to take such measures in similar situations also in the future – acts as a significant deterrent to member states (and individuals or groups). In this way consistent behaviour increases legitimacy and reduces the instances where harsher measures need to be taken.

In order to be certain that cases will be treated objectively by the regional institutions, it is necessary for the institutions to have autonomy in their actions. Autonomy, particularly autonomy from member states, requires first and foremost decisions by majority. Any form of decision-making which presupposes unanimity is detrimental to the autonomy of the organisation (states that feel that they would be treated badly would block decisions) and would damage objectivity. For this reason, autonomy of regional organisations implies that some form of bypassing national vetoes is enshrined in their texts. Autonomy also presupposes enforcement. Decisions that are taken without being enforced cease to bear respect and thus reduce the degree of legitimacy. Consequently, it is also necessary that the regional organisation is created with permanently functioning institutions rather than inter-state committees. Separate or independent, the traditional functionalist theory that integration institutions take a life of their own and promote the objectives for which they have been created seems correct in many instances, both in America (SICA) and in Africa (SADC).

The contrary example is also obvious. The intentional marginalisation of institutions in Mercosur in favour of inter-state commissions in particular during the first stage of its inception prevented any form of autonomous Mercosur action, reducing thus also its legitimacy. In Asia, the so called ASEAN way has been a challenge to cooperation, but several member states are battling with issues of their own legitimacy and challenges from within their borders and are thus reluctant to allow the regional integration organisation to become more interventionist. The states prefer to build mutual trust through "soft" means rather than curtailing their sovereignty and freedom of action.[527]

As pointed out above, autonomy also requires enforcement. Enforcement of decisions in most modern societies passes through the judicial branch. As a result the presence of regional courts which rule finally on relevant disputes is crucial. It is not coincidence that the degree of autonomy of different regional integration organisations increased when and to the extent that they instituted courts which ruled independently.

527 Weber (2013), pp. 352 and 355.

The issue of denying or deferring membership can have an important preventive effect. The example of Cambodia, in the otherwise so "interference shy" ASEAN shows an example of this. The country had to prove its credentials (it has never been a proper democracy although it now adheres to basic principles of constitutiinalism[528]) before being allowed to join ASEAN. From the EU area, the carrot and stick of membership negotiations are well known, primarily from the accession of East and Central European states since 2004.

Human rights courts can have an important influence over the legal systems of member states. Outside of Europe it is Africa that has the most important such organs. Not just the AU but also ECOWAS has a court of justice whose rulings are binding, which can have a positive effect on human rights in Africa and strengthen constitutional guarantees for rights. Levitt finds that in Africa a norm of pro-democratic intervention has crystallised through various mechanisms. The main one is consent, with states accepting such intervention through treaties or *ad hoc*. He also adds customary regional law, the principle of self-determination in addition to the emerging doctrine of democracy. He is aware that the existence of a norm of pro-democratic intervention is controversial – at least if by other means than consent.[529] Intervention by a regional organisation is a form of pro-democratic intervention that would fit under the description of consent, granted by giving the organisation such rights.

LEGAL TRANSPLANTS

Regional organisations learn from one-another and in particular, other regional organisations turn to the EU not just for inspiration but often for concrete assistance or models to use. The question of legal transplants is increasingly relevant in many areas of the law, as the process of globalisation as well as the transition of many states to market economy and democracy in a relatively short time period, mean that there are numerous situations in which countries use laws of other countries as models for their own new laws. The models may also be created by international organisations explicitly for the purpose of being models (like UNCITRAL model laws) or legal instruments applied by organisations may serve as models for national laws (the catalogue of rights of the European Convention on Human Rights). Even if especially construed model laws or other acts created by an international organisation may entail fewer problems than using the law of another country as a model, the basic issue of ensuring that a law fits with the general legal system of the state is the same. Legal transplants are not unproblematic as any

528 Hor Peng, "The Constitution of Cambodia and the Rule of Interpretation in Comparative Perspective" in *Cambodian Year Book of Comparative Legal Studies* 2010 IL Virtue Unions, Vol. 1, p. 25.

529 Levitt (2010), p. 106.

law is an element in an organic system and must be able to interact with the other elements of this system. An alien transplant may not be able to fulfil this role. The fact that situations of using many legal transplants often come at a time of upheaval generally in the country (Iraq, Bosnia Herzegovina, and Kosovo) does not make the exercise any easier. At the same time, there is nothing to gain from constantly re-inventing the wheel and legal transplants can support faster reform and closer integration into value systems of international organisations.

The regional integration body can serve as the link between the transplant and the user. If a legal transplant is distilled through an international (regional) organisation, its adoption into national law may become both more acceptable and easier than if it is taken from another country. The EU provides many examples of how countries have to adopt certain legislation to become members of the EU. The legislation may be modelled in some respects on that of certain countries but it directly comes from the organisation and furthermore its acceptance is a condition for membership of the organisation. In this context, for a country to adopt certain rules is a completely different issue than other countries (or the own government) just looking to foreign models as inspiration. For Turkey to accept rules against concentrations on ownership because its association agreement with the EU requires this is something rather different than a Turkish government suggesting that models from e.g. Germany or the Netherlands should be applied in Turkey because they appear to be good. For a country to accept the catalogue of human rights of the European Convention on Human Rights as its national law is not like suggesting copying the list of rights in the French constitution into national law. Bulgaria as one of the most recent and poorest EU member states shows many examples of how only through EU pressure, coupled with a more positive impression of EU than of national authorities, legal reforms can be made.[530]

The EU has a special role among regional integration organisations as the furthest reaching and most encompassing organisation and due to this role, the EU fulfils another role in relation to legal transplants than the mentioned distillation of the transplant before it is actually transplanted – the EU also provides its own transplants for other organisations to use. Institutional structure, specific legal instruments as well as substantive law have been copied from the EU into other regional organisations such as SICA or the AU (as discussed above). The benefits of doing this (again: why re-invent the wheel?) are the same as for transplants between countries, but the dangers are also the same. The EU is indeed a unique structure and the instrument of preliminary reference that works so well in the EU may not have any effect or even have detrimental effect (if it is not followed and thus the legitimacy of the organisation may suffer) in another regional organisation.

---

530 F. Trauner, "Post-Accession compliance with EU Law in Bulgaria and Romania: A comparative perspective" in Institute for European Integration Research Working Paper Series No. 1/2009, March 2009, pp. 12–13 and 23.

Catalogues of human rights have a special situation in the context of legal transplants as it is common for organisations to have such catalogues and that these are inspired from common constitutional traditions of countries as well as inspire new constitutions. A methodology and understanding of this particular aspect of legal transplants can be seen in different regions. The underlying idea of human rights catalogues and their general structure go back to the examples of the United States and France and their constitutions from the 1700's and could thus be claimed to be alien for most parts of the world, but as this transplant is so old and so widespread, having been adopted and later re-transplanted via international organisations, its origins are not normally seen as an obstacle. This said; the argument that the idea of human rights or at least the way they are interpreted does not take sufficient consideration of national traditions is raised every now and then, notably in authoritarian states with insufficient protection of rights.

V.2. REACTION

V.2.1. SUSPENSION

We have seen in the past that regional integration schemes did not include provisions on any form of sanction of undemocratic behaviour. Indeed, Latin American integration has instead been fraught with dictatorships joining and staying in the integration systems. Since the 1990s there has been increasingly some form of democratic clause in regional integration constitutional documents (statutes and treaties). In some cases this is explicit (like the Andean Pact). Other systems have more indirect forms of democratic consolidation. The most usual as well as the least invasive and in some respects perhaps most lenient – although it may still have important consequences – of such clauses is a provision on suspension from the organisation or its activities.

The EU did not have a suspension clause until the Treaty of Amsterdam (1997, into force 1999) when what is now Article 7 was added. Under this clause, some of the rights of member state including voting rights in the Council may be suspended if the state seriously and persistently breaches the principles on which the Union is founded (liberty, democracy, respect for human rights and fundamental freedoms, and the rule of law). Obligations remain binding and the suspension is just that – suspension – with no mechanism for expulsion. The Treaty of Nice (2000) added a preventive mechanism to this procedure. This consist of the possibility on a proposal by the Commission, the European Parliament, the Council (with a special majority and process) or one third of the member states to determine that there is a clear risk of a serious breach of fundamental principles by a member state in which case appropriate recommendations can be addressed to it. This means that the state can be asked what to do to avoid suspension, including any measures that are seen as relevant considering what the breach consists of. Despite its rather innocuous language, for an organisation with so many and so far-reaching powers as the EU, it is potentially a strong mechanism. It has not yet been used, but the EU has made use of its possibility to threaten *vis-à-vis* Bulgaria (for failure to complete reforms that it was obligated to complete in its accession agreement) and the liberal political groups in the European Parliament in September 2015 called on application of the procedure against Hungary for its handling of refugee issues.

In Latin American integration, suspension was used most recently in the case of Paraguay, which led among other things to the possibility of Venezuelan membership of Mercosur. From other continents, the examples of Madagascar as well as Fiji come to mind. Both these countries were suspended – from the AU and from the Pacific Forum and Commonwealth respectively – with Fiji later on also excluded from both organisations although it nominally remains on the membership list of the organisations, but is suspended from any activities. Due to development in 2014 and 2015 the countries have been readmitted.

Suspension is a political insult but it definitely in addition includes economic and trade- adverse measures. In the case of Honduras, which was simply not invited to meetings (so not formally suspended) it included the provisional interruption of free trade provision of the SICA treaty. The same development can be witnessed with Paraguay and Myanmar.

African organisations such as AU and ECOWAS have been quite active in using suspension, like against Mali and Guinea Bissau in 2012 – both countries allowed back in after some positive developments.

In most cases suspension or even threat of suspension has led to second thoughts for the violating country, leading to a smooth return to normality. The election of a new president in Honduras after an arranged agreement with President Selaya and his agreed return to the country allowed for the re-insertion of Honduras in SICA.

V.2.2. EXPULSION

If suspension may have a positive effect in that it encourages modification of behaviour in order to be let back into the system, expulsion may well prove to be counterproductive since it does not keep the leverage already in the hands of the regional organisations. As such it is more rarely used. Furthermore it is the ultimate measure and thus also of even greater political symbolic significance than suspension. From a legal point of view, very few integration organisations contain expulsion provisions. In addition expulsion, wherever existing, requires consensus among other member states.[531] This is yet another reason why this tool is rarely used.

531 Also suspension normally requires unanimity, which can be an obstacle also for this measure. As it is less far-reaching and also less sensitive, unanimity may however be easier to obtain.

In the past those few members that were expelled from international organisations – such as Cuba from OAS – were expelled mostly on political/ideological motives rather than in a genuine effort to protect democracy.[532] One of the arguments of Paraguay against its suspension was that it was not a consequence of democratic desire but rather revenge of the left-leaning regimes of Brazil and Argentina against the overthrow of leftist president of Paraguay. As such, expulsion is not really something that has been witnessed in regional integration organisations to support democracy. However, the mere threat of expulsion may be a powerful tool for democratisation if used judiciously as seen in Africa. It is understandable, however, that member states are in general reluctant to accept provisions that might be used against them, even in theory (like in the text of the regional treaty).

The example of Fiji shows how first suspension was used, with conditions to be fulfilled at a certain time, with expulsion following when the conditions were not met. In such cases it is important that expulsion really does follow, so the threat is not an empty one. States may gamble on that other members will be reluctant to push all the way to expulsion. For Fiji, it is interesting to note that it remained on the web-sites and in the list of members of both the Commonwealth and the Pacific Islands Forum. The 2009 chair of the Pacific Islands Forum, the Premier of Niue, explained the situation as follows: "*This decision does not amount to the expulsion of Fiji, as a nation, from its membership of the Forum. That proposition has not been considered by Leaders in their deliberations. As such, the Pacific Islands Forum remains a 16-member body and the Republic of the Fiji Islands continues to be part of the Forum group of nations, albeit with participation of the current regime suspended until further notice. A regime which displays such a total disregard for basic human rights, democracy and freedom has no place in the Pacific Islands Forum. Nevertheless, we look forward with great hope to Fiji's earliest possible return to constitutional democracy, through free and fair elections, when we will be able to restore this country to its rightful place among our family of Pacific Islands Forum nations. The Forum, as always, stands ready to assist Fiji's return to democratic rule, concerned, in particular, by the increasingly negative and wide-ranging impacts of events over the past two and a half years on the people of Fiji.*"[533]

This is an interesting illustration to the nature of regional integration as opposed to other international organisations. There is indeed an interest to have as many states as possible as members, to enjoy the advantages that there are of regional cooperation. The pressure states can exert on others is dependent on the strength of the organisation of which the extent of membership is one factor. Expulsion is thus not an easy solution as a means of pressure as it may be counterproductive.

---

532 The majority of the states that expelled Cuba were in fact dictatorships themselves.

533 Www.forumsec.org/pages.cfm/newsroom/press-statements/2009/forum-chair-on-suspension-of-fiji-military-regime-from-pif.html.

V.2.3 INTERVENTION

It is obvious that no international treaty provides for any form of intervention – military or other – without the consent of the Member State concerned. The only exception is the UN Charter Chapter 7. The principle of the inviolability and territorial integrity of sovereign states is a cornerstone of international relations. Nevertheless, interventions have been used to "restore" democracy. This has been always the privilege of the powerful. In the American continent the powerful has equalled the United States so all such intervention were conducted from the US with the support of the regional organisation concerned (the case of Grenada in 1983) or without it (intervention in the Dominican Republic 1965 and in Panama in 1989).

On other continents such interventions – few as they are – have had more disparate background. French intervention in Chad in 2008 did not have the blessing of the OAU whilst French intervention in Cote d'Ivoire in 2002 – which was in fact a peace-imposing intervention – was supported by ECOWAS. The intervention in Mali in 2013 was a more widespread intervention including not only French troops but also ECOWAS member state troops with the blessing of the African Union. The Australian pressure on Fiji from 2006 had the tacit support of the Pacific Islands Forum. Although in all these cases it was the powerful neighbour or regional potentate which took the initiative, there was an element of regional integration organisations participating.

It goes without saying that military intervention is not an easy option for the intervening force. A few casualties especially for Western powers might lead to a wide back-lash at home, like the US intervention in Somalia. For this reason, such interventions have been used when something of extra major importance was at stake. What such major interests were can roughly be grouped under a few points, like the "cleanliness" of the American backyard from the Communist threat, the stability of the region (Mali or Fiji), or major economic interests being at stake.

Oddly most such interventions have proven results in the sense that return to democracy has been achieved. Certainly the authors do not propose to institute interventionism as a means of democratisation, but merely to point out that on occasions the only way to deal with an authoritarian regime is force. From that point of view however, previous conclusions of this book are belied in the sense that rule of law cannot be imposed by peaceful means. Unfortunately observation of the countries where such forms of intervention have been used show that the causes of the undemocratic trends remain, even if the expressions of these trends are no longer there. In the long run it is not mere force that will institute democratic *societies*, but only – and for the short term – democratic *institutions*.

VI. ACHIEVEMENTS AND RESULTS

States are states according to international law, however unpleasant their regimes may be. At the same time, the idea of making demands on states as far as human rights, protection of minorities or democracy is concerned, is gaining ground and can be exercised in questions of recognition of states or – as shown in this book – membership of international organisations such as regional integration systems.

If the pressure from members of regional integration systems for democratic governance is strong enough and if there are many and good reasons to be a member of such a regional system, it is likely that states will exercise a certain element of self-restraint and the number of coups or other non-constitutional take-overs of power will be reduced. Such a trend can with some hesitation be observed. The hesitation is caused not so much by the fact that there are still coups – as a total end to such events would be difficult to imagine – but more as there may instead be other and more hidden non-constitutional changes of power. Still, all in all, it appears that regional integration organs have managed in different parts of the world to instil the understanding that there are limits to if and how states can violate their own constitutions and still be fully integrated in regional structures.

If this observed trend continues, direct breaches of the rules (as opposed to indirect) will become much less frequent because the potential perpetrators take as granted the external intervention, which in the past was not the case as it would earlier depend solely on bilateral power politics and national interests. Therefore self-restraint is exercised to a much higher degree than previously. This does not mean that we will end up in the best of worlds where democratic institutions will rule unimpeded; rather it means that breaches of the rule of law will acquire less violent and direct, but rather more surreptitious features. It depends on the regional integration grouping if they will be able and willing to deal with also such indirect violations of the principles they adhere to.

We see developments of changing or abusing constitutions to violate the principles set out in them in countries as different as Turkey, Bangladesh, Venezuela and Russia. In all these countries there has been no military intervention, no state organised coup or any other form of interruption of the constitutional and institutional order, but the governing structures have through a biased application of the law, intimidation of the media and political opponents managed to impose their will. This has happened without any form of external intervention to prevent it. It is not fortuitous that none of these countries is part of a strong regional grouping (even Venezuela has, in order to have a free hand, withdrawn from the Andean Community of Nations) and Turkey's trend toward covert authoritarianism was accelerated when chances of it joining the EU were much reduced. In Africa, where regional integration is growing in importance, cases like Madagascar and Cote d'Ivoire illustrate that regional bodies influence and exercise some restraint.

However, the various African bodies still suffer from a lack of acceptance of their legitimacy – at least if they take action to enforce decisions against states: in such situations, the states in question may instead question the legal basis for any decisions like Zimbabwe has done of the SADC Tribunal after its decisions condemning land confiscations in that country, which led eventually to the suspension of the Tribunal and the cessation of the possibility for individual complaints.

The American regional integration bodies have not attempted to take strong action for democratisation. Many regional integration schemes in the past did not include any provisions on sanctions for undemocratic behaviour as several member states were themselves dictatorships. In the Americas and elsewhere it is since the 1990s that some form of democratic clause in regional integration constitutional documents has become more common.

The nature of the regional integration body plays a role, both in the more direct manner of different organisations having different possibilities to influence the behaviour of member states, through its enforcement mechanism or other means to influence behaviour (like trade or other sanctions) and in an indirect manner, namely that in a closer integration system with various links between member states, they are more likely to be influenced by values and opinions from the other member states, than in a system where the reasons for the cooperation are more limited or strictly of a practical nature.

SADC is an example of a regional integration system where the countries in region are not (all) necessarily linked by very strong ties, neither as far as security or economy are concerned. When the predecessor of SADC was created it was the opposition against apartheid that linked the countries, so after the changes in South Africa (which then became a leading member of SADC) the *raison d'etre* of the organisation had to be recreated.[534]

The real effect of this perception of the importance of the organisation as well as its practical importance can be observed in the case of Madagascar. Although international organisations were at first somewhat confused over how to react to the unusual coup in the country, eventually sanctions were imposed and membership of SADC as well as the AU suspended. This has not been without importance, but indeed has been essential for efforts made in Madagascar to reach some kind of agreement between different parties, but at the same time,

534 Cawthra (2010), p. 10.

the negotiations have been protracted and the actions of the regional integration organisations have not managed to instil a sense of urgency into the leaders of the country. It can be speculated that similar kind of actions against an EU member would have led to much more serious and urgent measures taken by the member states in question, as in such a far-reaching organisation it is very difficult to be left out in the cold for any length of time.

Africa has interestingly gone from being a continent with a conservative view on international law notions such as sovereignty and non-intervention to being the first region to create a comprehensive regional collective security and intervention regime.[535] How effective it is, is another question. Article 30 AU means that governments that come to power by unconstitutional means are suspended from participation in AU activities. The AU may not be able to reverse military coups but governments that come to power in such way shall be excluded from the African diplomatic table, which should be a powerful tool of persuasion. This idea was not new in AU but was first introduced by the OAU in 1997 and applied since (against Sierra Leone, the Comoros, Cote d'Ivoire and Niger). This was also the reason why Madagascar could not participate in the summit where the AU was created. But the impact of such rules, especially against leaders that claim they came to power by democratic means, is still patchy.

Koefele Kole points to law-backed declarations and resolutions adopted by regional organisations as evidence that African states accept a customary international law right to political participation. This is an interesting assertion that democracy is an international right, something which is not universally accepted. If a state has accepted declarations or resolutions on democracy, the issue is of course different and there is a legal basis to also assert that the democracy should be real. Koefele Kole finds participatory democracy as an African regional customary law – an even more interesting interpretation as there are so many violations of it in Africa (something also recognised by Koefele Kole, who, however, finds that in more recent times Africa has indeed accepted participatory democracy as a regional element).[536] As important signals of the African acceptance of democracy Koefele Kole quotes the charter of the AU, especially Article 4 and Article 30 with the possibility to exclude unconstitutional states, and the Banjul charter. In the Charter, the taking of power by unconstitutional means is the only place where a sanction is prescribed.[537]

Although the institutional structure of regional integration authorities on its own does not necessarily matter so much for their ability to act effectively in promoting or supporting democracy, the question of what the longer term role

535 Levitt (2010), p. 111.
536 Koefele Kole (2008), especially pp. 234–235.
537 *Ibid.* pp. 237–238.

of the organisation can be may have an effect and here an organisation with an established structure and clear mandate has an advantage over a looser one.

One issue that challenges any conclusions on the importance of regional integration organisations for supporting democracy is that at times *ad hoc* groupings of states have fulfilled a similar role, quite without involvement of international organisations. This happened in 1997 in the case of the Central African Republic, where a group of states in the region came together specifically to condemn the coup and take measures against the state.[538] However, although both the action as well as the effect were similar to actions undertaken by organisations like ECOWAS, SADC or AU in other cases, the absence of an organisation and institutional structures is not insignificant. It makes the predictability and stability of the action questionable and in particular does not bode well for sustainability of any results achieved.

Although organisations can influence developments even without having a strong institutional structure, for the organisation to be able to play a decisive role and be able to deal consistently and determinately with regional crisis, a strengthened institutional structure and a more organised system is needed. ASEAN is an example of a body lacking this consistency and thus having taken measures to support democracy in a rather inconsistent manner. Commentators do not see it likely that ASEAN members would accept such more organised mechanisms. At the same time, this may depend on external pressures and events, as ASEAN showed a certain ability to act and take measures without the constant fear of violating the treasured non-intervention principle when some factors pushed for this, like the economic crisis or the environmental problems with the haze.[539]

More than acting directly to create post-conflict states – although this trend may be growing – regional integration systems can help prevent conflict. This does not just include defence and other security related systems that have as their task such conflict-avoidance, but it also includes economic integration or integration with multiple tasks that to a greater or lesser extent may influence states and have a positive effect in avoiding conflicts. What exactly it is in a regional integration system that allows it to play such a positive effect is a topic for analysis in its own right. It is clear that different systems have different kind of effect, the exact reasons are not clear but it is evident that the real influence is not linked to the statements and pronouncements made.[540] The role of institutions is clear in that a regional integration system must be able to act in order to gain respect and become a factor that states reckon with – in this the

538 Levitt (2010), pp. 132–133.

539 Caballero-Anthony (2006), especially at pp. 270–271 and 279.

540 For a thorough examination of different regional integration systems and what it is that influences their possibility to act to avoid conflict, see Y.Z. Haftel, "Designing for Peace: Regional Integration Arrangements, Institutional Variation, and Militarized Interstate Disputes", *International Organization* 61, Winter 2007, pp. 217–237.

current authors agree with Haftel[541] although may put even more emphasis on the actual institutional structures rather than informal settings (meetings etc.) within the systems. Although these are of course important and an institution or institutionalised meeting is not more important than what goes on at it, the current authors still see that a proper designated institution may be a better guarantee than just regular meetings for a regional system to play a significant role in mitigating conflict.[542] The more closely states are tied to one-another, the more is at stake to lose this relationship. This is important for violent conflict but it is also important for support – or incentives – to democracy, if lack of democracy would mean being left out of a desired cooperation.

The perception and credibility of the organisation play an important role. In this respect Madagascar can be used as an illustration and as Cawthra stresses,[543] the interventions of AU or primarily SADC (action for the AU) were not well received by the population that regarded it as intervention into the sovereignty of the state – without seeing justifications for such interventions. The traditional concept of sovereignty is in many ways changing, with closer interrelationship between states and correspondingly less of "total" sovereignty, but the basic perception of each state as sovereign entity with the right to determine its own affairs is not yet gone.

The question is also linked to the size of countries. If Turkey was the size of Kosovo it would not have this ability to such a wide extent. Dependency on other countries is also significant, due to geographical situation or dependency on imports especially of raw material.

The structure and institutional set-up of the regional integration system matter in the way that it gives certain predictability. If there is no strong system it will be an ad hoc decision if the organisation will take any action. Then the same kind of considerations that determine the matter in areas where there are no regional integration systems will be predominant. However, if there is a system, there is a predictability of intervention. In this matter, the more integrated the structure, the more predictable is the intervention. The more predictable it is, the more likely it is to act a deterrent for those who are contemplating unconstitutional actions.

As a result the level of intervention of the EU would be different than the intervention of the Arab league. The level of intervention of an organisation which is specifically aiming at political integration (the best example being of course again the EU) will thus likely be more effective than a cooperation organisation with vague political intentions. The development or evolution of regional integration schemes towards "deepening" inevitably leads to stronger involvement into each other's areas of competence. Often though not always

541 Haftel (2007).
542 *Ibid.*
543 Cawtrha (2010), p. 23.

deepening is accompanied by an approximation of political and social values. It is commonplace that integration especially political integration presupposes democratic institutions and the rule of law. As a result the stress on democracy is described in the legal texts governing the integration process. When integration takes a more political turn the relevant treaties mirror this development. EU after Maastricht and SICA illustrate this.

A number of elements are needed for the success of regional integration and these elements must be in the right constellation. The institutional structure is very important but it cannot on its own influence positively the entire integrative process if there is an absence of political will. Political will without a proper institutional and legal structure will, however, also be ineffective, as results will in such a situation not be sustainable but linked to personalities, to events or similar. Thus in addition to the institutional structure and the political will there is also a need for a capacity of the regional integration system to impose its decisions – a legal structure with legal bindingness and organs to impose this.

Regional integration can itself not be a way to deal with weakness of states as long as such integration is created by states and states are responsible for implementing it. In Africa the problem of weak states is well known and may mean that urging African states to respect international human rights and then monitoring that they do so, may not be the best way to achieve real impact of human rights. In certain countries there is a need for human rights mechanisms to control the powers of the state but e.g. in Africa the problem may instead be weakness of the state and a need for institutions that can implement rights. The government machinery may be just a shell at least outside of the capital city. In such a situation the government machinery needs to be strengthened but at the same time if rights are not well enough integrated into it, this machinery might be used for repression. Some commentators think that breaking with the traditional concept of the State could allow greater roles for ethnicities, as it has to some extent in the EU. However, an important issue is to get weak states to appreciate the role of constitutions for accountable government and for solving disputes between different groups. Successful constitution-making is as much about process as content and constitutional reforms can be a push for other reforms. In all of this, including to give away some of the role of the state to a regional integration organ, a strong enough state is needed.[544]

States that are part of democratic international organisations are more likely to democratise. In a regional grouping of democracies, it is more likely that states adopt democracy, which can be expressed as a tendency of clustering of democracies. With an increased frequency of democracies in a given region, the likelihood increases of non-democratic states in such a region democratising.[545]

---

[544] Manby (2004), pp. 1024–1025.

[545] A.J. Enterline & J.M. Greig, "Beacons of Hope? The impact of imposed democracy on regional peace, democracy and prosperity", *The Journal of Politics*, Vol. 67. No. 4 (2005), p. 1079.

Enterline and Greig state that there is indirect if consistent evidence that imposed democracy has a beneficial effect also from a regional viewpoint. West Germany after the Second World War and Japan are examples, but as so often in international relations it is difficult to find exact empirical examples that can be tested.[546] However, both Japan and Germany had positive impact not just for those countries but also regionally, as investors and as models. Regional peace and prosperity are indeed positively influenced by what Enterline and Greig call bright democratic beacons in a region, but democratisation as such is not, based on their study of a number of examples with specific criteria for comparison.[547]

There must be a minimum of interest from the member states to abide by regional integration instructions and some incitement to adhere to the decisions taken. If that is not the case (as in Fiji, described above) there is no influence of the regional integration system. Simply put, fear or money makes states work together. Objective necessity is another reason, not least for practical matters (as diverse as the Red Cross or ITU). There must be a minimum of mutual interest, an interest for states and for peoples – an added value of the integration. A problem is that there is nothing ensuring that the integration happens. In order to have a role on democratisation, the scheme must cover a substantial area. An organisation like the ITU will not promote democracy as it is not at all in the competence of the organisation which deals with only narrow technical interests. The organisation that can promote democracy must cover a sufficient number of different issues that can have a bearing on democratisation.

On the immediate or superficial level the connection between the effect of regional integration and democratisation or other positive reforms can be made rather easily: If authoritarian states join together in a regional integration body this fact will not *per se* change the nature of the states, any more than it could be expected that democracies that create a union would be willing to give up their democratic institutions and traditions to any major extent. The interesting question arises at the less obvious level. If mainly democratic states bring recent or unstable democracies to their midst, to what extent can they exert a positive influence on the weaker democracy? It is doubtless possible to exert such influence as the attraction of belonging to the union will be taken into consideration in the reforms in the recent or unstable democracy and if the attraction is great, it will be worth designing reforms in the way the union proposes or even demands. The institutional mechanisms of the regional integration will keep an eye on the unstable country and will be able to support as well as prevent different developments. This is seen in the EU with first the accession of Greece (1981), Spain and Portugal (1986) and later East- and Central European states (2005 and 2007) – but also with Cambodia in ASEAN. The means of influence are especially important in the membership process and

546 *Ibid*, p. 1080.
547 *Ibid*. p. 1095.

some commentators lament that the possibilities to influence states once they are already members are inadequate. However, even if the immediate carrot and stick will be most noticeable in the membership accession process, the EU does possess various important means of influencing members and the inadequacy (at times) of these means may be more a political question than that of the institutional structure as such and dependent on the fact that in many questions the member states as states rather than the institutional (imperfect federal) structures still carry major weight.

In the case of the African Union, as opposed to the EU and its enlargements, the AU consists of a number of unstable states, imperfect democracies or authoritarian states and only few well-functioning democracies. Here one cannot expect the positive influence of a majority of prosperous and successful democracies on a few less successful states but one must investigate how and if positive influences can be transmitted from the few successful ones or from the organisation itself, supporting the many weak states in their reforms. Can the organisation actually go further than its members? The African Union has been called an organisational framework for future political integration of the continent and as such it is very important.[548] The strength of this framework helps determine the success of the venture but it is not solely responsible for it.

In Asia the democratic transition in many countries from the 1980s onward meant that the interest for regional integration increased, albeit still resisted by authoritarian regimes. Especially the idea of independent institutional organs of the regional integration systems are opposed by the authoritarian regimes[549] – an indication that they do see a risk of such organs influencing the region in favour of democracy?

To some extent it is a fallacy to put such a question as an organisation created by its members – sovereign states in this case – cannot impose anything on its members that the same members do not decide it can do. However, the EU shows that at times states are indeed willing to go further together than they are alone. The EU can become the excuse to make reforms that would politically be sensitive in certain states. It can be the political excuse but it may also legitimately be so that something that makes sense at a European level would not be possible at the level of a single state. The environmental obligations under the Kyoto protocol may be one such example. The organisation can also simply take on a momentum of its own and provided that strong institutions are created, issues are indeed out of the hands of the member states. The jurisprudence of the European Court of Justice shows many such examples. The liberalisation of telecommunication in Europe was suggested by the European

---

548 Maluwa (2004), p. 196.

549 D. Webber, "Regionalism and EU-Asia Relations" (Chapter 6) in T. Christiansen, E. Kirchner and P. Murray, *The Palgrave Handbook of EU-Asia Relations* (Palgrave Macmillan 2013), pp. 93–107, at 99.

Commission, the organ that acts independently and does not represent the member states, and supported by the Court of Justice when challenged by several member states. This policy became the accepted and dominant policy for the EU and also for other European states, as part of agreements with the EU. It also inspired other states that often use the EU directives as models of modern liberalised telecommunications regulation. Thus the impact of a policy of a regional integration organisation, not immediately designed by states but by the organisation, can be very important indeed. This is, however, only possible when states have at some point agreed to create a strong organisation that can act in this independent manner. There is in the international legal situation of today no alternative to this initial will and ensuing decision of independent states.

The importance of the possibilities for intervention in African states as set out in the Constitutive Act of the African Union lies in the fact that then the collective body of states can maintain certain standards. The fact that the intervention is linked to observance of human rights is very interesting and opens wide possibilities for the organisation contributing to democratisation. The provisions against unconstitutional changes of government underline this role of the AU as a body to keep up standards of democratic governance in Africa. At the same time, the short history of the AU does not really show that member states intend to give much teeth to these possibilities. An organisation that is not strong enough to act anyway remains the sum of its parts and not more than that. In Africa as opposed to Europe, states have been unwilling to create that extra something that is more than the sum of its parts.

The African regional human rights system did contain several interesting aspects from its inception, but what was lacking was a strong enforcement mechanism. This meant that the system has not achieved the kind of integrating effect of creating a unified enforcement and implementation system as in Europe.[550]

As Maluwa says, the AU is supposed to be something new, not just old wine in new bottles. But the proof of the pudding is in the eating: that is what will show if the AU is a reflection of a new political will or a new false dawn. A gradualist approach to consolidate economic integration as a way to consolidate the foundation for a subsequent political integration may be a realistic way forward for Africa. For all the good things the OUA did, the real effect (or lack of it) still depends on the political will.[551] At least with the current structure, this will rests with the sovereign states.

What the European system with the European Court on Human Rights shows is that such an effective regional system does contribute to a common understanding of human rights, which in itself can have an integrating effect. The influence of the ECtHR cannot be exaggerated and the membership in the

550 *Introduction to the International Human Rights Regime* (2003), pp. 203–214.

551 Maluwa (2003), pp. 167–169.

ECHR of a state such as Russia that is not democratic and where violations of human rights are common and generally subject to impunity shows that even a good system cannot overcome such obstacles. But this said, even the states that violate the ECHR often show some restraint and states do not totally ignore the court's rulings. A common system of rights is created, even if it works best between like-minded states.

Even organisations that do not have a very strong mandate can select to play an important role when members agree and when the organisation turns out in some context to be a useful forum for a particular issue. The Commonwealth, as an organisation rather a weak structure but as a forum for different states held together by a common history (British domination) rather than current similarities, can be a forum where interesting views get to meet. These are brought together not because of their similarities, which has the positive effect that differences are brought to one table and can allow for a positive dynamism. It is not often that such organisations take an important role, however, and it is of course hard to imagine creating such an organisation as when an organisation is first created, the reason tends to be some form of similarities or more obvious shared interests.[552]

Because of the role of the Commonwealth to give or channel aid, even without a strong organisational structure, the organisation can be influential if it exercises its role to put pressure. In September 2009 the Commonwealth suspended Fiji for lack of progress in establishing democracy (after it having been suspended since 2006). The consequence of such a decision is that all Commonwealth aid will be cut off. The organisation has only once before taken such a decision.[553]

The issue of regional integration or at least regional impact of measures plays a role also in relation to issues of protection of international peace and security. This is seen in the UN Charter and the measures of use of force possible under this Charter, whether undertaken by the UN itself or by organs (like regional organs) given the mandate to undertake such measures. Regional issues are also used by states as reasons for certain action. The US led invasion of Iraq is an example, where the need to create a regional model of democracy was one element brought up as a reason for the intervention.[554]

Regional integration can be seen as an answer to globalisation, as protection against possible negative effects of globalisation. This was one of the reasons for the creation of the AU as put forward by Gadhafi and others discussing African Unity, but also European integration can be seen as an answer to globalisation.

---

552 Http://thecommonwealth.org. The Commonwealth commissioned an interesting report on civil paths to peace in 2007 (*Civil Paths to Peace: Report of the Commonwealth Commission on Respect and Understanding*) that presents ideas for how to mediate in conflicts. The Commonwealth is also known for supporting good works in different parts of the world, including such that may not get much attention in any other forum. See The Economist 10 November 2007.

553 Http://thecommonwealth.org. See also *The Economist*, 5 September 2009, 11 August 2012.

554 Enterline & Greig (2005), pp. 1075–1098.

European integration is in that case seen as a distinctive (west) European effort to counter the forces of globalisation, as regional governance with polity-like features to extend the reach of the values of this region and to avoid the line between national policies and relative anarchy of international rules.[555]

A "bad" institutional structure can work but only in a "good" system. If the constituent parts of an organisation are strong, share the same values and work towards common goals, the failures of the organisational structure will be an irritant rather than a barrier to positive results. Strong democracies that group together to promote certain values but that fail to establish a good organisational structure may still manage to promote the values, but weak states with unstable democracies can only achieve positive results of their cooperation if the system in which they operate is strong.

Failings in the institutional structure can lead to negative consequences also if the constituent parts are strong, but only once the integration has become strong enough for the organisation to lead its own life – good or bad. In the EU there are examples of negative consequences of the common agricultural policy or of bad implementation of competition law, handled by the EU institutions and not possible for the member states to immediately prevent even if they may observe that the results are not only not more than the sum of the constituent parts but even not equal to it, but less. Because the institutional structure of the EU is so strong, the only way to react to such negative consequences of the activities of the organisation is through the organisation's own structure and instruments (by changes to legislation using the established decision-making procedure or through complaints to the Court of Justice).

A positive institutional structure is more likely to have independent effects and achieve more than the sum of its parts. The dissemination effects are in this context stronger on the positive than the negative side, which is a further argument for the importance and beneficial role of regional integration. No African democracy has become weaker because of the African Union but there are examples of those that have become stronger.

Mattli believes that in economically hard times, leaders will be more open to accommodate demands from market players for regional rules and systems, as this may help them ensure their own survival in a manner that is not necessary in economically good times. As he puts it, why sacrifice national sovereignty when everything is going well and people (voters) are happy. Expected marginal political benefits are small in such a situation, whereas such benefits may look quite different in harder times.[556] This indicates that the recent global financial and economic crisis is a very interesting time for regional integration.

555 H. Wallace, "Politics and policy in the European Union: the challenge of governance" in Wallace & Wallace, *Policy-making in the European Union* (Oxford 1996). See also Maluwa (2003), fn. 10, p. 160.

556 Mattli (1999), p. 13.

VII. CONCLUDING REMARKS

The question if the success of regional integration (like in Europe) is dependent primarily on the methods of integration, including institutions, or on elements external to the process (history, culture, political systems) is a difficult one to give a clear answer to. A combination of factors is at hand and their respective weight appears to vary if changing the viewing position. This book provides many such viewing positions from all over the world, which illustrates the mentioned difficulties with drawing clear conclusions.

The Centre for Study of Federalism in its study on international democracy points out that the response of governments to globalisation has been to pursue international co-operation, not because it is their inclination, but because they have no other choice. With such an interpretation, the expansion of international organisation as a phenomenon is due to governments looking for solutions that they cannot find on their own. However, international organisations may not always provide the solution as they have their own limitations. The Centre in its report states that the most visible and serious such limits are to be found in their decision-making procedures, normally based on unanimity and national veto and ensuing lack of effective (limited but real) supranational powers.[557]

In the current global system where states maintain their role as the legitimate actors of international relations, regional integration systems are ancillary factors. Therefore significant issues that are very much still linked to national polities such as democratisation are mainly controlled by national politics and national institutions. In that sense regional integration cannot impose itself on states in order to establish democracy but it can act as a stabilising and enhancing factor when such forces (democratisation forces) or policies appear and try to be applied at national level. The regional integration system may be the essential supporting factor that determines the success or failure of a nascent democratisation. Furthermore regional integration systems can be important actors helping weak democracies fending off threats to democracy. This, however, puts a certain stress on the regional integration system: the EU does support its members remaining democratic but that is not the case for SICA *vis-à-vis* Honduras or ASEAN *vis-à-vis* Thailand.

In the last quarter century – a period including the creation or re-establishment of many sovereign states – demands of adherence to basic

557 Centre for Studies on Federalism, *International Democracy Watch (Draft Project)*, January 2009, at p. 3.

principles of democracy and respect for human rights have been made as a precondition for the recognition of states. The structure of the international system, consisting of states as the only unconditional actors, means that it is inevitable that this leads to higher demands for new states than for existing ones. Even if existing states cannot be de-recognised for violations of human rights or democracy, this ideological understanding of the right to be concerned about the internal order of other states supports that it is legitimate for the international community to react to violations of democracy.

There are some signs that states are more willing to adhere to regional rules on e.g. human rights than global such rules. The regional rules can take into consideration the special nature of a region and normally such rules would be more similar to national rules of member states, with specific characteristics already taken into account. National courts appear more inclined to use regional conventions even when they are reluctant to give direct effect to global instruments of international law.[558] In this way, regional human rights system can have a noticeable effect on the member states, which can support democracy in various ways. The step-by-step manner in which many regional instruments have developed also helps to make them acceptable and understandable to member states, in a way which global conventions often may not succeed in.

At the same time, the view in regional integration systems supporting democracy should not be overly optimistic. The emphasis may not be on ideological matters, but more pragmatic ones. Although the overview of different regional integration systems shows that the reasons for creating them do vary, economic and trade reasons often play an important role. Another key matter may be joint security against common enemies or threats. Integration based on such reasons can eventually translate into a deeper integration with a possibility to influence the democratic process, but such a development is not evident or inevitable.

But with this caveat, the authors have found examples that regional integration consolidates and supports democratisation on national level. Furthermore, the trend is of increased activities in this direction. The trend is not without exceptions and the strength of examples varies. However, the link between regional integration systems and support for maintained or increased democratization of member states is there.

[558] N. Abiad, *Sharia, Muslim States and Innternational Human Rights Treaty Obligations: A Comparative Study*, British Institute of International and Comparative Law, London, 2008, pp. 150–151.

BIBLIOGRAPHY

BOOKS

Abiad, N., *Sharia, Muslim States and International Human Rights Treaty Obligations: A Comparative Study,* British Institute of International and Comparative Law, London 2008

Alvarez, J.E., *International Organizations as law-makers,* Oxford University Press, Oxford 2005

Barthelemy, F., *Un continent en quête d'unité – l'au-delà du rêve,* Les éditions ouvrières, Paris 1991

Berry, D., *Caribbean Integration Law,* Oxford University Press, Oxford 2014

Burgess, M., *Federalism and European Union: The building of Europe, 1950–2000.* Routledge, London 2000

Burgess, M., *Comparative Federalism, Theory and Practice.* Routledge, London 2006

Burgess, M. & H. Vollaard (eds.), *State territoriality and European Integration.* Routledge, London 2006

Burrows, N. & R. Greaves, *The Advocate General and EC law,* Oxford University Press, Oxford 2007

Cawthra, G., *The Role of SADC in managing political crisis and conflict. The cases of Madagascar and Zimbabwe.* Friedrich-Ebert-Stiftung, Maputowthra 2010

Chesterman, S., *From Community to Compliance? The Evolution of Monitoring Obligations in ASEAN,* Cambridge University Press, Cambridge 2015

Falkner, G., O. Treib, M. Hartlepp, S. Leiber, *Complying with Europe. EU Harmonisation and soft law in the member states.* Cambridge University Press, Cambridge 2005

Focarelli, C., *International Law as Social Construct. The struggle for Global Justice.* Oxford University Press, Oxford 2012

Fukuyama, F., *The End of History and the Last Man,* Avon, New York 1992

Gardini, G.L., *The Origins of Mercosur. Democracy and Regionalization in South America* Series Studies of the Americas, Palgrave Macmillan February 2010

Ghani, A. & C. Lockhart, *Fixing Failed States: A Framework for Rebuilding a Fractured World,* Oxford University Press, Oxford 2008

Grabbe, H., *The EU's Transformational Power. Europeanization through Conditionality.* Palgrave, London 2006

Habermas, J., *The Structural Transformation of the Public Sphere. An Inquiry into a category of bourgeois society,* The MIT Press, Cambridge, Mass. 1991 paperback ed.

Harrisson, J. & L. Woods, *European Broadcasting Law and Policy,* Cambridge University Press, Cambridge 2007

Henkin, L., R.C. Pugh, O. Schachter, D. Smit, *International Law Cases and Material.* American Casebook Series, St Paul, Minnesota 1982

Horn, H., P.C. Mavroidis (eds.), *Legal and Economic Principles of World Trade Law*, Cambridge University Press, Cambridge 2013
Klabbers, J., *An Introduction to International Organizations Law*, Cambridge University Press, Cambridge 2015
Lasok, P. & T. Millett, *Judicial Control in the EU*, Oxford University Press, Oxford 2004
Lauranos, N., *Legal interaction between decisions of international organisations and European Law.*, European Law Publishing, Groningen 2004
Loades, D.M., *Politics and the Nation 1450–1660*, Fontana/Collins, London/Glasgow 1974
Majone, G., *Dilemmas of European Integration. The ambiguities and pitfalls of integration by stealth.* Oxford University Press, Oxford 2005
Mallat, C., *Introduction to Middle Eastern Law*, Oxford University Press, Oxford 2007
Mather, J., *Legitimating the European Union. Aspirations, inputs and performance.* Palgrave Macmillan, London 2006
Mattli, W., *The Logic of Regional Integration*, Cambridge University Press, Cambridge 1999
Micklitz, H.-W., *The politics of judicial co-operation in the EU. Sunday trading, equal treatment and good faith.* Cambridge University Press, Cambridge 2005
Nowak, M. (ed.), *Introduction to the International Human Rights Regime*, Martinus Nijhoff Publishers/ The Raoul Wallenberg Institute Human Rights Library, Leiden/ Boston 2003
Nyman-Metcalf, K. & I.F. Papageorgiou, *Regional Integration and Courts of Justice*, Intersentia, Antwerpen/Oxford 2005
Opazo Bernales, A. & R. Fernandez Vázquez, *Esquipulas II – una tarea pendiente.* Editorial Universitaria Centroamericana (EDUCA), San José CR. CSUCA 1990
Ovey, C. & R.C.A. White, *Jacobs & White The European Convention on Human Rights* 4th edition, Oxford University Press, Oxford 2006
Papageorgiou, I.F., *Éléments de supranationalité dans le processus d'intégration politique en Amérique Centrale à partir des années 1980.* Université Libre de Bruxelles, Mai 2001 (not published)
Rawls, J., *A Theory of Justice*, Harvard University Press, Cambridge, MA 1999
Rosamund, B., *Theories of European Integration.* (N. Nugent, W.E. Paterson, V. Wright (eds.) *The European Union Series)*, Palgrave Macmillan, London 2000
Schumpeter, J., *Capitalism, Socialism, and Democracy*, 3rd ed., Harper and Brother Publishers, New York 1950
Schütze, R., *From Dual to Cooperative Federalism. The Changing Structure of European Law*, Oxford University Press, Oxford 2009
Stetter, S., EU *foreign and interior policies. Cross-pillar policies and the social constructions of sovereignty.* Routledge, London 2007
Torres-Rivas, E. (ed.), *Historia General de Centroamérica.* 6 volumes. Sociedad Estatal Quinto Centenario, FLACSO, Madrid 1993
Vidmar, J., *Democratic Statehood in International Law*, Hart, Oxford/Portland 2013
Wallace, H., "Politics and policy in the European Union: the challenge of governance" in Wallace & Wallace, *Policy-making in the European Union*, Oxford University Press, Oxford 1996
Wiener, A. & T. Diaz, *European Integration Theory*, Oxford University Press, Oxford 2007 (reprint from 2004)

Zürn, M. & C. Joerges, *Law and governance in post-National Europe. Compliance beyond the nation state.* Cambridge University Press, Cambridge 2005

ARTICLES AND CHAPTERS

Abass, A., "The United Nations, the African Union and the Darfur Crisis: of apology and utopia" in *Netherlands International Law Review* 2007 Vol. LIV Issue 3 pp. 415-440

Abass, A. & M.A. Baderin, "Towards effective collective security and human rights protection in Africa: an assessment of the Constitutive Act of the new African Union" in *Netherlands International Law Review* 2002 Vol. XLIX, Issue 1 pp. 1-38

Acharya, A., "Europe and Asia. Reflections on a tale of two regionalisms" in B. Fort and D. Webber (eds.) *Regional Integration in East Asia and Europe. Convergence and divergence* pp. 312-321, Routledge, London, 2006

Agné, H., "Democratic Founding: We the people and the others", *International Journal of Constitutional Law* (2012) Vol. 10 No. 3 pp. 836-861

Altman, D., "Bringing direct democracy back in: toward a three-dimensional measure of democracy" pp. 615-641 in *Democratization* 2013 Vol. 20 No. 4 pp. 615-641

Andreosso, B. & O'Callaghan, "Market Access and Trade Facilitation" (Chapter 16) in T. Christiansen, E. Kirchner and P. Murray (eds.), *The Palgrave Handbook of EU-Asia Relations,* Palgrave Macmillan, Basingstoke 2013 pp. 263-276

Anstis, S., "Using Law to impair the Rights and Freedoms of Human Right Defenders: A case study of Cambodia", *Journal of Human Rights Practice,* 2012 pp. 1-22, (DOI:10.1093/jhuman/hus017)

Anwar, D.F., "Leadership in the history of Southeast Asian integration" in B. Fort and D. Webber (eds.), *Regional Integration in East Asia and Europe. Convergence and divergence* pp. 59-68, Routledge, London, 2006

Berman, S., S., "Lessons from Europe" in *Journal of Democracy* Vol. 18, No. 1, January 2007, pp. 28-41

Bieber, R., "The Lissabon-Urteil: An Association of Sovereign States" in *European Journal of Constitutional Law* 2009 (5) pp. 396-397

Caballero-Anthony, M., "Regional institutions and regional crises in East Asia" in B. Fort and D. Webber (eds.), *Regional Integration in East Asia and Europe. Convergence and divergence* pp. 265-285, Routledge, London 2006

Carothers, T., "The end of the transition paradigm", *Journal of Democracy* Vol. 13, No. 1, January 2002, pp. 5-21

Castaldi, R., "A Federalist Framework Theory of European Integration", Centre for Studies on Federalism, Turin 2005, www.csfederalismo.it/attachments/1360_a_federalist_framework_castaldi.pdf.

Chibundu, M.O., "NEPAD and the Rebirth of Development Theory and Praxis" in J.I. Levitt (ed.), *Africa. Mapping New Boundaries in International Law* pp. 257-295, Hart Publishing, Oxford/Portland, 2010

Christiano, T., "Self-determination and the Human Right to Democracy" (Chapter 25) pp. 459-480 in R. Croft, S. M. Liao and M. Renzo (eds.), *Philosophical Foundations of Human Rights,* Oxford University Press, Oxford 2015

Christiansen, T., E. Kirchner and P. Murray, "Conclusion" in T. Christiansen, E. Kirchner and P. Murray, *The Palgrave Handbook of EU-Asia Relations,* Palgrave Macmillan, Basingstoke 2013, pp. 618–642

Collins, R., "Constitutionalism as Liberal-Juridical Consciousness: Echoes from International Law's Past", *Leiden Journal of International Law* 22 (2009), pp. 251–287

Comini, N.M., "Union of South American Nations" in L. Levi, G. Finizio, N. Vallinoto (eds.), *The Democratization of International Institutions,* Routledge, Abingdon 2014, pp. 286–295

Cremona, M., D. Kleinmann, J. Larik, R. Lee, P. Vennesson, *ASEAN's External Agreements. Law, Practice and the Quest for Collective Action,* Cambridge University Press, Cambridge 2015.

Deng, F.M., "Africa's Internally Displaced and International Norms" in J.I. Levitt (ed.), *Africa. Mapping New Boundaries in International Law* pp. 65–101, Hart Publishing, Oxford/Portland, 2010

De Witte, B., "International Law as a tool for the European Union", *European Constitutional Law Review* (2009) 5, pp. 265–283

Dobrovoljec, D. & K. Nyman-Metcalf, "Enlargement of the European Union – A Regatta with Moving Goal Posts?", *European Journal of Law Reform* 2001 3(2), pp. 131–147.

Dosch, J., "Asia-Pacific Multilateralism and the Role of the United States" in J. Dosch and M. Mols (eds.), *International Relations in the Asia-Pacific* (St. Martin's Press, New York 2000) pp. 87–110.

Dri, C., "At What Point does a Legislature Become Institutionalized? The Mercosur Parliament's Path", *Brazilian Political Science Review* (BPSR) Vol. 2 n. 2 (2009).

Duffy, H., "Hadijatou Mani Korua v. Niger: Slavery unveiled by the ECOWAS Court", *Human Rights Law Review* 2008, pp. 1–20.

Enterline, A.J. & J.M. Greig, "Beacons of Hope? The impact of imposed democracy on regional peace, democracy and prosperity", *The Journal of Politics,* Vol. 67. No. 4 (2005)

Forere, M., "Is discussion of the United States of Africa premature? Analysis of ECOWAS and SADC integration effort", *Journal of African Law* 2012 56 (1) pp. 29–54

Franck, T., "The Emerging Right to Democratic Governance", *American Journal of International Law* 86 (1992)

Frändberg, A., "Legal Accessibility" in *Festskrift till Anders Fogelklou,* pp. 33–47, Iustus, Uppsala 2008.

Ghai, Y. & J. Cottrell, "A Tale of Three Constitutions: Ethnicity and Politics in Fiji", *International Journal of Constitutional Law* (2007) 5(4), pp. 639–669

Gil, L., D. Paikin, "Mapa de la integración Regional en América Latina." *Procesos e instituciones. Nueva Sociedad, Revista latinoamericana de ciencias sociales.* September 2013 www.nuso.org/upload/articulos/Analisis_mapa_de_integracion_regional.pdf

Haacke, J., "The development of ASEAN's diplomatic and security culture" in B. Fort & D. Webber (eds.), *Regional Integration in East Asia and Europe. Convergence and divergence,* pp. 150–169, Routledge, London 2006

Haftel, Y.Z., "Designing for Peace: Regional Integration Arrangements, Institutional Variation, and Militarized Interstate Disputes", *International Organization* 61, Winter 2007, pp. 217–237.

Hall, C., "Constitutionalism as Liberal-Juridical Consciousness: Echoes from international law's past", *Leiden Journal of International Law* 22 (2009), pp. 251–287

Hamilton-Hart, N., "The Chiang Mai Initiative and the prospects for closer monetary integration in East Asia" in B. Fort & D. Webber (eds.), *Regional Integration in East Asia and Europe. Convergence and divergence.* p. 109R, Routledge, London 2006.

Hauerstein, K., "Aspects of Administrative Law and its Reform in Cambodia" in K. Hauerstein & J. Menzel (eds.), *The Development of Cambodian Administrative Law,* Konrad Adenauer Stiftung, Cambodia 2014.

Hsien-Li, T., "Persistent engagement and insistent persuasion: the role of the working group for an ASEAN Human Rights Mechanism in institutionalizing human rights in the region" in H. Nasu & B. Saul (eds.), *Human Rights in the Asia-Pacific Region,* Routledge, London 2011, pp. 127–143

Higgott, R., "The theory and practice of region" in B. Fort & D. Webber (eds.), *Regional Integration in East Asia and Europe. Convergence and divergence,* pp. 17–38, Routledge, London 2006

Hong Tan, L., "Will ASEAN Economic Integration progress beyond a Free Trade Area?", *International and Comparative Law Quarterly* Vol. 53 Oct 2004, pp. 935–967.

Hor Peng, "The Constitution of Cambodia and the Rule of Interpretation in Comparative Perspective" in *Cambodian Year Book of Comparative Legal Studies,* IL Virtue Unions, Vol. 1 2010.

Jakab, A., "Neutralizing the Sovereignty Question: A new compromise formula", *European Constitutional Law Review* 2(2006), pp. 375–397

Joffé, G., "The Arab Spring in North Africa: Origins and Prospects", *The Journal of North African Studies* Vol. 16 No. 4 December 2011, pp. 507–532

Kissling, C., "The legal and political status of international parliamentary institutions" (Chapter 3) in L. Levi, G. Finizio, N. Vallinoto, *The Democratization of International Institutions,* Routledge, Abingdon 2014, pp. 25–52.

Koefele Kale, N., "Participatory Rights in Africa: A Brief Overview of an Emerging Regional Custom", *Netherlands International Law Review* 2008, pp. 233–258.

Koh, P.M.C., "Enhancing Economic Cooperation: A Regional Arbitration Centre for ASEAN", *International and Comparative Law Quarterly* No. 49 April 2000, pp. 390–412

Lake, D.A., "Regional hierarchy: authority and local international order", *Review of International Studies* 2009 (British International Studies Association), pp. 35–58

Levitt, J.I., "Pro-democratic Intervention in Africa" in J.I. Levitt (ed.), *Africa. Mapping New Boundaries in International Law* pp. 103–147, Hart Publishing, Oxford/ Portland 2010

Linz, J.J. & A. Stepan, "Toward Consolidated Democracies", *Journal of Democracy.* 7.2 1996 pp. 14–33

Loucel, R.R., "Integración centroamericana: evolución y perspectivas", *Integración latinoamerican,* Vol. 19, No. 201 (1994).

Luna Pont, M., "Southern American Common Market (MERCOSUR)" in L. Levi, G. Finizio, N. Vallinoto (eds.), *The Democratization of International Institutions,* Routledge, Abingdon 2014, pp. 261–285.

Lynch, G. & C. Crawford, "Democratization in Africa 1990–2010: an assessment", *Democratization* 18:2 (2011), pp. 275–310

Magliveras, K.D. & G.J. Naldi, "The African Union – A New Dawn for Africa?", *International and Comparative Law Quarterly* Vol. 51 Part 2 April 2002, pp. 415–425

Maluwa, T., "The Constitutive Act of the African Union and Institution-building in Postcolonial Africa", *Leiden Journal of International Law* 16 (2003), pp. 157–170

Maluwa, T., "Fast-tracking African Unity or making haste slowly? A Note on the Amendment to the Constitutive Act of the African Union", *Netherlands International law Review* Vol LI (2004), pp. 195–236

Manby, B., "The African Union, NEPAD and Human Rights: The missing agenda", *Human Rights Quarterly* 26 (2004), pp. 983–1027.

Manea, M.-G., "The Institutional Dimension of the EU/ASEAN Plus Three Inter-regional Relations" (Chapter 19) in T. Christiansen, E. Kirchner and P. Murray, *The Palgrave Handbook of EU-Asia Relations,* Palgrave Macmillan, Basingstoke 2013, pp. 313–329

Menzel, J., "Cambodia: From Civil War to a Constitution to Constitutionalism?" in C. Hill and J. Menzel (eds), *Constitutionalism in Southeast Asia,* Konrad Adenauer Stiftung 2008, pp. 42–46.

Möller, K., "Cambodia and Myanmar: The ASEAN Way ends here", *Asian Survey* Vol. 38, No. 12 (Dec., 1998), pp. 1087–1104.

Montinola, G.R. & R.W. Jackman, "Sources of Corruption. A Cross-Country Study", *British Journal of Political Science* Vol. 32, Issue 1, January 2002, pp. 147–170.

Nesadurai, H.E.S., "The Indo-Chinese enlargement of ASEAN" in B. Fort & D. Webber (eds.), *Regional Integration in East Asia and Europe. Convergence and divergence,* pp. 199–215, Routledge, London 2006.

Nguitragool, P., J. Rüland, *ASEAN as an Actor in International Fora. Reality, Potential and Constraints.* Cambridge University Press, Cambridge 2015.

Nicol, D., "Business Rights as Human Rights" in T. Campbell, K.D. Ewing & A. Tomkins, *The Legal Protection of Human Rights. Sceptical Essays,* pp. 229–243 (Chapter 11), Oxford University Press, Oxford 2011.

Nodia, G., "The Democratic Path", *Journal of Democracy* Vol. 13, No. 3, July 2002, pp. 13–19.

Nyman Metcalf, K., "Regional Integration and Sovereignty: The Sum is More than its Parts?" in P. Sevastik (ed.) *Aspects of Sovereignty,* pp. 83–100, Martinus Nijhoff, Leiden/Boston 2013.

Omerogobe, Y., "Functionalism in the UPU and ITU", *International Journal of International Law* Vol. 27, 1987, pp. 50–62

Orford, A., "Moral Internationalism and the Responsibility to Protect", *The European Journal of International Law* Vol. 24 No. 1 2013, pp. 83–108

Pachon, R., "La CAN y sus relaciones con Europa y Suramerica" in *Revista de la Integracion No 2 – La construcion de la integracion suramericana.* July 2008. Edition of the General Secretariat of the Andean Community

Papageorgiou, I.F., "The Role of Regional Parliaments in the Process of Regional Integration: The Case of the Central American Parliament" *The Federalist* 2002 XLIV(1), pp. 8–20.

Papageorgiou, I.F., "Central American Integration System" (Chapter 23) in L. Levi, G. Finizio, N. Vallinoto, *The Democratization of International Institutions,* Routledge, Abingdon 2014, pp. 299–315.

Pastori, A., "Inconsistencias jurídicas internas del Mercosur posteriores a la suspensión de Paraguay y a la Adhesión de Venezuela: ¿qué le hace una mancha más al tigre?". Study n. 6/2013. September 2013. Consejo Uruguayano para las Relaciones Internacionales.

Peter, F., "A Human Right to Democracy" (Chapter 26), pp. 481–490 in R. Croft, S. M. Liao and M. Renzo (eds.), *Philosophical Foundations of Human Rights*, Oxford University Press, Oxford 2015

Pham, J.P., "African Constitutionalism: Forging New Models" in J.I. Levitt (ed.) *Africa. Mapping New Boundaries in International Law*, pp. 183–203, Hart Publishing, Oxford/Portland 2010.

Price, M., "A Charter of Contradictions", *Arab Media and Society*, March 2008 at www.arabmediasociety.com/?article=648.

Renard, T., "The EU, the SCO and SAARC" in T. Christiansen, E. Kirchner and P. Murray (eds.), *The Palgrave Handbook of EU-Asia Relations*, Palgrave Macmillan, Basingstoke, 2013, pp. 359–373.

Sanahuja, J.A., "Multilateralismo y regionalismo en clave suramericana: El caso de UNASUR" in *Los desafíos del multilateralismo en América Latina. Pensamiento proprio*. No. 33, Year 16, January-June 2001, Edicion Cries. Buenos Aires, pp. 120–1.

Sanchez Rodriguez, D., "The Andean Community" in L. Levi, G. Finizio, N. Vallinoto (eds.), *The Democratization of International Institutions – First International Democracy Report* Routledge, 2013.

Saul, B., J. Mowbray & I. Baghoomians, "Resistance to regional human rights cooperation in the Asia-Pacific: demythologizing regional exceptionalism by learning from the Americas, Europe and Africa" in H. Nasu & B. Saul (eds.), *Human Rights in the Asia-Pacific Region*, Routledge, London 2011, pp. 107–126

Schmitter, P.C., "Central American Integration: Spill-Over, Spill-Around or Encapsulation?", *Journal of Common Market Studies* 1970 Vol. 9, No. 1.

Schneiderman, D., "Transnational legality and the immobilization of local agency" in *Annual Review of Law and Social Sciences* 2006, 2:387–408.

Sultan, N., "Al Jazeera: Reflections on the Arab Spring", *Journal of Arabian Studies 3.2*, December 2013, pp. 249–264

Tang, S., "Leadership in institution building. The case of ASEAN+3" in B. Fort & D. Webber (eds.), *Regional Integration in East Asia and Europe. Convergence and divergence*, pp. 69–82, Routledge, London 2006.

Terada, T., "The birth and growth of ASEAN+3", pp. 218–235 in B. Fort & D. Webber (eds.), *Regional Integration in East Asia and Europe. Convergence and divergence* pp. 218–235, Routledge, London 2006.

Trauner, F., "Post-Accession compliance with EU Law in Bulgaria and Romania: A comparative perspective" in Institute for European Integration Research Working Paper Series No. 1/2009, March 2009

Treisman, D., "The causes of corruption: A cross-national study", *Journal of Public Economics* 76 (2000), pp. 399–457

Tudoroiu, T., "The Arab Spring: Last Episode of the Cold War", *Contemporary Politics* 2013 19:3, pp. 304–320.

Umbrach, F., "ASEAN and Major Powers: Japan and China – A Changing Balance of Power" in J. Dosch and M. Mols (eds.), *International Relations in the Asia-Pacific*, St. Martin's Press, New York 2000, pp. 171–213.
Vervaele, J.A.E., "Mercosur and regional integration in Southern America", *International and Comparative Law Quarterly* vol. 54. April 2005, pp. 387–410
Vidigal, G., "Enforcing Democracy at the Regional Level: Paraguay's Suspension before the Mercosur Court", *Cambridge Journal of International and Comparative Law* (2)2: 337–349 (2013).
Von Bogdandy, A., "The European Union as Situation, Executive and Promoter of the International Law of Cultural Diversity – Elements of a Beautiful Friendship", *European Journal of International Law* Vol. 19 No. 2 (2008), pp. 241–275
von Bogdandy, A. & T. Makatsch, "Collision, Co-existence or Co-operation? Prospects for the Relationship between WTO Law and European Union Law" in G. de Búrca & J. Scott (eds.), *The EU and the WTO. Legal and Constitutional Questions* Hart, London 2001.
Webber, D., "Regional integration in Europe and Asia" in B. Fort & D. Webber (eds.), *Regional Integration in East Asia and Europe. Convergence and divergence*, pp. 289–311, Routledge, London 2006.
Weber, K., "The ASEAN Regional Forum" (Chapter 21) in T. Christiansen, E. Kirchner and P. Murray, *The Palgrave Handbook of EU-Asia Relations*, Palgrave Macmillan, Basingstoke 2013, pp. 344–358
Weithman, P., "John Rawls and the Task of Political Philosophy", *The Review of Politics* 71(2009), pp. 113–125.
Williams, A., "Philosophy of EU law", *Oxford Journal of Legal Studies* Vol. 29 Autumn 2009, pp. 549–577.
Wing, A.K., "Women's Rights and Africa's Evolving Landscape: The Women's Protocol of the Banjul Charter" in J.I. Levitt (ed.), *Africa. Mapping New Boundaries in International Law*, pp. 13–33, Hart Publishing, Oxford/Portland 2010.
Withaker, B.E., "Citizens and Foreigners: Democratization and the Policy of Exclusion in Africa", *African Studies Review*, Vol. 48 No. 1 (April 2005), pp. 109–126
Yoon, S.-J. & J.-J. Suh, "Nuclear Non-proliferation" (Chapter 25) in T. Christiansen, E. Kirchner and P. Murray, *The Palgrave Handbook of EU-Asia Relations*, Palgrave Macmillan, Basingstoke 2013, pp. 406–420

OFFICIAL DOCUMENTS *(IN CHRONOLOGICAL ORDER)*

Dossier IRELA, N° 11 "El plan Arias: una salida para el proceso de paz centroamericano?" IRELA, Madrid, February 1988
Advisory opinion of the Inter-American Court of Human Rights, July, 14 1989 (OC-10/89)
The Cairo Declaration on Human Rights in Islam, Organisation of Islamic Cooperation, 31 July to 5 August 1990, www.oic-oci.org/english/article/human.htm
Treaty Establishing the African Economic Community (The Abuja Treaty), 3 June 1991, www.uneca.org/itca/ariportal/abuja.htm

Tegucigalpa Declaration, Final Communiqué of the Meeting of Central American Presidents, 13 December 1991

ECOWAS Protocol A/SP1/12/01 on Democracy and Good Governance, 1991, www.comm.ecowas.int/sec/en/protocoles/Protocol%20on%20good-governance-and-democracy-rev-5EN.pdf

Presidential Declaration of Las Leñas, 26–27 June 1992, www.mercosur.int/innovaportal/v/273/1/secretaria/estructura_institucional_del_mercosur

Declaration and Treaty of Southern African Development Community, 1992, www.sadc.int

Additional Protocol to the Treaty of Asuncion on the Institutional Structure of Mercosur, Protocol of Ouro Preto, 17 December 1994,
www.sice.oas.org/trade/mrcsr/ourop/ourop_e.asp

Framework Treaty on Democratic Security in Central America, San Pedro Sula, Honduras, 15 December 1995 (Available at: www.state.gov/p/wha/rls/70979.htm)

Protocolo Modificatorio que crea la Comunidad Andina y establece el Sistema Andino de Integración, 8th Meeting of the Presidents of the Andean Pact, Trujillo 10 March 1996 (Protocolo de Trujillo).

Declaración del Consejo Presidencial Andino sobre Democracia e Integración, Bogotá 7 August 1998

Grand Bay Declaration of the Organisation of African Unity, 1999 www.achpr.org/english/declarations/declaration_grand_bay_en.html

Assembly of the Heads of State or Government, Thirty-sixth ordinary session/Fourth session of African Economic Community, 10–12 July 2000, Lomé, Togo, www.africa-union.org/Special_Programs/CSSDCA/cssdca-solemndeclaration.pdf

Constitutive Act of the African Union (by the Organisation of African Unity), Togo 10 July 2000,
www.oauoua.org/LOME2000/Africa%20Union%20Constitiutive%20Act%20ENG.htm

UNESCO Declaration on Cultural Diversity, 2 November 2001 http://unesdoc.unesco.org/images/0012/001271/127162e.pdf

Documents of the African Commission on Human and Peoples' Rights (ed. M. Evans, R. Murray) Hart, Oxford 2001

Ushuaia Protocol on democratic commitment in the Mercosur, the Republic of Bolivia and the Republic of Chile, Ushuaia, 24 July 1998. Entry into force: 17 January 2002. No 37341. UNTS. Treaty series. March 2002.

Andean Charter on the Promotion and Protection of Human Rights, Guayaquil, 23 July 2002

Declaración del Cusco sobre la Comunidad Sudamericana de Naciones. III Cumbre Presidencial Sudamericana. Cusco, 8 de diciembre de 2004. www.iirsa.org/admin_iirsa_web/Uploads/Documents/oe_cusco05_declaracion_del_cusco_eng.pdf

Unasur Constitutive Treaty, Brasilia 23 May 2008 www.comunidadandina.org/ingles/csn/treaty.htm.

UN General Assembly Resolution UN Doc A/RES/61/301 (2009) Honduras

UN Security Council Resolution S/RES/1973 (2011) Libya www.un.org/en/sc/documents/resolutions/2011.shtml

Protocolo de Montevideo sobre el Compromiso con la Democracia en el Mercosur (Ushuaia II). In www.mercosur.int/innovaportal/file/4827/1/protocolo_de_montevideo-ushuaia_ii_es.pdf. Adopted on 20 December 2011. (Not in force)

Decisión sobre la Suspensión del Paraguay en el Mercosur en Aplicación del Protocolo de Ushuaia sobre Compromiso Democratico, 29 June 2012 www.puntofocal.gov.ar/doc/comunicado_conjunto_presidentes_ep.pdf
Decisión sobre el Cese de la Suspensión del Paraguay en el Mercosur en Aplicación del Protocolo de Ushuaia sobre Compromiso Democrático, 13 July 2013. www.mercosur.int/t_generic.jsp?contentid=4506&site=1&channel=secretaria&seccion=3

CASE LAW

SADC (T) Case No. 2/2007 *M. Campbell and others and the Republic of Zimbabwe* www.sadc-tribunal.org/pages/decisions.htm
SADC (T) Case No. 7/2008 *L. M. Tembani and the Republic of Zimbabwe* www.sadc-tribunal.org/pages/decisions.htm
African Commission on Human and Peoples' Rights, *Dawda Jawara v. The Gambia, Comm.* Nos. 147/95 and 149/96 (2000)
ECOWAS Court, *Mme Hadijatou Mani Koraou v The Republic of Niger*, 27 October 2008, ECW/CCJ/JUD/06/08
ECJ Cases 60 and 61/84, *Cinéthèque SA v Fédérationnationale des cinémas français* [1985] ECR 2605
ECJ Case C-154/89, *Commission v. France (Tourist guides)* [1991] ECR I - 659
ECJ Case C-379/87, *Groener v Minister for Education and the City of Dublin Vocational Educational Committee* [1989] ECR I - 3967
ECJ Case C-148/91, *Vereniging Veronica Omroep Organisatie v Commissariaat voor de Media* [1993] ECR I - 487
ECJ Cases C-338/04, C-359/04, and C-360/04, *Criminal proceedings against Massimiliano Placanica (C-338/04),Christian Palazzese (C-359/04) and Angelo Sorricchio (C-360/04)* [2007] ECR I - 1891
ECJ Case C-402/05P, *Kadi* (2008)
Bundesverfassungsgericht (Germany): The Lissabon Agreement, 30 June 2009, www.bundesverfassungsgericht.de/entscheidungen/es20090630_2bve000208en.html

NEWSPAPER ARTICLES, INTERNET SOURCES AND OTHER MATERIAL

www.africa-union.org
www.african-court.org/en/
www.arableagueonline.org/
www.maghrebarabe.org
www.aseansec.org (ASEAN Secretariat)
www.asean.org/communities/asean-economic-community
www.forumsec.org (The Pacific Forum)
www.spc.int (Pacific Community)

www.gcc-sg.org/eng/ (Gulf Cooperation Council)

www.sectsco.org/EN/ (Shanghai Cooperation Organisation)

Centre for Studies on Federalism, *International Democracy Watch (Draft Project)*, January 2009, www.csfederalismo.it

Indicadores economicos de la CAN in http://estadisticas.comunidadandina.org/eportal/contenidos/indeco.htm (last access 2/1/2014)

The Economist, https://economist.com

www.dw.de/ecowas-summit-focuses-on-mali-guinea-bissau/a-16959010

www.eastasiaforum.org/2011/10/20/china-and-the-enlarged-east-asia-summit-the-makings-of-an-asia-pacific-community/#more-22346

www.britannica.com/EBchecked/topic/657790/Zollverein

www.opensocietyfoundations.org/voices/end-southern-africas-regional-human-rights-court?utm_source=Open+Society+Institute&utm_campaign=25ea45c3ba-justice-20120823&utm_medium=email

http://jurist.org/paperchase/2012/03/former-icj-judge-on-trial-for-madagascar-coup-plot.php

www.bernama.com/bernama/v6/newsworld.php?id=703832

www.hrw.org/news/2006/11/03/how-put-un-rights-council-back-track

www.arabmediasociety.com/?article=648

www.al-bab.com/media/charter.htm

www.dipublico.com.ar/9407/cumbre-del-mercosur-mendoza-2012-comunicado-conjunto-de-los-presidentes-de-los-estados-partes/

www.la-razon.com/mundo/Mercosur-confirma-reintegro-Paraguay-Cartes_0_1868213259.html. 12.07.2011.

www.telam.com.ar/notas/201312/45200-el-congreso-paraguayo-aprobo-el-ingreso-de-venezuela-al-mercosur.html

www.telam.com.ar/notas/201402/52158-el-parlamento-del-mercosur-condeno-la-violencia-en-venezuela-y-activara-un-observatorio.html

http://en.mercopress.com/2012/06/21/unasur-delegation-travels-to-paraguay-to-ensure-democratic-system-integrity

Opeal (Observatorio de Politica y Estrategia en America Latina) 11.09.2012 www.opeal.net/index.php?option=com_k2&view=item&id=12202:unasur-applies-"democracy-clause"-on-paraguay

www.lanacion.com.ar/1484248-lugo-se-juega-su-mandato-en-un-sorpresivo-y-veloz-juicio-politicov

www.telam.com.ar/notas/201312/45200-el-congreso-paraguayo-aprobo-el-ingreso-de-venezuela-al-mercosur.html. 18.12.2013.

El Clarin. 11.8.2013 in www.clarin.com/mundo/Unasur-anuncio-levanta-suspension-Paraguay_0_972502838.html

www.mre.gov.py/v1/Noticias/922-vii-reunin-ordinaria-del-consejo-de-jefes-y-jefas-de-estado-y-de-gobierno-de-la-unasur.aspx

www.ingramcontent.com/pod-product-compliance
Ingram Content Group UK Ltd.
Pitfield, Milton Keynes, MK11 3LW, UK
UKHW051922100926
8556IPUK00021B/1332

9 781780 683621